Partisan Gerrymandering and the
Construction of American Democracy

In *Partisan Gerrymandering and the Construction of American Democracy*, Erik J. Engstrom offers an important, historically grounded perspective on the stakes of congressional redistricting by evaluating the impact of gerrymandering on elections and on party control of the U.S. national government from 1789 through the reapportionment revolution of the 1960s. In this era before the courts supervised redistricting, state parties enjoyed wide discretion with regard to the timing and structure of their districting choices. Although Congress occasionally added language to federal-apportionment acts requiring equally populous districts, there is little evidence this legislation was enforced. Essentially, states could redistrict largely *whenever* and *however* they wanted, and so, not surprisingly, political considerations dominated the process.

Engstrom employs the abundant cross-sectional and temporal variation in redistricting plans and their electoral results from all the states— throughout U.S. history—in order to investigate the causes and consequences of partisan redistricting. His analysis reveals that districting practices across states and over time systematically affected the competitiveness of congressional elections, shaped the partisan composition of congressional delegations, and, on occasion, decided party control of the House of Representatives. In conclusion, Engstrom places recent developments in redistricting politics and scholarship within the larger historical context uncovered in this book.

Erik J. Engstrom is Associate Professor of Political Science at the University of California, Davis.

LEGISLATIVE POLITICS & POLICY MAKING

Series Editors

Janet M. Box-Steffensmeier, Vernal Riffe Professor of Political Science, The Ohio State University

David Canon, Professor of Political Science, University of Wisconsin, Madison

The Floor in Congressional Life
ANDREW J. TAYLOR

The Influence of Campaign Contributions in State Legislatures: The Effects of Institutions and Politics
LYNDA W. POWELL

The Evolution of American Legislatures: Colonies, Territories, and States, 1619–2009
PEVERILL SQUIRE

Getting Primaried: The Changing Politics of Congressional Primary Challenges
ROBERT G. BOATRIGHT

Ambition, Competition, and Electoral Reform: The Politics of Congressional Elections Across Time
JAMIE L. CARSON AND JASON M. ROBERTS

Partisan Gerrymandering and the Construction of American Democracy
ERIK J. ENGSTROM

PARTISAN GERRYMANDERING AND THE CONSTRUCTION OF AMERICAN DEMOCRACY

Erik J. Engstrom

The University of Michigan Press
Ann Arbor

Published in the United States of America by
The University of Michigan Press
Manufactured in the United States of America
⊚ Printed on acid-free paper

2016   2015   2014   2013   4   3   2   1

A CIP catalog record for this book is available from the British Library.

Library of Congress Cataloging-in-Publication Data

Engstrom, Erik J.
    Partisan gerrymandering and the construction of American democracy / Erik J.
Engstrom.
        pages   cm. — (Legislative politics and policy making)
    Includes bibliographical references and index.
    ISBN 978-0-472-11901-1 (hardback) — ISBN 978-0-472-02952-5 (e-book)
    1. Gerrymandering—United States. 2. Apportionment (Election law)—United
States. 3. Election districts—United States. 4. Voting—United States.
5. Representative government and representation—United States. 6. United States—
Politics and government. I. Title.

JK1341.E64   2013
328.73'073455—dc23

                                                                    2013015656

Acknowledgments

In writing this book, I have incurred many debts. At an early stage, Gary Cox, Mathew McCubbins, and, especially, Sam Kernell provided encouragement and insight. Janet Box-Steffensmeier and David Canon, the series editors for Legislative Politics & Policy Making, as well as the two anonymous scholars who reviewed the manuscript for the University of Michigan Press, offered careful readings and constructive advice. Jack Reilly and Matthew Pietryka conducted excellent research assistance. Georg Vanberg, Alan Wiseman, Chad Rector, Nathan Monroe, Chris Den Hartog, Charles Stewart, and Lee Sigelman provided helpful comments on various portions of the manuscript. In addition to commenting on aspects of the manuscript, Jamie Carson and Jason Roberts also shared in some of the research that forms the basis of chapter 7. Finally, I dedicate this book to my wife Mary and my daughter Emma for their love and support.

Contents

ONE

Gerrymandering and the Evolution of American Politics

This book evaluates the impact of congressional redistricting on elections and control of U.S. national government from 1789 to the reapportionment revolution of the 1960s. The motivating question is one that scholars seldom ask: what was redistricting like in the past? It turns out that the answer to this question is essential for understanding both the past and present of American politics.

Almost all previous research on congressional redistricting concentrates on the period after the 1960s. In the mid-1960s, the U.S. Supreme Court outlawed malapportioned electoral districts for both state legislatures and the U.S. House of Representatives. This transformative legal revolution produced a massive wave of redistricting across the nation that shifted the partisan landscape in state legislatures across the country and fundamentally redistributed power in American politics. In addition, this reapportionment revolution led to the creation of a large scholarly literature devoted to studying the causes and consequences of the modern decennial-redistricting process. In this now-vast literature, redistricting prior to the 1960s receives brief treatment, although the years before 1964 constitute nearly 75 percent of the United States' nearly 225-year history.

Such narrowly focused accounts suffer from two principal disadvantages. First, it has led political scientists and historians to radically underestimate the power of gerrymandering in shaping the development of American politics. Throughout the 19th century, partisan gerrymandering systematically structured the competitiveness of congressional elections, the partisan composition of congressional delegations, and, on occasion, decided party control of the House of Representatives. Gerrymandering roiled state legislatures across the country, and profoundly shaped the tumult of 19th-century politics and policy. The outcomes of these collisions continue to cast long shadows over modern American politics.

Second, the failure to examine the history of redistricting has led students of contemporary American politics to misunderstand the context in which modern redistricting takes place. Modern research has argued that redistricting produces, at best, only a minimal impact on the partisan balance of power in Congress. However, no consensus has emerged about why gerrymandering has had such little impact. Some scholars have argued that constraints on gerrymandering in the modern period—including court oversight, "one-person, one-vote" mandates, and demands by congressional incumbents for secure seats—have made it virtually impossible to engage in a full-blown partisan gerrymander. Others contend that the partisan gains to be had from gerrymandering are limited, regardless of the institutional configuration under which redistricting takes place. Moving beyond the relatively fixed institutional and political context of modern redistricting provides a powerful opportunity to assess these competing explanations.

Some of the most interesting questions in the study of American politics, therefore, concern the differences between the past and the present. Understanding the causes and consequences of these differences prove essential for understanding both the historical development and contemporary practice of American democracy.

The Electoral Development of Congress

Although the basic constitutional architecture of the federal government has remained largely constant since 1789, the day-to-day conduct of American politics has changed dramatically over time. Nowhere are these differences more visible, and more consequential, than in the House of Representatives. Nowadays, elections to the House are characterized by extremely low levels of competition. Incumbents dominate election outcomes. Most incumbents who run for reelection win, and win big. One consequence of low competition is that membership in Congress is relatively stable from one year to the next. Another consequence is that the partisan seat distribution in the House tends to respond slowly to changes in public preferences. Indeed, a large and influential literature on congressional elections is motivated by trying to understand the causes and consequences of low competition and candidate-centered congressional elections.

Congressional elections of the mid-to-late 19th century, by contrast, were characterized by rabid partisanship, intense voter interest, massive turnout, and fever-pitched competition. For example, between 1870 and 1890, nearly 45 percent of House elections were decided by a vote margin of 10 percent or less (Dubin 1998). Compare that to House elections in the 2000s, in which only 22 percent were decided by such a narrow margin (Jacobson 2009, 32). The deep competitiveness of district-level congressional elections also reflected, and reinforced, intense battles over control of the national government.

Throughout most of the 19th century, the national vote in House elections was very close. As a result of the fever-pitched local and national competition, party ratios in the House could, and often did, change dramatically. For example, in 1854, Democrats lost a monumental 74 seats. The House only had 234 members total, so the seat swing accounted for nearly 30 percent of the membership. In 1874, Republicans were on the losing end of another massive wipeout—surrendering 94 seats. In 1894, Democrats lost 114 seats (in a chamber of 357). These impressive seat swings reflected, and reinforced, intense competition between the parties for control of national government. Notably, from 1870 to 1900, each party controlled the House exactly half of the time.

The fierce competition for elected office radiated down to the individual career decisions of representatives. Today, Congress is filled with career politicians. In a typical year, nearly 95 percent of incumbents run for reelection and win. By contrast, in the 19th century, many fewer incumbents ran and fewer won. In 1852, for example, only 52 percent of incumbents sought election. Consequently, tenures in Congress tended to be brief. Representatives tended to serve one or two terms before perhaps returning to their home state to pursue local office, receiving a federal appointment, or returning to the private sector. The result was immense turnover in the membership of the House. At the beginning of the 28th Congress in 1843, for example, 73 percent of the members were freshmen. This rapid turnover shaped both the internal structure of the House and the legislative process. For example, committee memberships and committee chairs were incredibly fluid, making the reciprocal tit-for-tat relationships necessary to forge durable policy coalitions incredibly difficult to foster.

While these facets of 19th-century electoral and legislative politics constitute agreed-upon facts, the reasons for them remain uncertain and controversial. Unfortunately, past scholarly research fails to provide a fully satisfying explanation for the tumult of 19th-century politics and its replacement by the professionalized politics of the 20th century. The dominant scholarly narrative emphasizes realignment and critical elections. According to this narrative, American political history can be divided into long periods of electoral normalcy and brief periods in which traditional voting patterns and ideological cleavages are abruptly overturned. Though considerable debate exists within the realignment literature about what exactly constitutes a critical election, some common patterns in the literature can be identified.

According to its foremost proponents—V. O. Key (1955), Walter Dean Burnham (1970), and James L. Sundquist (1983)—critical elections feature abrupt, permanent changes in traditional voting patterns. These changes in mass-voting behavior are accompanied by intense battles at the elite level over party nominations, party platforms, and ideological alignments. Finally, the realignment of ideological coalitions creates "a unified majority party capable of enacting major policy shifts" (Brady 1988, 29). Critical elections thus are defined by sudden shifts in voting patterns, reshaped party platforms, and sweeping changes in public policy.

Although considerable ink has been spilled debating whether or not certain elections meet the criteria of a critical realigning election, the general consensus is that, at a minimum, the elections of 1828, 1860, 1896, and 1932 deserve a spot on the electoral equivalent of Mount Rushmore. These elections, according to the chief advocate of the realignment narrative, constitute the "mainsprings" American politics (Burnham 1970); they reshaped electoral and policy coalitions for succeeding generations. The realignment narrative also serves as a normative baseline against which many political observers judge modern American politics. Moreover, the supposed absence of transformative elections in the post–World War II era provides the evidence that many commentators, in and out of academia, have used to impugn modern U.S. politics.

The realignment narrative also provides a potentially satisfying explanation for the modernization of American politics—and the House in particular—in the 20th century. Again, the dominant scholarly storyline follows in the footsteps of Burnham. In particular, the election of 1896, so the argument goes, swept aside the fever-pitched party competition of the 19th century and replaced it with low turnout, less partisan elections, and professionalized political institutions. By turning the North into the preserve of the Republican Party and the South into the preserve of the Democratic Party, the tumultuous partisan elections of the 19th century were gradually replaced by candidate-centered elections.

In the context of congressional elections, the consequences of the 1896 realignment meant that members of Congress could control their own district in a way that had been previously impossible. Fewer representatives suffered electoral defeat. Moreover, the creation of single-party dominated districts also drastically reduced voluntary retirements from Congress. Incumbents increasingly decided to run for reelection and win. The result was to transform the House from a body of amateurs to a body of professionalized, careerist politicians. The consequences of this transformation cannot be overstated. Indeed, the vast literature on congressional politics—including research on the incumbency advantage, the electoral connection, the vanishing marginals, committee powers, campaign finance, pork-barrel politics, etc.—can be framed as the search for the causes and consequences of candidate-centered elections. Thus, the realignment narrative provides a sweeping explanation for the dynamics of American political history. It offers an account for both the turbulence of 19th-century politics and its replacement by the professionalized politics of the 20th and 21st centuries.

Yet this traditional narrative suffers from a number of problems. One problem is that the critical election perspective downplays the importance of other elections. Noncritical elections are typically subsumed into the category of "normalcy." Yet one does not have to look far to find other 19th-century elections that were rife with hot-button campaign issues and significant policy consequences: consider the election of 1874. The congressional seat swings in this election easily matched those of other elections typically deemed realigning. Nor was the election of 1874 without profound long-term policy consequences (Mayhew 2004). This election brought Democrats to power for the first time since the late 1850s. With majority control of the House, Democrats rolled back the federal government's commitment to Reconstruction in the south. The impact of these policy decisions are hard to overstate. The actions halted Reconstruction in its tracks—fundamentally altering the trajectory of American politics for the next century.

One can readily tell similar stories about other elections. Consider, for example, the election of 1888. Although mostly ignored in the vast realignment genre, the election of 1888 produced dramatic changes in both parliamentary procedure and economic policy. The subsequent 51st Congress featured a fundamental reworking of the legislative process (i.e., Reed's Rules), an elaborate extension of the tariff system (i.e., the McKinley Tariff), and a radical manipulation of the currency market (i.e., the Sherman Silver Purchase Act). Each of these legislative acts looms large in the United States' political and economic history. Yet the election that selected this Congress rarely musters notice in the realignment narrative. Delving even further back into American electoral history, one could point to the election of 1802. In this election, Republicans gained 38 seats, solidified their grip on the national government, and set about reversing a decade worth of pro-Federalist public policy. Notably, the subsequent Congress voted to fund the Louisiana Purchase (see chapter 2), which altered the course not just of American history, but of world history. Yet despite the dramatic influence the 1802 election had on the future trajectory of American history, this election garners nary a mention in the realignment narrative.

One could easily point to other examples of transformative elections and pivotal legislative sessions throughout the 19th century. But even if we were to allow for a more expansive definition of "critical elections," the notion that some elections are more consequential than others, and elicited more excitement among voters, raises more questions than it answers. Even more problematic is that when scholars have gone looking for evidence of the massive swings in popular opinion that a critical election explanation would predict, the evidence has been far from clear-cut. Indeed, in the context of congressional elections, the vote swings of the 19th century were not especially large when compared to the corresponding seat swings. For example, in the congressional election of 1854–55, Democrats lost only 4 percent of their vote share from the previous election, yet lost a stunning 74 seats. In 1894, Democrats lost 11 percent of the vote from the previous election, but lost 114 seats. These massive seat swings do not square well with the notion of critical elections being driven by equally large swings in popular opinion.

In an influential modification of the realignment narrative, David Brady (1985; 1988) first uncovered this striking pattern of 19th-century House elections. He found evidence that in two of the "realigning eras" of the 19th century—the Civil War and 1890s realignments—big seat swings were brought on not by big shifts in mass opinion, but a systematic small shift in the vote being reproduced across a number of highly competitive districts. The result was an avalanche of legislative turnover. Based on this evidence, Brady argued that the Civil War and 1890s realignments were the result of "structural factors" rather than "the result of changes in mass voting behavior" (1985, 29).

Brady went on to argue that in a realigning period elections are dominated by an overriding national issue (i.e., slavery in 1860; the economy in 1896). Because the parties take clear-cut, distinct positions on issues in these elections, voters are presented with stark alternatives. This nationalization produces a systematic vote swing across districts, a corresponding seat swing, and, ultimately, large tranches of legislative turnover. The result is the election of a new majority party that then enacts bold new policies on the dominant issue cleavage. According to Brady, both the Civil War and 1890s realignments meet these criteria. Thus, Brady provided a major refinement of the realignment narrative for the tumultuous patterns of 19th-century elections and policy.

While Brady's argument and evidence are persuasive, they beg a series of important—and unanswered—questions. First, falling into the same trap as prior work on critical elections, the argument implicitly dismisses other elections as irrelevant or inconsequential. But other elections such as 1802 and 1874 display a strikingly similar pattern—small swings in the vote leading to large swings in seats. In 1802, for example, Republicans' seat share in the House increased from 59 percent to 71 percent, although their vote share only increased from 56 percent to 57 percent (Rusk 2002, 215–17). In 1874, Republicans' vote share dropped from 53 percent to 45 percent, yet their seat share collapsed—falling from 69 percent to 37 percent (matching the losses suffered in 1854 and 1894). Thus, lumping elections into only one of two categories—critical and noncritical—does too much violence to the nuanced patterns of American political history.

Second, one is left wondering why, in some years, electoral outcomes become nationalized, and not in others. The historical record of the 19th century is chock-full of national issues that dominated electoral campaigns and party rhetoric: war, western expansion, national banks, the extension of slavery, Reconstruction, suffrage, currency, tariffs, economic regulation, and civil-service reform. All of these issues, at one time or another, pervaded 19th-century electoral campaigns. Beyond the much-discussed programmatic elections of 1860 and 1896, one finds national issues permeating campaign platforms and contemporary newspaper coverage (Bensel 2000; Gerring 2001; Kernell 1986). To put this in the language of statistics, there is little to no variation on the independent variable. National issues permeated 19th-century campaigns. Thus, nationalization alone cannot serve as a satisfactory explanation for variation in party swings and legislative turnover.

Third, even if we were to allow for a more expansive definition of "nationalized" congressional elections, a much larger puzzle remains unanswered. Why did small shifts in the vote lead to massive legislative turnover in some elections, but not others? Why were 19th-century congressional electoral results, and subsequent policy outcomes, so tumultuous? Why are modern congressional elections tame, compared to their 19th-century counterparts? These questions cut to the heart of how we understand American political institutions—past and present.

Gerrymandering and the Construction of American Democracy

To answer these questions, this book turns the spotlight on partisan ger-rymandering. The rest of this book is devoted to showing that the strate-gic manipulation of congressional districts played a fundamental but, until now, ignored role in shaping the historical trajectory of American politics and public policy. Aside from a few initial forays by political historians, research on American electoral development has radically downplayed dis-trict design. Yet politicians of this era often acted as if little else beyond ger-rymandering mattered. Redistricting roiled legislatures across the country, biased electoral outcomes, made and ruined political careers, and funda-mentally shaped political control of the national government.

In this era, before the one-person, one-vote doctrine and the Voting Rights Act, state legislators had nearly free reign over *when* and *how* to redistrict. Congress occasionally added provisions to various apportion-ment acts mandating that district populations be as equal as possible, but there is little evidence that these provisions were ever enforced, much less achieved. Aside from the requirements that districts maintain geographical contiguity, and after 1842 that districts select only one representative, there was almost no oversight of the districting process.[1] Thus, mapmakers of the 19th century had a much broader strategic menu to choose from than do their modern counterparts.

Political parties in control of state government took full advantage of this freedom. Unlike the modern period in which states redraw congres-sional boundaries at regular 10-year intervals, in the 19th century, states redistricted almost whenever they wanted. In every year from 1862 and 1896, with one exception, at least one state redrew its congressional district boundaries. Ohio, for example, redrew its congressional district boundar-ies six times between 1878 and 1890. Other states went long stretches with the same boundaries. Unless prodded by a reapportionment, which added or subtracted seats to a states' congressional delegation, state legislatures could opt out of redistricting altogether. Connecticut, for instance, kept the exact same congressional district lines for 70 years (1842–1912).

The importance of incumbency and careerist aspirations among con-gressional incumbents, although on the rise, had yet to fully take root. The norm of using seniority in allocating committee chairmanships had yet to emerge. Thus, protecting incumbents was less important than simply cap-turing as many seats for your side as possible. As a result, parties were will-ing to push partisan advantage to the edge. To do so, partisan mapmakers carved states into districts with narrow, yet winnable, margins. For example, consider the pro-Democratic redistricting of Indiana in 1852 where Democrats carved the state into a remarkable 10 (out of 11) Democratic districts despite only garnering 53 percent of the statewide vote.

These state-level redistricting decisions aggregated together to shape party ratios in the House. For much of the 19th century, and especially in the period after the Civil War, the national division of the congressional vote was razor thin. With electoral mobilization at its maximum, parties looked in other directions for electoral advantage. Redistricting offered one such tool. The timely partisan shift of a few seats could make the difference between majority and minority status in the House. In 1878, for example, the mid-decade redistricting perpetrated by Democrats in Ohio and Missouri created just enough seats to allow Democrats to hold onto the House. Similarly, in 1888, Republican legislators in Pennsylvania engineered a last-minute redistricting that helped ensure a narrow Republican majority in the House.

By making districts competitive in the quest for short-term partisan advantage, parties were often able to wring a disproportionate number of seats out of their vote share. Yet this strategy sometimes backfired. By manufacturing competitive districts, state parties, at times, created an electoral system where small swings in the national vote could lead to immense swings in seats. For instance, in 1874, the Republican percentage of House seats dropped from 69 percent to 36 percent (94 seats) despite their national vote dropping only 7 percent. The explanation for these dramatic reversals in electoral fortunes lies with the highly competitive congressional districts of the 19th century. And, pushing the argument back one step further, this competitive electoral system was, to a large extent, the product of strategic mapmaking.

The consequences of highly partisan, and unpredictable, redistricting also extended to the career decisions of politicians. Because states drew such competitive districts, political careers were often cut short. Incumbent members of Congress faced a more variable redistricting schedule, and one that was more partisan when it happened. These two factors provide part of the explanation for the short tenure of 19th-century representatives. Directly, the partisan redrawing of districts could end a career. Indirectly, because redistricting was less predictable, planning for a long-term career in the House was hampered. The uncertainty surrounding when, and if, one would be redistricted likely decreased the willingness of members to make long-term investments in a congressional career.

Not only does redistricting provide a key to unlocking the puzzle of 19th-century electoral patterns, subsequent changes in the frequency and nature of redistricting help explain the emergence of candidate-centered politics in the 20th century. By the 20th century, the frequent and highly partisan redistricting gave way to an era of limited redistricting. Where redistricting in the 19th century was frequent, in the 20th, redistricting became comparatively infrequent. Because the courts had yet to enter the political thicket, there was no compulsion for states to redraw district boundaries. As competition for the state legislatures declined from their earlier heights during the early to mid-20th century, the incentives to frequently redistrict for partisan advantage lost much of its steam. Many states consequently opted out of the redistricting game altogether.

As I show in chapter 8, redistricting became less frequent, less partisan, and, hence, less transformative in its consequences. Representatives could plan and build careers in the Congress without having to fear that their district would be redrawn at any moment. And as careerism took off, changes in the internal distribution of power in the House—and, by implication, American national politics—radically shifted. With more members serving for longer, norms of seniority emerged to allocate positions of power such as committee chairmanships. The net result of these changes in redistricting practices was to lay down the building blocks for the rise of candidate-centered elections.

Gerrymandering and Public Policy

While this book is ultimately about political history, its subject is of tremendous political and practical importance. The collisions between party elites during the 19th century profoundly shaped the policy landscape, and the reverberations of these collisions continue to roil American politics.

To take one example, the American South is still emerging from a legacy of Jim Crow laws and one-party domination. The federal abandonment of Reconstruction and African-American suffrage rights in the 1870s and 1880s shaped Southern, and national, politics for succeeding generations. Indeed, it is little exaggeration to say that much of national elections and policy making between the 1870s and 1960s revolved around the dynamics of Southern politics. The one-party South guaranteed Democrats a nearly 100-seat head start in the race for majority control of the House, and, for much of this period, gave the southern wing of the Democratic Party a de facto veto over national policy making (e.g., Katznelson and Mulroy 2012; Key 1949). The subsequent transformation of Southern politics and society that has taken place since the 1960s has shaped not just policy and society in the South—it has also transformed American politics at the national level.

While this part of the narrative of American politics is well known, I show in chapters 4 and 5 that gerrymandering played a central role at pivotal junctures in Southern history. For example, gerrymandering strategies in the early 1870s helped bring Democrats to national power for the first time since the Civil War. In Southern states, gerrymandering was used as a tool to oust Republicans and bring Democrats into power both in the state legislatures and Southern congressional delegations. In the North, highly responsive gerrymanders swept Democrats into power for the first time since the Civil War.

Back in control of the House, the Democratic majority proceeded to undermine the foundations of Reconstruction policy. The result was to return the South to Democrats. In 1892, Democratic gerrymanders helped Democrats gain a majority in the House. With majority control, they were able to put the final nail in the coffin of African-American suffrage rights in the South by officially repealing the federal statutes that had been created to enforce the 15th Amendment. The federal abandonment of suffrage protection would profoundly shape Southern politics and society for the next century. It would be another 70 years before the federal government would intervene in Southern electoral politics. The legacies of these events continue to cast a long shadow over American politics and society.

Gerrymandering also shaped other foundational policy trajectories of the 19th century. As we will see in this book, the Louisiana Purchase, the Kansas-Nebraska Act, tariff regimes, and currency policy were all influenced by political alignments that had been manufactured by gerrymandering. Similarly, in the 20th century, district design fundamentally altered the policy priorities of the federal government. For example, malapportionment in House districts in the early to mid-20th century consistently produced rural majorities in the House. The result was to bias federal policy making toward agricultural interests at the expense of policies favored by metropolitan interests. From sugar subsidies to funding of school lunches, gerrymandering and malapportionment was implicated.

Gerrymandering also played a starring role in the parliamentary evolution of the House. Consider, for example, the passage of Reed's Rules—arguably the most consequential parliamentary development in the history of the House (Binder 1997; Cox and McCubbins 2005; Strahan 2007; Vallely 2009). In the 51st Congress, following the 1888 election, the Republican Speaker of the House, Thomas B. Reed (R-ME), successfully enacted a series of parliamentary rule changes that allowed the majority party—

and the speaker in particular—to break the ability of the minority party to obstruct and delay legislation.

Reed's gambit centralized legislative scheduling in the hands of the Speaker and reduced the power of minorities to obstruct legislative business; in effect, transforming the House into the highly partisan institution that it is to this day. Indeed, prominent congressional scholars like Gary Cox and Mathew McCubbins (2005) have argued that the history of the House can be divided into two periods: before and after Reed's Rules. Left out of the story, however, is that Speaker Reed, and his fellow Republicans, owed their narrow majority to a timely pro-Republican gerrymander in Pennsylvania just prior to the 1888 election. Without the strategic gerrymander in Pennsylvania, Republicans likely would have been in the minority in the 51st Congress. The subsequent development of the House—and American politics—would have been quite different.

In addition to these long-term policy and parliamentary reverberations, the evolution of redistricting created political and legal reverberations that continue to mold modern redistricting politics. The current set of laws and regulations surrounding redistricting emerged directly out of the consequences of redistricting politics in the mid-20th century. In the final chapter, I examine the current political and legal nature of modern redistricting and how it has been directly shaped by the earlier history of redistricting.

Gerrymandering Dismissed?

It is natural at this point to ask: if district design has been so influential throughout political history, why have students of U.S. politics missed its importance? I believe that the primary reason is because modern political science research has radically underestimated the importance of gerrymandering. For most political scientists, gerrymandering has more bark than bite when it comes to explaining electoral outcomes. Indeed, the majority of political-science research concludes that congressional redistricting has "minimal effects" on elections and the national distribution of seats. Bruce Cain and David Butler (1991) summarize this conventional wisdom among political scientists: "Virtually all the political science evidence to date indicates that the electoral system has little or no systematic partisan bias, and that the net partisan gains nationally from redistricting are small" (Cain and Butler 1991).[2]

Past research has offered a number of explanations for these modest effects. These explanations generally fall into one of two camps. The first focuses on the legal constraints under which modern redistricting takes place. The second argues that gerrymandering is inherently a limited tool for achieving political power. These two perspectives are not incompatible, but they do put different emphasis on the reasons why modern gerrymanders have been limited in impact.

Turning first to the legal constraints, modern mapmakers face a number of hurdles that may limit their ability to pursue full out partisan gerrymanders. Perhaps most important is that states must create congressional districts with equal population. This requirement is the outgrowth of a series of Supreme Court decisions handed down in the mid-1960s that outlawed the malapportionment of legislative districts in both House and state legislative districts. The aftermath of these cases fundamentally reshuffled political power in both the state legislatures and in Congress (Ansolabehere and Snyder 2008; Cox and Katz 2002). Across the country, political power was redistributed away from rural areas to urban and suburban regions (Ansolabehere and Snyder 2008; Cox and Katz 2002; McCubbins and Schwartz 1988).

Beyond the immediate impact on political alignments in the 1960s, the legal doctrine set down in these cases, and elaborated upon in subsequent litigation, continues to shape contemporary redistricting controversies. First and foremost, the reapportionment revolution fully enmeshed judges in the redistricting process. Redistricting nowadays takes place under the watchful eye of the courts. Although partisan gerrymandering per se has not been ruled unconstitutional, there are a number of judicially enforced rules that place limits on the creativity of partisan mapmakers. The ruling that districts must contain nearly equal population presumably has narrowed the strategic options of partisan mapmakers. Moreover, the need to adjust for intrastate population inequalities compels every state (with more than one representative) to redraw districts once a decade. Prior to the 1960s, states had much more leeway over when, and even if, to redraw district boundaries. One result was that in many states, district lines remained frozen for decades—often leading to gross inequalities in district populations and substantial partisan biases.

Alongside the one-person, one-vote doctrine, the Voting Rights Act has also given the judiciary and the Department of Justice the statutory basis for overseeing parts of the redistricting process (Canon 1999). Section 5 of the Voting Rights Act requires states with a history of discrimination against minorities—most in the South—to preclear their redistricting maps with the Department of Justice or with courts. Moreover, Section 2 of the Voting Rights Act allows the Department of Justice or private parties to challenge a redistricting plan that would dilute the voting power of racial minorities. The upshot of these various constraints is that full-blown partisan gerrymanders may be difficult to engineer without running afoul of some established statute or legal doctrine.

A second perspective argues that the partisan gains to be had from redistricting are simply limited. Politicians are often more interested in protecting themselves than in knocking off members of the opposition. This leads incumbents of both parties, it is argued, to collude with each other and create electorally safe districts for both sides. Moreover, the frequency of divided government in the states—where both parties hold a veto over any new plan—creates further conditions favorable to pro-incumbent plans. Finally, a pro-Democratic gerrymander in one state may be cancelled out by a pro-Republican gerrymander in another state, cumulating into a minimal nationwide effect. Thus, for many scholars, the political conditions for gerrymandering to matter nationally are very hard to produce.

Overall, then, the dominant view in scholarly literature is that redistricting has minimal impact on elections and public policy. Yet this research is based on the redistricting cycles that have occurred since the court-led reapportionment revolution of the 1960s. This narrow focus has led to three disadvantages. First, it has caused a huge blind spot for students of American political history. If one is told by modern researchers that gerrymandering does not matter in the present, it becomes natural to assume gerrymandering failed to matter in the past as well—this would be a fallacious conclusion. By moving beyond the relatively fixed institutional and political context of modern redistricting, 19th-century elections provide a unique opportunity to assess the competing explanations for the supposed minimal effects of contemporary redistricting.

The second disadvantage concerns contemporary efforts to reform the politics of redistricting. Contemporary politicians, Supreme Court justices, appellate judges, lawyers, and citizen-reform groups wrestle with these complex issues every decade. Too often, however, current debates over reforming redistricting are devoid of any historical context. It is my hope that this book will add some much-needed historical clarity to these debates.

The third disadvantage of this narrow focus is that a failure to understand the history of gerrymandering has led to an underestimation of gerrymandering on contemporary politics. Modern political science has been asking the wrong counterfactual. The standard approach to assessing gerrymandering is to ask whether electoral competition changes immediately after a redistricting. Because of the preoccupation with short-term, year-to-year changes, scholars have missed the long-term structural impact of districting. Did redistricting in one year alter the partisan balance nationally? But this is not the only, and maybe not the best, way to frame the counterfactual. Another, reasonable, counterfactual is to ask: what would elections to Congress look like if districting returned to pre-*Wesberry* standards?

Modern studies of redistricting analyze marginal year-to-year changes. For example, a typical study will ask: did electoral competition in Congressional elections shift between 2000 and 2002 in relation to party control of state legislatures? If not, many scholars conclude, gerrymandering does not matter. But this focus on marginal changes ignores the "base." Think of the districting system as like an iceberg. Studying electoral changes over a simple two-year cycle is like looking to see if the iceberg alters its course if a few ice chips are taken off. But this misses the impact of the iceberg itself.

Thus, one also needs to consider other counterfactuals beside a change from one year to the next. Another counterfactual is what gerrymandering and its consequences would be like if we returned to pre-*Wesberry* standards. Once we begin to look at gerrymandering through this lens, it throws into sharp relief the idea that strategic district design has, and will continue, to shape American politics. We need to ask: what is the full range of districting possibilities, and how does that stack up against contemporary practices?

Thus the wide variation in 19th century districting practices provides for a powerful and unique research opportunity. This variation can allow us to test whether the conventional political-science wisdom of minimal effects holds generally, or reflects the institutional constraints peculiar to modern redistricting. In analyzing redistricting plans and their electoral results before the 1960s, this book demonstrates substantial consequences of gerrymandering. In both the original decision by Congress to mandate single-member districts, and the subsequent state-level discretionary decisions to redraw district boundaries, the strategic calculations of political parties drove the nature and timing of institutional choice. In turn, the redistricting plans drawn by state governments in this era systematically shaped the competitiveness of congressional elections, the career paths of representatives, the partisan composition of congressional delegations, and, on occasion, even decided party control of the House of Representatives.

Plan of the Book

This book is divided into three sections. The first section (chapters 2 and 3) analyzes the causes and consequences of districting during the early republic—from 1789 to 1842. In chapter 2, I examine how district design and the rise of political parties interacted to shape the trajectory of electoral politics in the early republic. This chapter shows that districting became a partisan weapon almost from the very beginning of the republic. Moreover, some states opted not to use districts at all. Although we now take election by single-member districts for granted, the Constitution makes no mention of them. In fact, during the early republic, a number of states elected their House representatives in a system of statewide at-large elections, known as the "general ticket." Under this system, each voter cast as many votes as there were House seats to fill; the winners were the top M vote-getters, where M was the number of seats to fill. Congress banned the practice in 1842 when, as an amendment to the decennial Apportionment Act, they mandated that all states use geographically contiguous, single-member districts.[3]

Chapter 3 examines the politics behind this pivotal, but often overlooked, transformation in America's electoral structure. The majority party in Congress at the time—the Whigs—calculated they would be the losers in most general-ticket states heading into the upcoming midterm election (1842). By carving up general-ticket states into districts, Whigs stood to gain extra seats in the election and preserve their narrow majority status. The analysis of floor debates, electoral returns, and roll-call votes reveals how short-term political calculations led to the creation of this defining and enduring electoral institution.

The second, and longest, section of this book (chapters 4 through 7) examines the causes and consequences of redistricting between 1842 and 1900. This 60-year period overlaps with what political historians have dubbed "the partisan-factional" era of American politics (Silbey 1991). These years constituted a distinct political era, with unique political and partisan characteristics. The historian Joel Silbey summarizes these features: "To put it broadly, what happened in the era between 1838 and 1893 was the replacement of a political nation based on personal, family, and clan ties, and deferential informal structures, with one based on collective behavior and regularized, impersonal institutions. . . . Most critically, the political world now became deeply partisan. The primacy of political parties was the dominant fact of this political era (and of no other). Parties defined the terms of political confrontation and shaped the behavior of most participants in the many levels of political activity" (1991, 8–9).

Nowhere was the primacy of partisan politics more fully prevalent than in the design of congressional district maps. State legislatures in the 19th century did not hesitate to redistrict whenever they wanted. Some states redistricted frequently—often more than once a decade—while other states opted out of redistricting altogether. Chapter 4 investigates the timing of redistricting events during the 19th century. When a new majority party captured state government, and the existing districts were drawn by the out party, the probability of redistricting dramatically spiked up. On the other hand, when there was divided party control, or one-party domination—and the state neither gained nor lost seats at the decennial apportionment—the probability of redistricting was close to zero.

Once a state party chose to redraw district boundaries, it then faced the decision over *how* to redistrict. Chapter 5 examines the effects of redistricting on state congressional delegations and the resulting partisan composition of the House. Using statewide electoral data, the first section of this chapter shows that when a single party controlled the districting process, they were able to systematically engineer a favorable statewide partisan bias. The second part chapter 5 turns to a detailed district-level investigation of redistricting. Using county-level electoral data, the chapter demonstrates that when a single party controlled the districting process, they used districting to systematically stack the electoral deck in their favor. These partisan biases systematically structured the partisan composition of state congressional delegations and, at times, even determined party control of the House.

Chapter 6 examines competition in congressional elections. 19th-century congressional elections are notable for their intense competitiveness. Modern research argues that redistricting either reduces competition or has no effect. The results from the 19th century show that redistricting was actually used to *increase* competition. In an attempt to maximize their seats, parties carved states into districts with narrow, yet winnable, margins. The result was to manufacture competition. This chapter also explores the consequences of these strategic decisions and shows that redistricting helped contribute to the landslide elections of 1854, 1874, and 1894.

Chapter 7 explores how the variegated redistricting cycle of the 19th century shaped the decisions of congressmen to run for reelection. One of the long-noted features of the 19th-century House of Representatives, which distinguishes it from the modern Congress, is the substantial turnover in membership. This chapter shows that redistricting was a significant contributor to the high levels of 19th-century turnover. When districts were redrawn, incumbents were much less likely to run for reelection. Through a series of counterfactuals, I show that redistricting acted as a drag on the development of careerism in the House.

Chapter 8 examines the causes and consequences of malapportionment (i.e., unequal district sizes). It was the inequality of legislative districts, after all, that finally goaded the judiciary into action in the 1960s. This chapter examines the level of malapportionment and the causes of malapportionment. I show that while malapportionment did indeed exist, it accounts for only a small portion of partisan biases in the 19th century.

The final section of the book (chapters 9 and 10) carries the story forward to the present. Chapter 9 explores redistricting between 1900 and the 1960s, when the federal courts finally entered the redistricting arena. Chapter 10 concludes the book by reviewing what this research implies for the modern theory and practice of redistricting. I conclude chapter 10 by discussing the lessons provided by this book for recent developments in redistricting politics.

PART I

The Early Republic, 1789–1840

TWO

Districting and the Construction of Early American Democracy

Students of U.S. politics have long viewed political parties as essential in making a large-scale republican democracy work. Political parties coordinate the collective actions of elites and citizens. They provide for a modicum of collective responsibility that the constitutional separation of powers otherwise makes so difficult. Because political parties hold this prominent place in U.S. politics, the study of the early development of America's parties remains of much interest to political scientists and historians. In this large literature, the traditional narrative has focused heavily on contestation for the presidency (e.g., McCormick 1982) and the construction of legislative coalitions within Congress (e.g., Aldrich 1995; Hoadley 1986). The larger-than-life personalities and dramatic stakes of these battles provide much of the scholarly fodder for studies of the creation and evolution of America's first political parties.

But to a much greater extent than has been recognized by students of American political parties, congressional redistricting played a vital part in the evolution of party politics in the early republic. Although Governor Elbridge Gerry's remap of Massachusetts in 1812 is deservedly enshrined in the American political history hall of fame—and, subsequently, has become the textbook example of electoral manipulation—district design for partisan gain was not isolated to this one incident. Partisan collisions over districting pervaded the early republic, and even had antecedents in the colonial legislatures. Indeed, the construction of the first congressional districts elicited howls of protest and claims of manipulation. In Pennsylvania, for example, Federalists in the state legislature eschewed districts altogether. Instead, they made provisions to select all of Pennsylvania's congressmen in a statewide election. The result was a clean sweep for Federalist congressional candidates (Tinkcom 1950). In Virginia, Anti-Federalists in the state legislature, led by Patrick Henry, attempted to prevent James Madison's bid for a seat in the U.S. House. Henry placed Madison's home county (Orange) in "a Congressional district otherwise composed of counties considered heavily antifederal" (Ketcham 1971, 275).[1] Although Madison narrowly eked out a victory over James Monroe, the episode highlights that from the very outset of the new Constitution, party politicians—or their factional predecessors—looked to district design in the quest for political power.

Because the Constitution left to state governments the principal decisions about how to elect members of Congress, the state legislatures became primary agents in the partisan pursuit of national power. The resulting battles shaped party politics and legislative outcomes in a way that reverberated over the next two centuries and created legacies that we are still living with today. As party elites collided over district design, they forged the foundations of Congress and set the country on a fully partisan trajectory.

Choosing Districts

In forging the Constitution, the framers left many of the knotty decisions about election administration to the states. Nowhere was this more evident than in the rules governing congressional elections. Aside from specifying membership requirements and term lengths, the Constitution is otherwise silent on the specifics of how members of the U.S. House are to be elected. Although Article I, Section 5 provides Congress with the power to regulate the "times, manner, and places" of congressional elections, for much of the 18th and 19th century the federal government left it to the states to determine the mode of election. In particular, the Constitution makes no mention of House representatives being elected from geographically defined districts.

As a result, the means by which members were elected to the House differed considerably across states. Notably, a number of states elected their House representatives through a system of statewide, at-large elections, known as the "general ticket." In the first Congress, for example, five states chose to use districts and five states chose the general ticket (the other three states were allotted only one representative). In general-ticket elections, voters cast as many votes as there were seats to fill and all candidates were listed on a single slate. The winners were the top M vote-getters, where M was the number of seats to fill. Consequently, a party that garnered over 50 percent of the vote statewide could expect to win all of the congressional seats. In contrast, states divided into single-member districts allowed smaller, geographically concentrated constituencies to gain representation, reducing the chances of a party sweep of the delegation. Thus, the choice between the general ticket and districts often meant the choice between a unified or divided state party delegation.

Between 1789 and 1840, over a quarter of the states in any given Congress used the general-ticket method of electing representatives, yielding an average of 15 percent of the House membership (see fig. 2.1). Under the general ticket, candidates campaigned statewide in at-large elections. Each voter was allotted as many votes as there were seats to fill, but could not give any candidate more than a single vote.[2] If a majority of voters in the state preferred one party over the other, the result would almost always be a one-party sweep of the delegation (Calabrese 2000; Scarrow 1999). A stylized depiction of the winner-take-all nature of general-ticket elections is illustrated in figure 2.2. This figure plots a hypothetical vote-seat curve for general-ticket elections. As can be seen, the translation of votes into seats is an all or nothing affair. Parties polling over 50 percent of the two-party vote receive everything while parties polling anything less than 50 percent can expect to receive nothing.

By contrast single-member districts fail to reward larger parties nearly as much (at the state level). A party that polls less than 50 percent still has a fighting chance of winning some seats—provided their supporters are geographically concentrated enough to constitute a majority in one or more districts. The s-shaped curve in figure 2.2 represents a stylized depiction of the single-member district votes-to-seats translation. This figure presents the familiar cube law, which the modern electoral-systems literature uses to serve as a rough approximation of the vote-seat translation in regimes using first-past-the-post single-member districts (King 1989; Rae 1967; Tufte 1973). As the two curves illustrate, a party winning, say, 40 percent of the statewide vote can expect to get roughly a quarter of the state delegation under single-member districts, whereas under the general ticket, they would get nothing.

The depictions of the vote-seat curves in figure 2.2 are, admittedly, theoretical. How well do they stack up against actual congressional election results during the early 19th century? Figure 2.3 plots the actual Demo-

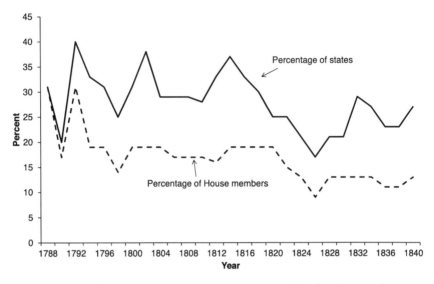

Fig. 2.1. Percentage of states and congressional membership using the general ticket, 1788–1840. (Data compiled by the author from information in Martis 1982, table 2, 4–5.)

cratic statewide vote share against their statewide seat share for both districts and general ticket from 1800–1840.[3] The pattern largely conforms to what one would expect. The all-or-nothing nature of the general ticket is abundantly clear with almost all of the seat shares falling at the extremes of zero or one. The vote-seat plot for districts, on the other hand, is more evenly distributed.

More detailed evidence of the consequences of these two systems for the partisan composition of state delegations can be seen by examining the incidence of unified delegations under both districts and general ticket. Table 2.1 presents these percentages for all congressional elections, for states with more than one representative, from 1800 to 1840. Over 95 percent of the elections held under general ticket resulted in unified party delegations, while only 28 percent were unified under districts. As these numbers indicate, a general-ticket election did not always guarantee a unified delegation, but compared to districts, the probability of a party sweep was significantly greater.

Given the striking differences between the two electoral systems, one would reasonably suspect that choosing the rules would create a ripe opportunity for either partisan gain or partisan retrenchment. We can more clearly see the impact of partisanship on the decision to adopt dis-

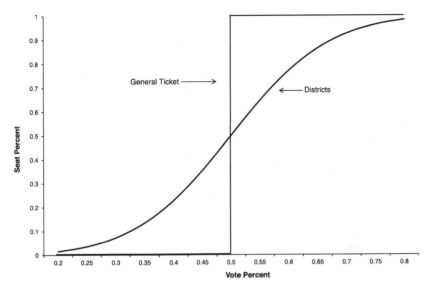

Fig. 2.2. Hypothetical vote-seat translation under general ticket and single-member districts

TABLE 2.1. The Incidence of Unified House Delegations, 1800–1840

	Districts	General Ticket
Unified Delegation	74 (27.7%)	116 (95.1%)
Nonunified Delegation	193 (72.3%)	6 (4.9%)
Total	267	122

Source: Rusk 2001.
Note: Column percentages in parentheses.
$\chi^2 = 152.1; p < .01.$

tricts or the general ticket by considering the logic which would produce changes in the electoral laws governing congressional elections at the state level. Changing the electoral system required both an opportunity and a motive. On the opportunity side, we would expect any changes to the electoral system to only occur when there was unified partisan control of state government. During periods of divided control, each side can block the others' schemes. Thus, one would expect changes in the electoral laws to occur only when there was unified party control of state government.

But of course there were a large number of cases of unified party control that failed to produce a switch in electoral system. Hence the next

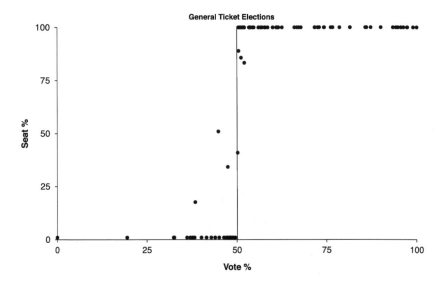

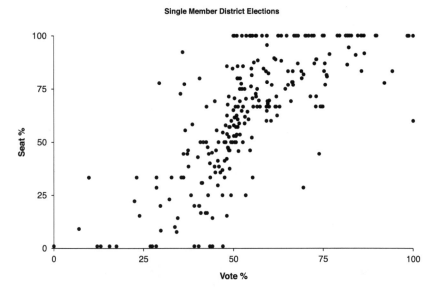

Fig. 2.3. Vote-seat distribution under general ticket and single-member districts, 1800–1840

question is: what motivated parties to either alter the electoral system or continue with the status quo? The logic would be that in states where a one faction could expect to consistently outpoll the opposition in a statewide vote, the general-ticket mode of election would maximize their seat share. In effect, they could turn a majority vote into a winner-take-all electoral system. On the other hand, where parties (or factions) might anticipate their vote share to decline in the future, switching, or maintaining, districts would make more sense.

Ideally, one would like to test these expectations with an empirical model, but the absence of reliable data on party ratios in the early state legislatures makes a straightforward empirical test difficult. Nevertheless, one can find ample anecdotal evidence of political shenanigans driving the choice of electoral system in various state histories. For example, in Pennsylvania, the system for choosing representatives to the national government emerged as a major source of contention within the state legislature. The Pennsylvania legislature chose to adopt the general ticket for the first federal elections. In doing so, Federalists in the state legislature sought to ensure a unified Federalist delegation to the House. Prior to the next election, the state switched to districts. The switch to districts passed by a single vote and was prompted by concerns of western Pennsylvanians—the site of growing Republican sentiment—that they were underrepresented by the general ticket (Hoadley 1986, 36; Tinkcom 1950). The switch passed by a single vote in the assembly with Republican-leaning legislators siding in favor. In 1792, the state again switched back to the general ticket on a closely divided vote within the legislature (Tinkcom 1950, 51), and then finally settled on districts in 1794.[4]

New Jersey provides another interesting case. From 1788 to 1840, New Jersey operated primarily with the general ticket. But two attempts to move the state onto the district system illustrate the political machinations that the freedom of district design created. The early decision to adopt the general ticket was pushed by factions in west New Jersey who were primarily supportive of the Federalists. Confident that they would win the statewide vote, they saw a clear advantage in employing the general ticket (McCormick 1953, 107). In three subsequent legislative sessions, Anti-Federalists attempted to pass a districting plan, "but met with defeat in the legislature" (McCormick 1953, 108). Republican forces finally succeeded in carving the state into districts for the 1798 election. The effort paid off as Republicans converted a 0–5 deficit in the previous election into a 3–2 majority of the congressional delegation. Federalist forces in the state legislature, two years later, responded by switching the state back to the general ticket. The switch, although motivated by partisan concerns, backfired on the Federalist Party as they narrowly lost a statewide majority, and, therefore, lost all of their seats in Congress. As the political historian Richard P. McCormick wryly noted, "Once in control the new party [Republicans] abandoned its earlier advocacy of district elections and capitalized to the fullest extent on its power" (1953, 108).

Partisan jockeying over electoral systems was not confined to Northern states. In 1841, the Democratic-controlled state legislature in Alabama passed a general-ticket law, seeking to convert a narrow 3–2 Democratic advantage in the congressional delegation into a 5–0 advantage in the subsequent congressional elections. The effort succeeded. As we see in the next chapter, the actions in Alabama prompted members of the Whig Party in Congress to respond in-kind and outlaw general-ticket elections altogether.

These anecdotes provide ample evidence that state politicians, early on, realized the potential gains from the manipulation of electoral law. As we see in the next chapter, it was only with federal intervention in 1842 that put an end to the widespread use of the general ticket.

Designing Districts

For states that opted to divide their state into districts, the decision became how and where to place district lines. The entry of the term "gerrymandering" into the political vernacular, in 1812, can lead to the mistaken impression that partisan monkey business started in 1812. However, one can easily find examples of district manipulation well before 1812 and Gerry's map. In this era before court supervision, states were free to construct districts largely as they sought fit. The maps were codified through the standard statutory process, which meant that the two chambers of the state legislature had to jointly agree to pass a redistricting bill and that bill then had to be signed by the governor. Where a single party had majority control of the state legislature and the governorship—or had a large enough majority to override a gubernatorial veto, or the governor lacked a veto—they were in prime position to draw maps to greatly advantage their congressional brethren.

In designing districts for partisan advantage, mapmakers typically chose from one of two recipes. One was to pack as many of the opposition voters into a single district while spreading their followers into narrow, yet winnable, districts. This strategy concedes one or more districts to the opposition, but in such a way as to force the opposition to waste many of their votes. While the packing strategy has many advantages, it has one drawback: it concedes one or more districts to the opposition. Thus, a second gerrymandering strategy is to turn each district into a microcosm of the statewide vote. Where the dominant party can expect to win the statewide vote in the near future, an optimal strategy is to have each district mirror this favorable statewide vote (Cain 1984, 1985; Owen and Grofman 1988). By efficiently distributing its supporters in marginal, but winnable, districts, this "efficient gerrymander" strategy allows the controlling party to win every seat in the state.

Were state parties of the early republic using redistricting to alter the partisan tilt of their state congressional delegations and possibly alter the partisan composition of the House of Representatives? One way to answer this question is to analyze the effect of districting partisanship on the translation of votes into seats. Applying standard reasoning in the redistricting literature, one can think of districting plans as affecting two elements of the vote-seat translation: partisan bias and electoral responsiveness (e.g., Gelman and King 1994; Tufte 1973). Partisan bias is defined "as the difference between the expected seat share that the Democrats would get with an average vote share of 0.5 and their 'fair share' of 0.5 (half the seats for half the votes)" (Cox and Katz 1999, 820). A districting plan that packed Federalist voters into a few safe districts and placed Democratic-Republicans in a number of marginal, yet winnable, districts, would produce a pro-Democratic-Republican bias. In other words, they would win more than their fair share of seats given their overall vote.

Electoral responsiveness—or the swing ratio—is the change in a party's aggregate seat share given a 1 percent change in their vote share. For example, a responsiveness value of three indicates that a shift in the statewide vote from 50 percent to 51 percent would produce a corresponding three-percentage-point seat shift. A districting plan with a number of marginal, highly competitive districts will have a high value of responsiveness (i.e., a small swing in the statewide vote will generate a large swing in seats). A plan with numerous safe seats will have a lower level of responsiveness because it will take a large swing in the statewide vote before seats start changing hands.

With these twin concepts in hand, one can model the impact of differing redistricting plans on electoral outcomes. Data on the timing of redistricting events comes from Martis (1982) which lists the precise date when every redistricting plan became law. Matching these dates with party control of state government allows us to classify the partisanship of redistricting plans. The data on party control of the state legislatures during this period comes from Dubin (2007). In the small number of cases where Dubin's information on the partisanship of the state legislature was missing, the winner of the U.S. Senate election served as a proxy for party control of the state legislature. Because state legislatures chose senators during this era of indirect elections, the victor of the Senate contest should provide a close approximation of party control of the state government.

Using the information on the date of redistricting and partisanship of state government at the time of redistricting, redistricting plans from 1800 to 1824 were classified into one of three categories: Democratic-Republican, Federalist, or Bipartisan. From 1826 to 1832, plans were classified as Democratic (Jacksonian), National Republican, or Bipartisan. Then, from 1834 to 1840, new plans were coded as Democratic, Whig, or Bipartisan. Bipartisan plans were plans passed during periods of divided government. This happened either when there was split partisan control of the legislature or when there was a unified party legislature, but the legislature lacked sufficient votes to override the veto of an opposition party governor. It is worth noting that during this period there were few bipartisan plans; almost all were passed by unified partisan majorities.

Following standard practice in the electoral systems literature (e.g., Grofman 1983; Tufte 1973), one can estimate the bias and responsiveness of districting plans using the following vote-seat equation:

$$ln(s_{it}/(1 - s_{it})) = \lambda + \rho(ln(v_{it}/(1 - v_{it}))) \tag{1}$$

where s_{it} is the proportion of seats won by the Democratic-Republicans, and v_{it} is their vote share in state i at time t.[5] The model includes a constant, λ, measuring partisan bias, and an independent variable, $ln(v_{it}/(1 - v_{it}))$, with the coefficient ρ measuring electoral responsiveness.[6] Like Cox and Katz (2002), the measures of bias (λ) and responsiveness (ρ) were estimated separately for each type of districting plan. In addition, anticipating that congressional elections within a state might affect one another, the model was estimated with an extended beta-binomial distribution (Cox and Katz 2002; King 1998).[7] This model is appropriate given that the dependent variable is a proportion and that there is potential correlation in the probability across districts (within a state) of a Democratic-Republican victory.

The estimates of partisan bias and electoral responsiveness are displayed in table 2.2. The top panel displays the results from 1802 to 1820. They show that Republican dominance of the House was greatly aided by districting regimes. Partisan Republican plans produced a bias of 8.66 percent in favor of Republican candidates. In other words, with 50 percent of the statewide, Republicans won 58.66 percent of the congressional seats. Interestingly, bias for Federalist plans was not significantly different than zero. The likely explanation is the relatively small number of Federalist redistricting plans. Moreover, in states where Federalists had drawn the maps, Republicans continued to perform well. Nevertheless, the strong bias produced by Republican plans coupled with the larger number of Republican-drawn plans helped produce Republican dominance of the Congress from 1802 to 1820. Aside from a brief resurgence of Federalists in the early 1810s, following a negative public reaction over the War of 1812, the Federalists were relegated to permanent minority status.

From 1822 to 1840, one finds a strong bias in favor of Democratic (and later Jacksonian Democratic) plans. Indeed, the bias was staggering. With

TABLE 2.2. The Vote-to-Seat Translation in the Early Republic

	1802–20	
Plan Type	Partisan Bias	Electoral Responsiveness
Democrat-Republican	8.66*	1.70*
	(3.00)	(.19)
Federalist	5.72	3.44*
	(4.98)	(.87)
γ	.006	
	(.01)	
Log-Likelihood	−631.64	
Number of Observations	108	
	1822–40	
Plan Type	Bias	Responsiveness
Democrat-Republican/Jackson	17.92*	.85*
Democrat	(2.99)	(.21)
Bipartisan	21.30	5.08*
	(14.11)	(2.16)
National Republican/Whig	−1.99	2.32*
	(17.92)	(.64)
γ	.12	
	(.03)	
Log-Likelihood	−995.58	
Number of Observations	159	

Note: The table presents maximum likelihood estimates of partisan bias and electoral responsiveness using an extended beta binomial distribution. Standard errors are in parentheses.

*$p < .05$.

50 percent of the vote, Democrats could expect to win 67.92 percent of the statewide seats. Moreover, the responsiveness of Democratic plans was almost one. In other words, Democratic plans during this period produced very low levels of competition and substantial level of bias. On the other side, National Republican (and later Whig) plans produced insignificant amounts of bias. Although the coefficient on bias was negative, indicating a small amount of pro-National Republican/Whig bias, it was nowhere near statistical significance. Again, like the results for the Federalists, these insignificant results partially reflect the small number of redistricting plans that were drawn by National Republicans or Whigs.

Turning to the estimates for electoral responsiveness, one finds relatively low levels of responsiveness for all of the partisan redistricting plans. These results show that it took a fairly large change in the vote to produce a big swing in seats. Some of this may have reflected the comparatively modest levels of competition for control of the House of Representatives. Rather than scouring for extra seats, by boosting the swing ratio, the maps appeared to lock in the gains that Republicans had already made. This strategy contrasts with the one pursued by parties later in the 19th century. As we see in later chapters, as mass-based political parties emerged in the 1840s, mapmakers adjusted their strategies; pursuing plans with much higher swing ratios and more competitive district margins, with the aim of ratcheting up their seat shares. As we will see, this shift in strategies toward hyperresponsive gerrymanders reverberated across the political landscape, producing fiercely fought congressional elections and rapid turnover of the congressional membership.

Redistricting and Reapportionment

The previous section shows that parties—and, in particular, the Democratic-Republicans (and later the Jackson Democrats)—successfully used district design to drastically bias electoral outcomes in their favor. Coupled with the strategic use of district design was the interaction with federal reapportionment. Then as now, following each census, the states are reallocated seats in the House proportional to their state population. Nowadays, because the size of the House has remained fixed at 435 (since 1911), seats are simply reshuffled among the states; with some states gaining a few seats and some state losing a few. Because modern population shifts within the country over the course of a single decade tend not to be overly dramatic, the number of seats gained or lost by a state tends to be modest. But in the

19th century, the size of the House was not fixed. Typically following a census, Congress voted to increase the size of the House to adjust for both the admittance of new states into the Union and overall population growth. Consequently, most states received additional seats following a census. And some states received a large bounty of new seats. Following the 1801 reapportionment, for example, New York saw its House delegation increase from 10 to 17. Ten years later, New York's allotment increased again, rising from 17 to 27.

These sizable increases in seat delegations provided crafty mapmakers with ample material to radically increase their partisan seat shares. By packing opponents into a few safe districts and shoehorning the new seats into favorable territory, state parties could quickly and dramatically ramp up their House delegations. To see what extent the interaction of partisanship and reapportionment influenced election results, table 2.3 presents a model predicting increases in partisan seat shares. The dependent variable is the difference in Democratic-Republican seats, within a state, between the current and prior election. Thus, the dependent variable tells us whether, and by how many, Democratic-Republicans increased (or decreased) their seat shares within a state in a given election. The key independent variable indicates what type of redistricting plan was implemented when a state gained seats: Democratic-Republican, Federalist, or Bipartisan. From 1826 to 1834, plans were classified as Democratic (Jacksonian), National Republican, or Bipartisan. Then, from 1834 to 1840, new plans were coded as Democratic, Whig, or Bipartisan. The type of partisan plan was then interacted with a variable indicating whether the state redistricted or not in a given year. This interactive variable tells us whether redistricting increased seat shares conditional on the type of redistricting plan that was drawn.

The results in table 2.3 demonstrate a clear impact of partisan districting on electoral outcomes. Setting the prior seat share and change in vote share at their average values, the model predicts that when Republicans redistricted, their seat shares increased by an average of 2.16 seats. The model also predicts that in non-redistricting years, under Republican-drawn maps, the change in seat shares were statistically indistinguishable from zero. This suggests that the big marginal impact of redistricting and reapportionment happened right after a new map was drawn. Put together with the prior estimates of partisan bias, the results show that parties typically maintained this seat boost over the course of a redistricting plan. Given that the model controls for changes in Republican vote shares, the seat increases can fairly be attributed to redistricting.

Interestingly, the model predicts that Federalists (and later Whigs) gained little marginal increase from reapportionment and redistricting. In both cases, the predicted increase in seat shares following a Federalist or Whig redistricting was statistically indistinguishable from zero. Given that most of the growth in population happened in western regions, which tended to be rich with Democratic-Republican (and later Jacksonian Democratic) votes, it is little surprise that Federalists found little aggregate gain in the reapportionment process. Thus, federal reapportionment and control of redistricting at the state level reinforced the dominance of the Democratic-Republicans following the election of 1800. This advantage held for the next 40 years. As we see later, in the rest of this section, the gains made by Democratic-Republicans from redistricting reapportionment put them in a position to not only further enhance their own fortunes, but to fundamentally alter the trajectory of American history.

1802: Reapportionment, Redistricting, and the Louisiana Purchase

Perhaps nowhere was the impact of redistricting and reapportionment more pivotal than in the 1802–03 congressional elections and the subse-

TABLE 2.3. Redistricting, Reapportionment, and Seat Gains, 1800–1840

Independent Variable	Coefficient
Redistricting	2.39*
	(.61)
Redistricting × Federalist (or National Republican or Whig) Plan	−1.96*
	(.89)
Redistricting × Bipartisan Plan	3.35*
	(.62)
Federalist (or National Republican or Whig) Plan	−.98*
	(.44)
Bipartisan Plan	−1.25*
	(.17)
Vote Change	.08*
	(.02)
Previous Democratic-Republican Seat Share	−.03*
	(.005)
Constant	2.13*
	(.42)
Number of Observations	258
R^2	.35

Note: The dependent variable is the change in Democratic-Republican seat shares between the prior and current election. Robust standard errors, clustered by state, are in parentheses.
*$p < .05$.

quent 8th Congress. In the 1801 reapportionment, Congress made provisions to increase the House from 106 to 142 members.

Because growth in southern and western regions of the country far outpaced growth in the Northeast, states with significant western land saw their seat shares radically increase. Table 2.4 reports that the states gaining seats tended to be more Democratic-Republican than other states. States where Democratic-Republicans controlled the redistricting process saw their total seat share in the House increase from 61 seats in 1800 to 98 seats in 1802. The biggest gains came in states like New York (+7), South Carolina (+3), and Pennsylvania (+5), which all had significant population

TABLE 2.4. The Joint Impact of Reapportionment and Redistricting

	1802					
Type of Plan	Total Seat Change			Democratic-Republican Seat Change		
	1800	1802	Change	1800	1802	Change
Democratic-Republican	61	98	+37	45	71	+26
Federalist	14	17	+3	5	7	+2
General Ticket	21	27	+6	10	15	+5
	1812					
Type of Plan	Total Seat Change			Democratic-Republican Seat Change		
	1810	1812	Change	1810	1812	Change
Democratic-Republican	104	137	+33	79	89	+10
Federalist	6	6	0	6	2	−4
General Ticket	28	33	+5	15	14	−1
	1822					
Type of Plan	Total Seat Change			Democratic-Republican Seat Change		
	1820	1822	Change	1820	1822	Change
Democratic-Republican	105	134	+29	90	87	−3
Federalist	20	13	−7	4	6	+2
General Ticket	27	36	+9	24	26	+2
	1832					
Type of Plan	Total Seat Change			Democratic Seat Change		
	1830	1832	Change	1830	1832	Change
Democratic	75	118	+16	75	88	+13
National Republican	53	57	+4	17	21	+4
Bipartisan	3	7	+4	3	6	+3
General Ticket	28	30	+2	14	22	+8

growth in the western parts of their states; areas which tended to favor Democratic-Republicans. The Federalists, on the other hand, only gained three total seats.

Second, Democratic-Republicans controlled redistricting in most of the states slated to gain the largest number of seats. They were able to use their control to enhance their numbers in Congress. The effectiveness of Republican district maps can be seen in the second panel of table 2.4, which lists the number of seats gained by Republicans across the different redistricting regimes. Of the 37 total House seats gained in states where Republicans controlled redistricting, 26 elected Republicans to Congress. The lopsided results in big states where Republicans controlled the redistricting process—that is, Pennsylvania, New York, and Virginia—swung the national political balance firmly in Republicans' favor.

So potent was the impact of Republican redistricting efforts that Republicans achieved that *rara avis* of American politics—a presidential gain in midterm elections. Republicans increased their share of House seats from 60 percent to 71 percent despite an increase of only 1.2 percent in vote share (Rusk 2002). Most of this gain can be directly attributed to the federal reapportionment and how the resulting districts were redrawn.

The added seats, moreover, transformed what had been a modest Republican majority in the prior Congress into a formidable legislative machine bent on reversing a decade worth of Federalist policy (Cunningham 1963; Smelser 1968). Nowhere was the legislative power of the Republican majority more fully exercised than in the decision to expand the United States into a continental power. During the 8th Congress, the primary legislative battle was over whether to accept, and approve a funding plan for, the Louisiana Purchase. Arguably no federal action had a more dramatic impact on the trajectory of American history than the Louisiana Purchase. The acquisition of the Louisiana territory from France for $15 million doubled the territory of the United States and removed France as a rival in the western interior. The purchase opened the western continent to the United States, and, thereby, fundamentally altered the future of American history.

Although the story of the Louisiana Purchase is now told as a bravura act of negotiation by Thomas Jefferson—or, more accurately, his diplomatic delegates James Monroe and Robert Livingston—over Napoleon Bonaparte, the purchase generated considerable domestic opposition. In particular, a formidable resistance to the purchase arose in Congress. Although the Jefferson administration had taken the lead in negotiating the treaty, Congress still played an essential role in making the purchase happen. While the Senate was responsible for ratifying the treaty, the purchase also required a funding plan. As a result, assent from the House was necessary if the purchase was to go through.

When the issue came before Congress, it met with considerable opposition. In particular, the battle lines were refracted through the polarized partisan atmosphere of the time. As Theriault has argued, the two parties "were *the* organizing units behind the Louisiana Purchase debate" (Theriault 2006, 310–11). A number of Federalist leaders in Congress, in particular, were vocal in their opposition to the purchase. The central rhetorical plank of the opponent's argument was that France had no legal basis to sell the land to the United States in the first place. These opponents argued that the land belonged to Spain, and that France was therefore not in a legal position to sell the territory.[8]

There were four votes in the House related to the purchase. But two stood out. First was a vote in the House on a resolution to require President Jefferson to turn over all his documents related to the retrocession of the Louisiana Territory. The motivation behind the request was an attempt by Federalists to challenge whether Spain had actually ceded the Louisiana Territory to France. The amendment, offered by the New York Federalist Gaylord Griswold, called upon Jefferson to produce a copy of the original treaty between France and Spain, and the deed ceding the territory from to France. Griswold, and other Federalists, contended that Spain had never ceded the land to France, and therefore, "Napoleon had concocted a fraudulent sale to squeeze money out of the United States" (DeConde 1976, 189). The political motive behind this legislative maneuver was to nullify the purchase and ultimately embarrass the president (DeConde 1976, 189–90).

Defeating this resolution, therefore, was a necessary step in the Republicans' path to approving the purchase and appropriating the requisite funds. The vote failed by a mere two votes: 57 to 59. All but one Federalist voted against, while Republicans split. Thus, had there been more Federalists in the House the resolution likely would have passed and created a major stumbling block to congressional approval of the purchase and subsequent appropriations.

A second vote on approving the act also narrowly passed (Theriault 2006, 312). This vote too broke down largely along party lines. The Federalists, looking for a wedge issue to distinguish themselves from the Jefferson administration, voted against the purchase, while Republicans almost uniformly voted in favor. Again, the padded Republican majority gave them enough votes to secure passage of the appropriations bill. On both of these pivotal roll-call votes, we can see the vital role played by gerrymandering. Absent the additional seats picked up in the 1802 round of redistricting, Republicans likely would have failed to defeat the Federalist attempts to block the purchase. It is an understatement to say that the course of American history would have been radically different had the purchase deal fallen through.

From the perspective of national party politics, the Louisiana Purchase "guaranteed a further lightening of New England's relative weight in the national scale" (Smelser 1968, 76). More pointedly, it further lightened the relative weight of Federalists in national politics. Thus, the purchase signaled the beginning of the end for the Federalists as a viable national party. Although they would continue to win the occasional congressional and state election in the Northeast, their time as an effective nationwide party was soon to come to an end.

1812: War and the Original Gerrymander

The interaction between party fortunes, electoral rules, and policy outcomes continued throughout the next decade. The 1811 reapportionment provided for an increase in the size of the House from 142 to 182 members. As table 2.4 shows, states where Republicans controlled the redistricting process gained the lion's share of these new seats. However, before Republicans could fully translate their control of maps into seats, political events intervened. Voter dissatisfaction with the War of 1812 led to significant Republican vote losses in the 1812–13 election. Their seat share in the House dropped from 70 percent to 61 percent. Yet Republican dominance of mapmaking staved off a full-blown electoral disaster. Without the cushion given to them by redistricting, Republican seat losses likely would have been a lot worse. The Republicans' total share of the national vote was 49.9 percent while the Federalist share was 48.7 percent. In other words, a dead heat. Despite the virtual tie in vote shares, Republicans still captured control of the House, winning 110 seats to the Federalists' 72 (Rusk 2002, 215–18).

The extra boost in seats provided Republicans with a solid working majority in the House despite evenly splitting the congressional vote with Federalists. And they needed every one of these votes to pursue their policy agenda. The 13th Congress took place in the middle of the war with the British Empire that had started in 1812. House Federalists, generally opposed to President Madison's prosecution of the war, sought to draw a strong contrast with both congressional Republicans and President Madison (Ketcham 1971, 591–92). The end product of this strategy was fierce partisan polarization. Indeed, the 13th Congress was one of the most polarized in U.S. history. Of the 352 roll-call votes in the House, 303 met the traditional definition of a party unity vote, where at least 50 percent of the membership of one party voted in opposition to at least 50 percent of the other party. Thus, 86 percent of roll-call votes split along party lines. In fact, this Congress had the second-highest level of party unity voting in the history of the House (second only to the 58th Congress, which was elected in 1902).

Congress fought over a number significant issues ranging from appropriations to the military, whether to shut down domestic ports to prevent supplies reaching British forces in the states, how to respond to British impressment of seamen on American ships, and whether to recharter the temporarily defunct national bank. Each of these issues was decided in close votes along partisan lines. Congress even split along party lines over the appropriate response to the burning of the Capitol Building. In a narrowly decided vote, Republicans defeated a bill that would have temporarily removed the seat of government from Washington, DC, until the end of the war.

One place where Republican districting efforts may have backfired was the redistricting in Massachusetts—the original "gerrymander." The now-famous map, and much of the outrage, concerned the districting of the state senate by Republicans. But congressional districts were also crafted with an eye toward boosting Republican seat shares in Congress. The map, however, failed to prevent a Federalist triumph in the 1812 election. Federalists won 80 percent of the House seats in the 1812 election and recaptured control of the state legislature. Presaging events in Texas 190 years later, the new Federalist majority set about remapping congressional districts to further enhance the prospects of Federalist congressional candidates in the 1814 election. The remapping efforts succeeded as Federalists captured 18 of the state's 20 seats. With 66 percent of the statewide vote, Federalists won 90 percent of the congressional seats.

Outside of northeastern states like Massachusetts, however, the prospects for the Federalists as a national party remained bleak. Growing population in the West and South, combined with the partisan crafting of congressional districts by Republican mapmakers ultimately doomed the Federalists in congressional elections. By the late 1810s, Federalists ceased to exist as an effective party competing on a national scale.

1822: Redistricting in the Era of Good Feelings

The demise of the Federalists ushered in the so-called Era of Good Feel-ings. This ironic title denoted the brief period in which Republicans dominated the government. Given the absence of interparty competition, the incentives to gerrymander for partisan gain briefly lost some of their steam. In a few places, however, mapmakers still found room and reason to manipulate district lines. In particular, where the last vestiges of Federal-ism still existed, they sought to mold districts to shut out Republicans. In Massachusetts, notably, Federalists still controlled the state government. Prior to the 1822 election, Federalists "sought to shut out their opponents in the congressional election by resorting to partisan districts" (Griffith 1907, 101). Their efforts paid off. Federalists, despite being knocked down nationally, held onto 7 of the 13 districts in Massachusetts in 1822. Out-side of Massachusetts, however, Republican dominance of the redistricting process helped reproduce their dominance in congressional elections (see table 2.4).

1832: Redistricting and the Bank War

The emergence of the Democratic Party behind the candidacy of Andrew Jackson in the presidential election of 1828 reenergized two-party com-petition both across the country and within the House. By the time a new reapportionment was scheduled to take place in 1831, two-party competi-tion had reemerged in many parts of the country. The rise of party com-petition also reignited redistricting battles across the states. Reapportion-ment aided Democrats in greater numbers than the National Republicans. States where Democrats controlled the redistricting process gained 16 new seats in the reapportionment compared to 4 in National Republican-controlled states. This increase in seats combined with partisan control of the mapmaking process greatly reinforced Democrats' hold on the House. In Massachusetts, for example, the bill to redistrict congressional districts was subject to four weeks of heated debate in the legislature (Griffith 1907, 106). National Republicans in the legislature sought not just to dilute the Democratic vote, but also to snub the upstart Anti-Masonic vote. The map worked, as Republicans won 11 of the 12 congressional seats with 57.9 per-cent of the statewide vote. The map also put an end to any hope the Anti-Masons had of establishing themselves as a viable opposition in the state. As Griffith writes, "Not long after this election, the Antimasonic party in Massachusetts began to be merged in other parties and gradually lost its identity" (Griffith 1907, 108).

Outside of the Northeast, however, the vast bulk of districting plans worked to the advantage of Democratic congressional candidates. As the estimates of partisan bias indicated, Democratic plans in this period heavily favored Democratic candidates. The product of this bias can be seen in the 1832 congressional election. In the election, Democrats won 60 percent of the House seats despite garnering a slim 51.4 percent of the national vote (Rusk 2002, 222).

The majority in the House proved decisive during the subsequent Congress. The 23rd Congress was extremely turbulent. Prior to the election of 1832, President Andrew Jackson had, in a highly controversial decision, vetoed the rechartering of the Bank of the United States. Following his reelection in 1832, President Jackson continued his battle against the bank by unilaterally withdrawing federal funds from its control (Remini 1967). The decision created a massive uproar and roiled the 23rd Congress. The Senate, in particular, was not inclined to sit back and support the president's actions. The Senate was controlled by anti-Jackson forces led by Senator Henry Clay. Indeed, the Senate, for the only time in its history, formally censured the president. Given Senate hostility toward Jackson, Democratic control of the House became essential in providing political cover for Jackson's decision to withdraw funds from the bank. Democrats in the House were by no means fully supportive of Jackson's decision. However, they did eventually line up behind the president, passing a series of resolutions supporting the funding withdrawal. Absent a majority in the House, the Bank War likely would not have been won by Jacksonians. The consequences were enormous and reverberated beyond the narrow confines of economic policy. As the historian Daniel Feller has written, Jackson's victory in the Bank War "shaped the new Whig and Democratic parties and reshaped the balance of power within the federal government" (Feller 2004, 164). As we will see in the rest of this book, the emergence of fierce competition between these two mass-based political parties ushered in an entirely new era of redistricting politics.

Parties and Institutional Choice in the Early Republic

A vast literature in political science has analyzed the profound impact of voting rules and the translation of into seats on the behavior of legislatures and parties. Electoral rules profoundly shape the behavior of legislators and the structure of party systems. In the contemporary United States, political parties compete within a relatively well-defined and regulated institutional framework. Federal elections are held on the same day. Balloting rules are nearly similar across states. Rules for financing federal campaigns are standardized across jurisdictions. Thus, it can be easy for modern observers to miss the pervasive influence of electoral rules on political competition.

During the early republic, however, the rules were themselves objects of violent contestation. Parties arose not just in response to the incentives provided by electoral rules, but also as a means to bend and influence the rules for personal and partisan gain. The high-stakes politics of the early republic included fights over the rules themselves. The result was great variance across states over how elections were conducted. Nowhere was this more evident than in the decisions over how to elect congressmen. Whether to elect members in geographic districts or in statewide at-large elections constituted one choice. States choosing to use districts then faced a second-order choice: where to place district boundaries. The result of this freedom was wide diversity in how members of the House were elected and how they behaved in the legislature.

By 1840, however, diversity began to give way to uniformity. This quiet revolution in electoral laws has gone largely unnoticed, but it is essential to understanding the early development of American politics. According to the historian Richard L. McCormick, "To put the matter simply, the rules under which the political game was to be played changed greatly between 1800 and 1840. The most obvious development was a trend from diversity to uniformity in governmental structures and electoral procedures from state to state. The magnitude and significance of this quiet revolution in the electoral environment has generally been ignored, except for a curious preoccupation with modification in suffrage qualifications" (McCormick 1967, 110). The next chapter explores one of the transformational moments in this institutional revolution—the decision by Congress to mandate single-member districts for all House elections.

THREE

The Origins of Single-Member Districts

As we saw in the previous chapter, between 1789 and 1840 over a quarter of the states in any given Congress used the general-ticket method of electing representatives. But in 1842, Congress abruptly voted to end the practice. Why did Congress change the rules of the game and why did it happen in 1842? Given that the electoral rules had clear partisan consequences, one might suspect that reform was ripe for strategic manipulation. By the election of 1840, the second-party system had reached full steam (Aldrich 1995; McCormick 1966; Silbey 1991). The parties had developed into large-scale electoral machines focused on winning mass-based elections and capturing control of the national government. The intense competition to win elections on a nationwide scale further increased the incentives for parties to seek out every possible advantage, including manipulating the rules of the game.

This incentive was evident in the switch to single-member districts. The census of 1840, which formed the basis for reapportioning state representation in the House, indicated that most of the general-ticket states where Democrats were strong would be gaining seats, while the general-ticket states where Whigs were strong would be losing seats. Single-member districts gave Whigs a greater chance of winning some seats in Democrats' general-ticket bastions. By outlawing the general ticket, Whigs were trying to pick up extra seats—or, at the least—minimize the potential loss of seats that the new apportionment promised. In addition, Whigs had the opportunity to make such a change. For the only time in their brief history, Whigs had control of both Congress and the presidency. Thus, the switch to single-member districts was the result of the newly dominant Whigs manipulating the rules of the electoral game to try and maintain their majority in the House.

Beyond highlighting this pivotal, but often forgotten, transformation in the American system of representation, this chapter makes a broader contribution to our understanding of the origins of electoral rules. A vast body of research demonstrates the consequences of electoral institutions on party systems and representation. Electoral institutions, however, are not preordained (e.g., Bawn 1993; Cox 1997; Remington and Smith 1996). They are fashioned by politicians who have a vested interest in their effects. The results presented in this chapter remind us that even the seemingly most fundamental of political institutions can be created out of short-term political considerations.

The Apportionment Act of 1842

Political historians generally acknowledge the election of 1840 as a watershed moment in the development of American political parties (McCormick 1966; Silbey 1991). The famous campaign of "log cabins and hard cider" marked the culmination of party development that began with the rise of the Jackson-led Democratic party in the 1820s and emergence of the Whig Party as Democrats' main competitor. By the election of 1840, Whig and Democrat organizations were fighting on an even basis in almost every state. By 1840, nearly 80 percent of the states had a competitive two-party system, compared to only 10 percent in 1824 (see fig. 3.1).

Coupled with this rise in competitive elections was the nationalization of party labels and party organization. By 1840, national elections were carried out under the banner of two strong political labels commanding a habitual following among voters. As opposed to the shifting factionalism of early American politics, voters in the second-party system responded "to candidates and issues as Whigs or Democrats" (McCormick 1975, 102). According to the political historian Michael Holt (1984), the transition between 1836 and 1840 "was also marked by the elaboration of party machinery and by the emergence of impressively high levels of internal party cohesion and interparty disagreement. . . . For the first time . . . the parties articulated coherent and contrasting platforms regarding proper governmental policy at the state and national levels" (17). Rampant partisanship also pervaded the legislative process. Offices within Congress—

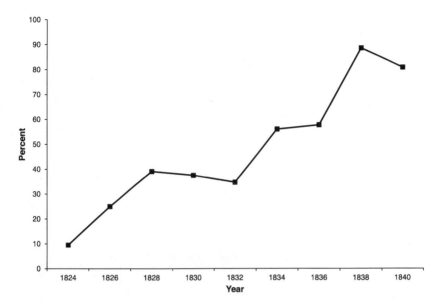

Fig. 3.1. Percentage of states with competitive congressional elections, 1824–40. This figure presents the percentage of states where the statewide margin between the top two parties was less than 10 percent in congressional elections. (Data compiled by the author from data in Rusk 2002.)

such as the Speaker of the House—were recognized as the property of the majority party. It was also accepted that the majority party would use its position to dole out federal jobs and contracts based on party affiliation. Thus, by the 1840s, voting behavior, campaign organization, and winning office had become thoroughly linked by political parties.

Against this backdrop the 27th Congress, which assembled in 1841, faced the decennial ritual of reapportioning the House of Representatives. The election of 1840 had thrust the Whig Party into control of both the White House and Congress (Holt 1999). Riding the coattails of their victorious presidential candidate—the military hero William Henry Harrison—Whigs wrested control of both the House and Senate from the long-dominant Democrats. Upon the opening of the 27th Congress in 1841, Whigs held 142 seats to Democrats' 98, while the split in the Senate was 29–22 in their favor.[1]

Most of the first and second sessions of the 27th Congress were spent attending to the nation's economic crisis and the financial troubles afflicting the states (Holt 1999, 122–61). The completion of the census in January of 1842, however, meant that Congress would have to turn some of its attention to the constitutional obligation of reapportioning the House. In the House, the task of crafting an initial apportionment bill was given to a special committee chaired by Horace Everett (W-VT). The committee reported at the end of January, but the full House did not take up consideration of the bill until April (Shields 1985, 365). The bill contained two provisions. The first called for a ratio of 68,000 people per representative. The second required that every state with more than one representative divide its seat allotment into geographically contiguous, single-member districts.

Debate on the floor revolved around these two features of the bill. First, there was substantial disagreement over the appropriate ratio of people per representative, and, hence, the size of the House.[2] After flirting with various ratios, the House finally agreed on 50,179 people per representative, which would enlarge the House from 242 to 255. Second, the House also spent a week contentiously debating the merits and constitutionality of the districting provision. The vote to include districting into the final bill passed by a razor-thin margin of two votes (101–99), while the vote to pass the entire bill and send it to the Senate was 113–87 (*Congressional Globe*, 27–2, 471).

In the Senate the Judiciary Committee, chaired by Georgia Whig John Berrien, considered the Apportionment Bill. The Senate modified the House version, however, increasing the ratio for apportioning the House to the much higher 70,680 people per representative. The immediate implication was that the House would be reduced in size from 242 to 223. The Senate also agreed to keep the districting provision, despite numerous attempts on the floor to pass amendments that would limit its reach. The penultimate vote striking the districting provision fell 19–24, after which the entire bill passed 25–19 (*Congressional Globe*, 27–2, 614).

The Senate's alterations did not initially sit well with many House members. Upset that it had tinkered with the apportionment ratio, the House nevertheless agreed to the Senate version, and, in June 1842, sent the bill to the White House. President Tyler, despite initial concerns of Whig congressmen that he might veto, grudgingly signed the bill into law.[3] Thus, the House was to be reduced in size, and any state using the general ticket would now be required to carve up their state into districts.

The decision to reduce the size of the House is intriguing (and will be relevant for the rest of the story), but the main interest here concerns the districting provision.[4] Section 2 of the act stated:

> That in every case where a state is entitled to more than one representative, the number to which each state shall be entitled under this

apportionment shall be elected by districts composed of contiguous territory equal in number to the number of representatives to which said state may be entitled, no one district electing more than one representative. (5 Stat. 491 (1842))

Why did Congress mandate this requirement? One explanation found in the historical literature is that it was a good government reform aimed at creating uniform electoral standards to protect the interests of minority constituencies. The general ticket limited geographically concentrated minorities from gaining seats commensurate with their vote share. Districting, according to this argument, would increase the chances of minority interests to receive some representation. As Shields observes, "while each party's members insisted that the other would corrupt any system, most legislators agreed that equality of representation was a desirable goal and that uniform districting might increase the fairness of elections" (1985, 362).

A second explanation, offered by Calabrese (2006), presents a partisan-centered rationale. Calabrese argues that when there is a newly dominant party—defined as one which controls both the presidency and Congress—they have an incentive to mandate single-member districts. Parties with unified control of national government, typically elected at a presidential election, should anticipate a loss at the midterm elections and thereby have an incentive to switch to single-member districts. This switch, he argues, will help insulate incumbents of the dominant party from adverse political tides. This argument offers a potentially satisfying explanation for the switch to single-member districts. It certainly fits the surface details of the period. Yet there is a problem. The glitch is that the argument mispredicts the timing of the switch to single-member districts. If the argument is right, then the transition to single-member districts should have happened prior to 1840. Why didn't the Jeffersonian Democratic-Republicans mandate single-member districts following their sweep of the 1800 election? Why didn't the Jacksonians do the same following their triumph in 1828? There had to be something more than a new regime taking power in 1840 that finally triggered the change.

A third explanation centers on battles between large and small states. Zagarri (1989), for example, argues that the districting law was the result of a coalition of Whigs and small-state representatives. Prior to 1842, small states were the primary users, and main defenders of, the general-ticket system. But, according to Zagarri, Whigs were able to peel off some of these small-state members by playing on their fears that, absent universal districting, large states might adopt general-ticket elections, producing unified delegations that would then act against small state interests (130–31). "In the end," Zagarri argues, "the support of senators and representatives from small states such as New Hampshire, Georgia, Missouri, and Mississippi, which still had general-ticket elections, was crucial to the passage of the bill" (131). There is, however, a serious problem with this story—the members from these states overwhelmingly voted against the districting provision.

In contrast, one might reasonably surmise that, as the majority Whigs surveyed the political landscape, they observed an opportunity to pick up extra seats in the next House elections by carving up general-ticket states into districts. Whigs recognized that general-ticket elections greatly improved the prospects that a majority party could sweep a state's entire delegation and shut out the minority party. As they recently saw in Alabama, in 1840, their party garnered 43 percent of the statewide vote, yet did not receive a single seat (Holt 1999, 155; Thornton 1978, 94). Moreover, Whigs discerned that under the new apportionment they were going to be net losers in the states using the general ticket. Whigs had done well in general-ticket states that were slated to lose seats in the new apportionment. Democrats, on the other hand, had done well in general-ticket states that were slated to gain seats. A switch to districts would provide Whigs a chance, in the strong Democratic general-ticket states, to win seats more commensurate with their vote share. Thus, it was not that the general ticket merely punished minority constituencies. Nor was it simply that Whigs were a new party in power; there had been newly dominant parties before. Instead, what the new census numbers revealed was that any new federal apportionment was going to hurt Whigs' primary constituency—themselves.

How the General Ticket and the New Apportionment Affected Whigs

The proponents of districting argued that it was necessary in order to protect the interests of minority constituencies and prevent large states from overrunning small states. During the debates, however, a number of members charged that the districting provision had nothing to do with protecting "minority interests" and everything to do with simple party politics. These charges of partisanship originated from Democrats' side of the aisle. Democrats dismissed the proponents' (i.e., Whig) arguments as subterfuge, claiming that Whigs were simply trying to boost their prospects in the upcoming election. For example, Senator Lewis Linn (D-MO), after dismissing the proponents' arguments, leveled the following accusation—as summarized by the *Congressional Globe*:

> It seemed to him, therefore, the question assumed a political aspect—a party one. He would not disguise his opinion upon this point; he believed it was a party question. He believed—and he chose to speak plainly—that the Whig party would derive a positive advantage from this particular clause of the bill. (*Congressional Globe* 27-2, 596)

Senator Arthur Bagby (D-GA) went one step further, equating districting with the French "Reign of Terror" (*Congressional Globe* 27-2, 612). Democratic protests, such as these, suggest that partisan motives may have played a central role in the switch to single-member districts.

At first glance, however, it would appear that Democrats' claims of partisan manipulation were unjustified. Seven states elected their representatives to the 27th Congress via general ticket—New Hampshire (5 seats), Rhode Island (2), New Jersey (6), Missouri (2), Alabama (5), Georgia (9), and Mississippi (2). Of these seven, three—Rhode Island, New Jersey and Georgia—returned unified Whig delegations for a total of 17 members. The other four states all went against Whigs, resulting in 14 seats for Democrats. Among general-ticket states, Whigs actually had a slight (3 seat) advantage. Thus, from this cursory counting of seats, it appears that Whigs would lose by banning the general ticket.

The results of the census and the consequent redistribution of House seats under the new apportionment, however, fundamentally altered this political accounting. Politicians knew the recent census' reshuffling of seats to the general-ticket states would advantage Democrats. Recall that the House and Senate had each proposed different bases for apportionment; the House version called for an increase; the Senate, a decrease in the size of the House. The Senate version was the one finally agreed upon (and the one I will work with here). The first four columns of table 3.1 lists each general-ticket state, their old apportionment, the number of seats they were entitled to under the upcoming apportionment, and the net change.

Using past election results, Whigs could categorize the partisan direction of each state. Presumably, in this pre-polling era, the best information politicians had about the upcoming election were the results of the previous election (Kernell and McDonald 1999, 803). Thus, Whigs in 1842 could anticipate which way a state was expected to go based on the most recent election returns. The fifth column of table 3.1 lists how each state voted in the elections to the 27th Congress (the elections of 1840 and 1841). Based on these results, New Hampshire, Missouri, Alabama, and Mississippi could safely be called strong Democratic states. New Jersey, Rhode Island, and Georgia fell into the Whig camp. By combining the partisan direction of each state with the future gain or loss in seats, Whigs recognized how the general ticket disadvantaged them. Since these states returned unified delegations, Whigs could reasonably calculate the resulting aggregate partisan breakdown. In the strong Democratic states, there were potentially seven new seats that would fall into the Democratic column: New Hampshire (−1), Missouri (+3), Alabama (+2), and Mississippi (+3). On the Whig side, there was going to be a net loss of two seats: Rhode Island (no change), New Jersey (−1), and Georgia (−1). Thus, Democrats were poised to gain seven seats, while Whigs dropped two. According to this political arithmetic, under the new apportionment, Whigs would have 15 seats in general-ticket states, compared to Democrats' 21.

These estimates, while bad for Whigs, are conservative. Whig politicians had reason to consider even worse scenarios. They had suffered a crushing defeat in the recently held Georgia state elections (August 1841), when Democrats captured both the state legislature and governor's office (Debats 1973; Holt 1999). If, as appeared likely, Georgia swung away from Whigs in the next congressional election, this eight-seat shift would provide Democrats a new general ticket advantage of 29–7.[5]

Moreover, during congressional deliberations, word trickled in from Maine that the state legislature had recently ended its session by passing a contingent redistricting plan. Unsure how many seats it was going to receive in the next election (it currently had eight), Maine's legislature drew up a districting plan for an apportionment of eight seats. If, however, the new apportionment gave it seven or nine seats, the plan called for election by general ticket (*Niles National Register*, April 9, 1842, 85; *Congres-*

TABLE 3.1. The Partisan Distribution of Seats in General Ticket States

State	Old Apportionment	New Apportionment	Net Change	Statewide Democratic Vote	Party Controlling State Government
New Hampshire	5	4	−1	58.1	Democrats
Rhode Island	2	2	0	0	Whigs
New Jersey	6	5	−1	48.2	Whigs
Missouri	2	5	+3	58.1	Democrats
Alabama	5	7	+2	58.3	Democrats
Georgia	9	8	−1	42.5	Democrats
Mississippi	2	5	+3	53.4	Democrats

sional Globe 27-2, 590). Congressional members in both parties knew that the new apportionment allotted seven seats to Maine, thereby triggering a switch there to a general-ticket election. The current Maine delegation was evenly split four to four, but in the recent state elections (September 1841), Democrats won in a landslide.[6] Hence, if the general ticket were installed, the ominous political winds blowing in from Maine would cost Whigs another three, possibly four, seats under the general ticket. Thus, if one added Georgia and Maine to the Democratic column, the split among general-ticket states was now 36–7 against Whigs. In short, Whigs were about to suffer large losses and possibly lose control of the House.

Carving the general-ticket states up into districts gave Whigs a chance to avoid this huge swing of seats toward Democrats. Although Democrats were in control of state government in all the general-ticket states, except New Jersey and Rhode Island, there are constraints on the districting process—geographic distribution of voters, respect for county lines, incumbent protection, etc.—which limit the ability of strong parties to gerrymander clean sweeps (Cain 1985; Cox and Katz 1999). Thus, Whigs saw districting as a way to stave off complete electoral disaster. While Whigs were judiciously circumspect about speculating on their reform's partisan affects, Democrats were quite willing to reveal Whigs' political motivation. The following summary of Senator Alfred Cuthbert's (D-GA) speech in the *Congressional Globe* illustrates that Democratic politicians keenly understood the workings of electoral institutions:

> Mr. Cuthbert observed that it may operate for the benefit of a party—he would not say what party. But he would explain what he meant. Suppose Alabama was entitled to nine members; while under the general-ticket system, she would have the whole nine of the party now in the minority in Congress; but, under the district system, the same party would have probably but five; would not that be proof that this clause acted for the benefit of the party forcing the bill now with this clause? (*Congressional Globe* 27-2, 590–91)

In the next section, we see that each side acted as if it had thoroughly grasped these lessons in institutional manipulation.

State Competition versus Party Strategy

Was the districting mandate a result of competition between large and small states or was it an attempt by Whigs to take away seats from Democrats? Fortunately, we can test these competing explanations using the roll-call results on districting in the House and Senate.

Evidence in the House

The clearest way to test for the effects of partisanship and state size is to examine how each member voted on the amendment to include districting in the final bill (H.R. 73). If Whigs were the driving force behind districting, then we should find them overwhelmingly voting in favor of reform, and Democrats in opposition. To test for the effects of state size, the most straightforward measure is the population of the state in which the member resides. One might also expect that individual members would differ in their support for districting based on the manner in which they were elected. House members from general-ticket states, all else being equal, should be less likely to vote for districting since their jobs were directly threatened. To account for this possibility, I included a dummy variable indicating whether or not the member was elected by general ticket.

The results, estimated via logit and presented in table 3.2, indicate the strong influence of partisanship. Even after controlling for state population and manner of election, Whigs, as expected, were significantly more likely to vote for districting. The coefficient on the state size variable is insignificant. In addition, members from general-ticket states were less willing to vote for districting ($p < .01$).

TABLE 3.2. The Determinants of Voting for Districts in the U.S. House (logit estimates; dependent variable = vote on districting provision)

Variable	Coefficient (standard error)
Whig	5.50*
	(.78)
General Ticket	−1.61*
	(.71)
State Population	.0003
	(.004)
Constant	−3.58*
	(.92)
N	200
Log-Likelihood	−56.43

*$p < .05$.

To see the differential effects of partisanship and electoral structure more clearly we can convert the coefficients into probabilities of voting yea. Combining party with electoral structure gives us a two by two matrix of possible combinations. The predicted probabilities for each combination are displayed in table 3.3. Democrats were overwhelmingly opposed to districting, regardless of how they were elected. The probability of a Democrat voting yea was near zero (.04 and .01, for district- and general-ticket based representatives, respectively). Whigs, on the other hand, had a much higher probability of voting yea, as expected. Whigs chosen by general ticket, however, were less likely to favor the reform than were their district-elected brethren. The probability of a district-based Whig voting yea was .86, while for general-ticket Whigs, it was only .56.

Examining the general-ticket Whigs more closely illustrates how collective interests competed with individual interests. The general-ticket Whigs came from two states: Georgia and New Jersey. The Whigs from Georgia all voted against districting, while the New Jersey contingent voted in favor. What might be driving this differential result? The clearest answer seems to hinge on which state party would be controlling the process of drawing the new districts. Democrats, as noted earlier, had captured control of Georgia's state government, while Whigs were the majority party in New Jersey. Although we lack direct testimonial evidence, these patterns are consistent with the conjecture that congressional members from these states were calculating the expected utilities of life under districts versus general ticket. With fellow Whigs in control of drawing districts, New Jersey congressmen could count on securing favorable districts (Levine 1977; McCormick 1953). Whig representatives from Georgia, on the other hand, facing an opposition state legislature, could expect much less friendly treatment. Thus, taking their chances under the general ticket may have seemed a better proposition.

TABLE 3.3. Probability of Voting Yea in the House

	Whigs	Democrats
General Ticket	.56	.01
	(.29, .80)	(.0007, .04)
Districts	.86	.04
	(.71, .95)	(.004, .14)

Note: Predicted probabilities with population set at its mean value; 95% confidence intervals in parentheses.

Evidence from the Senate

Voting on districting in the Senate was even more clear-cut in terms of partisanship. Unlike the House, the Senate entertained a number of proposed amendments to the districting provision. Most of these were put forward by Democrats attempting to exempt particular states from districting, or trying to postpone its implementation. The penultimate vote on districting was an amendment offered by Senator Allen (D-OH) to eliminate the provision from the bill altogether. The vote on this amendment failed 19 to 24. As can be seen in table 3.4, the vote to keep districting broke straight down party lines. No Democrats defected, and the only Whig to cross party barriers was the states-rightist Berrien, of Georgia (Debats 1973). Thus, the results in the Senate further confirm a party-centered explanation for the single-member-district mandate.

The Best-Laid Plans . . .

Two events conspired to mute the impact of the Whig plan. First, they "suffered one of the most staggering reversals in off-year congressional elections ever witnessed in American history" (Holt 1999, 151). Their representation in the House plummeted from 59 percent to 36 percent. Factional battles in Congress, bickering between President Tyler and Whig congressmen, and the failure to enact adequate legislation to cope with the nation's economic crisis all contributed heavily to their losing control of the House. Second, four of the general-ticket states—New Hampshire, Georgia, Mississippi, and Missouri—did not obey the districting mandate, electing their representatives to the 28th Congress via general ticket. These states sent a combined 22 members, all Democrats, to the House. Whigs contested their seating, but Democrats, now with a 61-seat majority, held to party lines and voted to ignore the districting law. Thus, the general-ticket Democrats defied the districting mandate and took their seats.

TABLE 3.4. The Senate Vote to
Eliminate the Districting Provision

	Yea	Nay
Democrats	18	0
Whigs	1	24

$\chi^2 = 39.11; p < .01.$

One reason why the partisan explanation offered in this chapter may have previously been overlooked is because of the initial failure of the districting act. This does not mean, however, that the act did not matter. Congress now had the statutory basis to unseat members elected by general ticket. The critical factor was a congressional majority finding it in their political interests to enforce the law. Indeed, the hold-out states may have switched to districts in anticipation of having their delegation unseated. While Georgia shifted to districts in December 1843, after Whigs recaptured the state government, the other three states—New Hampshire, Mississippi, and Missouri—did not switch until the election of 1846. Democrats in these states anticipated that Whigs would recapture the House, and, hence, not seat their representatives. Throughout 1846, Whigs mounted an unprecedented nationwide midterm election campaign, eventually winning back majority control of the House (Holt 1999, 236–45). Thus, Democrats in the holdout states likely discerned that national political tides had turned against them and, fearing that their delegations would not be seated, preemptively switched to districts. The convergence to single-member districts in congressional elections was now complete.[7]

PART II

The Partisan Era, 1840–1900

FOUR

The Strategic Timing of Congressional Redistricting

Following the 2002 election, Republicans in Texas' state legislature found themselves in an unfamiliar position: the majority. The combination of a new state House majority and the reelection of Republican Governor Rick Perry produced the first unified Republican government in Texas in more than a century. Many credited the efforts of then House Majority Leader Tom DeLay with the Republican victory, noting that he had been instrumental in candidate recruitment and fundraising. DeLay's efforts ended up personally damaging—DeLay was convicted of money laundering in the state legislative elections—but the political effects of the redistricting clearly benefited Republicans nationally.

One of DeLay's primary goals in helping the Texas Republicans secure a state legislative majority was the redrawing of the state's U.S. House districts. Following a legislative stalemate over congressional redistricting in 2001, a federal-court panel had designed a districting map for Texas that produced a 17–15 Democratic advantage in the state's congressional delegation. This Democratic advantage occurred despite a statewide vote of 56.6 percent for Republican candidates and Republican control of all 29 statewide elected offices. DeLay and many Texas Republicans saw their newfound majority as a golden opportunity to devise a plan that would accurately reflect the partisan leanings of Texas voters and enhance the Republican majority in the House of Representatives.

DeLay's redistricting gambit consumed the Texas legislature in 2003. Democrats sought to block the new plan—first by fleeing to Oklahoma and later to New Mexico to prevent a quorum, and to avoid being detained by the Texas Rangers. The stalemate was finally broken and a new plan enacted after Democratic state senator John Whitmire abandoned the quorum boycott and returned to Austin. The new plan produced a dramatic shift in the partisan composition of the Texas delegation. Five Democratic incumbents were defeated, and the 109th Congress began with Republicans holding a 21–11 advantage over Democrats—a net shift of six seats to Republicans. These six seats allowed Republicans to hold onto their slim majority in the House of Representatives.

The Texas case drew nationwide attention and scorn from many politicians, pundits, and press members, who labeled it unprecedented, antidemocratic, and illegal. The *Washington Post*, in an editorial entitled "The Soviet Republic of Texas," chastised the Texas legislature for violating a "longstanding tradition" against mid-cycle redistricting, calling the plan "a new low . . . [that] will aggravate the triumph of extremes in Washington while further sovietizing America's already-fixed electoral game."[1] The issue eventually ended up in front of the U.S. Supreme Court. A divided court upheld the constitutionality of mid-decade gerrymanders and partisan gerrymanders more generally (*League of United Latin American Citizens v. Perry*, 2006).[2] Democrats vowed to seek revenge in other states, giving rise to fears of a redistricting arms race.

Had Democrats looked back in history, however, they may have been chagrined to find out that what goes around comes around. In the spring of 1878, the Speaker of the House, Samuel J. Randall (D-PA), sent out an urgent missive calling on Democratic-controlled state legislatures to redistrict and manufacture additional Democratic seats. Terrified that Republicans were on the brink of capturing the House in the upcoming midterm elections, Speaker Randall decided that drastic action was in order. In April 1878, the *New York Times* reported:

> Samuel J. Randall, Speaker of the House of Representatives, has written to leading Ohio Democrats that it is of the utmost importance to the Democratic Party that the Ohio Legislature should redistrict the state. Mr. Randall gives as a reason that the indications point to Republican success in carrying the next House unless some effort of this kind is made by Democrats where they have power. (*New York Times*, April 23, 1878)

Democratic leaders in the Ohio and Missouri state legislatures heeded Randall's call for a new redistricting. The resulting maps crucially swung nine seats to Democrats, and helped Democrats maintain their slim majority in the House.

The Texas Democrats of 2002 were also not the first group of politicians to flee a legislature while trying to block an unfavorable redistricting plan. In 1861, for example, Democratic legislators walked out of the Indiana State Senate to prevent the passage of a pro-Republican congressional districting map. According to a historian of Indiana politics, after Democrats bolted from the chamber, the following exchange occurred:

> "I saw them pretty nearly all in a batch, and the answer was, 'Tell them to go to hell,'" said the Republican doorkeeper who tracked down the absentees. "I move that we don't do that [go to hell]," said Senator Michael D. White with levity. After White's motion was agreed to, Republicans dropped redistricting, and Democrats returned. (Walsh 1987, 217)

Indiana was unable to redistrict until 1867, when Republicans secured a large enough majority to overcome the continuing threat of Democratic bolts.

Thus, the practice of mid-decade redistricting had many precursors in the 19th century. The impetus to redraw districts became even greater following the congressional decision in 1842 to mandate single-member districts in every state. Political parties in the states quickly seized upon the potential for partisan gain that followed from this switch to single-member districts. In New Jersey (one of the states affected by the 1842 law), the Whig-controlled legislature, in 1843, quickly passed a districting law intended to maximize their share of the congressional delegation. When Democrats regained control of the state legislature, in 1845, they returned the favor and drew up new districts favorable to Democratic congressional candidates. Whigs, in 1847, once again back in charge of the legislature, none too surprisingly, imposed another new plan (Levine 1977).

This back-and-forth redistricting may strike modern observers as quite peculiar. Nowadays, congressional redistricting takes place at regular 10-year intervals following the census. Indeed, part of what made the recent Texas mid-decade remap so newsworthy was its seemingly exceptional occurrence. In the context of recent history, it was. Yet in the 19th century, states displayed few qualms about redistricting mid-decade. To visualize the near constancy of redistricting during the partisan era and how it compares to other eras of American politics, figure 4.1 plots the number of states redrawing district boundaries between 1790 and 2010. Between 1862 and

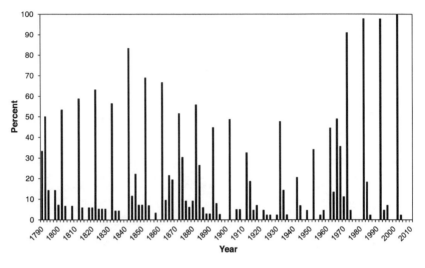

Fig. 4.1. The percentage of states redistricting, 1790–2010. States with only one congressional seat were excluded. (Data compiled by the author from information in Martis 1982.)

1896, there was only one election year in which at least one state did not redraw its congressional districts (fig. 4.1). Ohio, for example, redistricted seven times between 1878 and 1892—at one point conducting six consecutive congressional elections with six different plans.

While some states redistricted frequently, others went decades without writing a new districting plan. In addition, states sometimes threw newly gained seats into at-large elections or chose their entire congressional delegation on a statewide ballot. In this chapter, I examine the logic behind the variation of redistricting events in the 19th century. The central argument is that party competition drove state decisions to rewrite the rules of the electoral game. When a new party came into power, and the current districts were drawn by the out party, the probability of redistricting sharply increased. These gerrymandering arms races typically happened in competitive, battleground states like Ohio and Indiana, where the closeness of the statewide vote greatly increased the payoffs to manipulating district boundaries. At other times, party competition led states to freeze their districts for long stretches of time. As long as a state's representation in the House went unchanged, strong parties often found it in their interest to keep the congressional districts dormant. These silent gerrymanders, to borrow V. O. Key's (1956) evocative phrase, normally happened when there was divided partisan control of state government or one-party domination, such as in the post-Reconstruction South and the Northeast after the elections of the mid-1890s. It is worth also noting the sharp decline in redistricting during the early to mid-20th century and the subsequent changes in redistricting patterns following the 1960s. We will return to these important trends in chapter 9.

In addition to shedding light on the factors inducing institutional change, the diversity of 19th-century redistricting highlights the importance, for the legislative elections literature, of looking beyond the modern era of redistricting. Almost everything we know about the politics of redistricting comes from research inspired by the wave of court-ordered redistricting in the mid-1960s. The conventional finding of this work is that redistricting has a minimal impact on the partisan makeup of congressional delegations (Abramowitz 1983; Campagna and Grofman 1990; Niemi and Winsky 1992).[3] The inference normally drawn from this finding is that state legislators prefer to protect incumbents of both parties rather than increase their party's share of the House delegation. Moving beyond modern redistricting allows us to ask whether this finding holds more generally. How do politicians behave when freed from the shackles imposed by courts? Do they more aggressively pursue partisan interests?

Uncovering the logic behind the timing of 19th-century redistricting events can also illuminate contemporary decisions by state parties to redistrict. The courts have set the floor on the timing of redistricting—states must readjust their district boundaries at least once a decade. But the courts have yet to impose a ceiling—states can still redistrict more than once a decade, unless prohibited by their state constitution (Cox 2004). This was affirmed by the recent Supreme Court decision—*League of United Latin American Citizens v. Perry* (2006)—which upheld mid-decade redistricting. Thus, identifying the conditions which prompted mid-decade redistricting in the 19th century may provide important insights into understanding recent mid-decade redistricting efforts.

The Timing of Redistricting Before One-Person, One-Vote

In the modern era, the nature and timing of districting choices available to states are relatively circumscribed. The court enforced one-person, one-vote doctrine induces regular redistricting. Because population naturally shifts over the course of 10 years, states are compelled to bring the equality of their districts back into line. The Voting Rights Act—and its subsequent amendments—serves as another major constraint on contemporary map-makers. States, or localities, covered by the Voting Rights Act (i.e., those with a past history of discriminatory barriers in the electoral process) must submit any proposed maps to the Justice Department or a federal district court for preclearance.

Redistricting in the 19th century, by contrast, was largely unfettered. Although the reapportionment of congressional seats following the decennial census often prompted states to redistrict, there was much broader discretion available to states. A state could find itself in one of three scenarios depending on whether or not the size of their congressional delegation stayed the same, grew, or shrank.[4]

If a state did not gain any seats then, absent a new redistricting plan, the old districts stayed in place. Nothing legally compelled states to redistrict. As long as a state's representation in the House went unchanged, its district boundaries could remain untouched. On the flip side, there were also no restrictions on how often a state could redistrict. States were free to redistrict in years other than those immediately after a census and could redistrict more than once a decade.

If a state gained seats, it faced slightly different options. Before 1872, if a state gained seats, and failed to redistrict, they reverted to their current plan and forfeited the representation of any newly gained seats. Because states naturally disliked losing representation they almost always redrew their maps to incorporate additional seats. This changed, however, in 1872 when Congress attached a provision to the Apportionment Act allowing gaining states to keep their old plan intact and elect any new seats in a statewide, at-large election until a new redistricting plan could be passed. The at-large provision was repeated in every following Apportionment Act until 1929 (and remained in force until 1967).[5]

Finally, when a state lost seats the choices were more drastic. Although states infrequently lost seats during the 19th century, it did occasionally happen (see column 3 of table 4.1). Prior to 1882, federal law did not stipulate what would happen if a state lost seats and failed to redistrict. Apparently these states faced the unacceptable threat of their delegation not being seated in the House. Consequently, every state that lost seats between 1842 and 1880 redistricted. In 1882, Congress passed a provision allowing a losing state to temporarily elect its entire delegation in statewide, at-large elections (i.e., general-ticket elections) (22 Stat. 5).[6] This momentarily lifted the ban on general-ticket elections. Although this provision was not part of the Apportionment Act of 1892—presumably because no states lost seats in that years apportionment—it was included in both the 1901 and 1911 Apportionment Acts and stayed in force until the 1960s.

All told then, a state could find itself in one of three scenarios depending on whether or not the size of their congressional delegation stayed the same, grew, or shrank. Since each scenario had a varying effect on the decisions faced by state legislatures, and the strategic choices faced by political parties, it is necessary to analyze each separately.

Unprompted Redistricting

This section examines unprompted redistricting—that is, redistricting that was not triggered by changes in a states apportionment of seats. This encompasses both non-census years and those years following a census, but where a state did not gain or lose seats during the congressional reapportionment. The key question is why some states redistricted frequently while others went decades without redrawing district boundaries. The answer lies in the interaction between the party currently in control of state government and the party that had last drawn the districts.

The first condition that had to be in place was unified party control of state government. Although parties may have wanted to gerrymander in order to solidify and extend partisan gains, they first had to be in a position to pass the requisite legislation. Their ability to do so hinged on whether they could overcome the separation of power constraints laid out in their state constitution. The procedural requirements for passing legislation—specifically, the constitutional provisions for a gubernatorial vetoes and legislative overrides—varied considerably across states. Many states simply mirrored the U.S. Constitution, providing for an executive veto and a

TABLE 4.1. The Reapportionment of Seats in the U.S. House, 1840–1900

Apportionment Decade	Number of States with No Change	Number of States Gaining Seats	Number of States Losing Seats
1840	1	8	13
1850	11	9	7
1860	6	5	7
1870	6	26	1
1880	9	22	3
1890	20	18	0
1900	20	18	0

Source: Martis 1982.

super-majority override requirement (usually two-thirds, but in some cases three-fifths). A number of state constitutions, however, broke from the federal mold, requiring only a simple majority in each legislative chamber to override a veto, while others dispensed with an executive veto altogether. In these states, when one party controlled both chambers, the legislature did not need the assent of the governor. In what follows, I assume that a state was under unified control if one party controlled all the formal veto points, and divided party control otherwise.

The distinction between unified versus divided control is crucial for understanding the baseline conditions that produced an unprompted redistricting. If both parties controlled at least one branch of the state government, then any new plan had to be agreed upon by both parties. Since redistricting typically involves zero-sum change (i.e., there is no plan that simultaneously makes both parties better off), each party would naturally veto the others schemes. Hence, as long as a states' delegation size was unchanged, one would not expect to see a redistricting event during divided government.

This expectation is borne out by the historical record. Between 1840 and 1900, only twice did a state, unprompted by a seat change, redistrict when there was divided partisan control. The exceptions occurred in Georgia in 1850 and Tennessee in 1880. In both cases, third parties held a substantial number of seats in the legislature, and perhaps formed a majority coalition with one of the other parties.

What, then, triggered redistricting? We can think of state parties as surveying the political landscape and weighing the costs and benefits of redistricting.[7] Negotiating a new district plan, appeasing congressional incumbents, satisfying local party organizations, and agreeing on how best to allocate partisans into new districts were among the many transaction and opportunity costs that had to enter into any party's utility calculation. When the net benefits of switching to a new plan outweighed the political costs of crafting a new plan, a state party should have found it profitable to redistrict. This most likely should have happened when the gap between the dominant party's ideal plan and the status quo plan was fairly large. When there was little difference between the dominant party's ideal plan and the status quo their motivation to redistrict would have been low, but as this gap widened, their incentive to redistrict would have increased.

What considerations might have altered the utility calculus in such a way to increase the probability of a redistricting event? Two conditions, in addition to unified government, had to be met before the probability of redistricting became substantial. The first condition was when one unified party surrendered to another. When a new party came into power, we might suspect that it would want to adjust congressional districts to solidify or extend any partisan gains. In Indiana, for example, Republicans captured control of the state government from Democrats in the 1866 election and promptly redrew congressional districts.

However, not all new majority parties wanted to redraw congressional districts. When new majorities discerned that the possibilities were highly discrepant with the current districts, one would expect increased incentives to redistrict. This most likely occurred when the out party crafted the current districts. Here the gap between the status quo and the in-party's ideal plan was relatively wide. Consider the story of New Jersey described in the opening of this chapter. Democrats took control of the state legislature from Whigs in 1845. Whigs had drawn the existing districts; thus, Democrats had both the opportunity and motive to redistrict. The shoe was on the other foot two years later when Whigs retook control of the state legislature. They too were a new unified party facing an unfavorable reversion plan and promptly redrew more favorable maps.

Thus, we should expect a spike in the probability of redistricting when there was both a party turnover and an out-party districting plan. On the other hand, when the current districts were drawn by the in party, the current majority's interests should have been reflected in the status quo. Here, the majority party should have been happy to keep the districts as is.

To test these predictions, I collected all of the relevant data for every state legislative session from 1840 to 1900. We first need to know when states redistricted. Fortunately, Martis (1982) lists the precise date when each redistricting statute was passed into law. These passage dates were then matched with the partisan composition of the state legislature and governor using Burnham's (1985) data on state legislatures and various state histories. I coded each legislative session into one of three governmental types: Unified Democratic, Divided, or Unified Republican/Whig. The coding took into account the veto provisions of each state. To see how this worked, consider a state that only required a simple majority to override a gubernatorial veto. If, for example, the state had Democratic majorities in each legislative chamber, but a Republican governor, the state would still be coded as Unified Democrat. If, on the other hand, the state gave the governor a veto and Democrats did not have sufficient majorities to override a veto, then the state was coded as Divided.

The dependent variable is whether a state passed a redistricting plan or not during a given legislative session. Between 1840 and 1900, there were 32 unprompted redistricting events. I exclude all state-years in which a state gained or lost seats, or had only one congressional member. In addition, for the former Confederate states, I exclude the first plan passed after the Civil War because new congressional districts were a precondition of their readmittance placed on them by the federal government.

The two critical conditions suspected to prompt redistricting are whether or not there was a party turnover of state government and whether the out party controlled the last redistricting. Combining these two factors together produces four possible categories: (1) party turnover and an out-party redistricting, (2) party turnover and an in-party redistricting, (3) no party turnover and an out-party redistricting, and (4) no party turnover and an in-party redistricting. I expect the largest probability to occur when there is both a party turnover and an out-party reversion. When only one or neither of these conditions is met, I expect the probability to be comparatively smaller.

Given that the unit of analysis is a state legislative session, the appropriate statistical model is a binary time-series cross-sectional model—or, equivalently a grouped duration model (Beck, Katz, and Tucker 1998). To control for any duration dependence, I included dummy variables for every year since the most recent redistricting (Beck, Katz, and Tucker 1998). The standard errors are clustered by state to account for any nonindependence within states.

The results are presented in table 4.2. Consistent with expectations, when there was a new unified regime and the current district were written

TABLE 4.2. Estimating the Likelihood of an Unprompted Redistricting, 1840–1900 (logit estimates; dependent variable = redistricting)

Variable	Coefficients (robust standard srrors)
Party Turnover and	2.31**
Out-Party Reversion	(.39)
Party Turnover and	1.23**
In-Party Reversion	(.48)
No Party Turnover and	.19
Out-Party Reversion	(.59)
Years since Last Redistricting	−.008*
	(.025)
Constant	−3.35**
	(.39)
N	828
Log-Likelihood	−175.61

Note: Robust standard errors (clustering by state) in parentheses.
**$p < .05$, *$p < .10$.

by the out party, the probability of a redistricting was positive and significant. In addition, the coefficients for the other two regimes were insignificant. The impact of no party turnover and an in-party reversion is reflected in the intercept and is negative.

To more clearly see the substantive impact of the independent variables, I converted the results into the probability of a redistricting event. Setting *Years Since Last Redistricting* at its median value of eight years, we see striking evidence, presented in table 4.3, of parties strategically timing their redistricting events in response to their electoral circumstances. The largest probability of redistricting arose when there was both a switch in party control and the previous districts were written by the out party. Here, the probability of a redistricting spiked to .25. Yet when there was neither a party turnover nor an out-party reversion, the probability plummeted to .03. The near-zero probability in the lower right cell of table 4.3 indicates that once a favorable plan was in place parties tended to pursue a strategy of neglect.

Ohio

As noted in the introduction to this chapter, between 1878 and 1892, Ohio redistricted a remarkable six times. The key to understanding this redistricting frenzy begins by considering Ohio's peculiar rules for apportioning the state legislature. Ohio had an interesting system where apportionment of state-legislative districts was conducted by a three-person commission: the governor, lieutenant governor, and state auditor. They conducted this apportionment under fairly strict guidelines laid out in the state constitution. The upshot was that state legislators were proscribed from crafting their own districts. This prevented parties from using district maps to create a single-party hegemony in the state legislature. The even balance

TABLE 4.3. The Effects of Party Turnover and Reversionary Districts on the Probability of Redistricting

Party Turnover	Current Districts Written by the Out-Party	
	Yes	*No*
Yes	.25	.10
	(.18, .35)	(.05, .18)
No	.04	.03
	(.01, .10)	(.02, .06)

Note: The cells contain the simulated probability of a redistricting event; 95% confidence intervals in parentheses.

between the two parties statewide thereby produced shifting, and often precarious, legislative majorities.

While the state constitution strictly limited partisan shenanigans regarding state legislative districts, no limits were placed on the design of congressional districts. Moreover, Ohio's state constitution did not provide the governor with a veto. As long as party loyalty held, whichever party captured the state legislature could, if it wanted, implement a congressional district map of their choosing. Table 4.4 displays the combined effects of party turnover and out-party districts for Ohio between 1878 and 1890. In every case where there was party turnover and an out-party redistricting plan, a new replacement map was promptly put in place. Each new regime then made it one of their first orders of business to redraw the states' congressional districts (Argersinger 1982). The only exception was 1882 when Ohio gained a seat in the federal apportionment and was required to redistrict anyway.

Party leaders sometimes went to great legislative lengths to pass a new redistricting plan. In 1886, for instance, Republicans engineered a plan to unseat four Democratic state senators from Cincinnati based on charges of electoral fraud. These four seats gave Republicans a firm majority in the state Senate, to go with their majority in the lower House, and opened the door for Republicans to replace the pro-Democratic congressional map that been put in place two years earlier. According to the *New York Times*, "The ousting of the four fraud representatives from Cincinnati means a redistricting of the State, or rather the undoing of the Democratic gerrymander" (*New York Times*, May 3, 1886). As we see in the next chapter, these maps were partisan to the hilt. The results were district maps that at times determined partisan control of the national government. Indeed, it would not be an exaggeration to say that during the Gilded Age, as Ohio's district maps went, so went Congress.

TABLE 4.4. The Impact of Party Control on Redistricting Decisions in Ohio, 1878–90

Year	Previous Control of State Government	Current Control of State Government	Partisanship of Previous Plan	Redistricting?
1878	Republican	Democratic	Republican	Yes
1880	Democratic	Republican	Democratic	Yes
1882[a]	Republican	Republican	Republican	Yes
1884	Republican	Democratic	Republican	Yes
1886	Democratic	Republican	Democratic	Yes
1888	Republican	Republican	Republican	No
1890	Republican	Democratic	Republican	Yes

[a]Gained seats in the 1882 apportionment.

Connecticut

At the other end of the spectrum was Connecticut. The state redrew its congressional districts after the 1842 reapportionment and did not redistrict again until 1910. Just as in Ohio, the interaction between the constitutional structure and party control of the state legislature drove the frequency of redistricting. But whereas in Ohio these factors led to frequent redistricting, in Connecticut they combined to forestall redistricting for 70 years.

The first thing to note is that Connecticut neither gained nor lost seats in any of the federal reapportionments between 1850 and 1900. The state had exactly four congressional representatives for this period. As a result, there was no outside prod that compelled the state to redistrict. If congressional districts were to be redrawn, the motivation had to come from within the state legislature itself. But the state legislature—and, in particular, the Republicans who dominated the state legislature—found little reason to consider redrawing the congressional map.

Connecticut, like many northeastern states, used a town-based representation system for the lower house of the state legislature. The rule, written into the state constitution, required that every town receive a representative—regardless of the town's size. The result was egregious malapportionment. According to C. K. Yearley, in the late 19th century, "Four of the states smallest towns with a total population of 1,500 enjoyed four representatives against only twice that number to represent the 407,715 inhabitants of the four largest cities. Thus, Tolland County with 3% of the State's population in sparsely settled farming country sent 8.3% of the representatives to the legislature although New Haven, by contrast, with 30% of the population supplied only 16.6% of the representation" (Yearley 1970, 40). These "rotten boroughs" inflated Republican (and Whig) numbers in the legislature given their strength in the rural, small towns. Even in pro-Democratic election years, Democrats found it nearly impossible to overcome the unfavorable electoral bias of the lower house.

Thus, with a congressional district plan that favored Republican congressional candidates and Republicans in firm control of the lower house of the state legislature, there was little motivation in the state legislature to adjust the congressional district boundaries. And Democrats could not gain the necessary majorities to pass a new plan. Over time, this led to stunning discrepancies in House district populations. In 1842, the districts had actually been roughly equal in population—the largest district had 90,000, and the smallest had 72,543. This difference, although not strictly equal, was minor by 19th-century standards. By 1900, however, the population differences had reached enormous levels. In 1900, the largest district (the 2nd) had nearly three times as many people as the smallest (the 3rd)—310,923 to 129,619. Perhaps not surprisingly, the most populous district—the 2nd, which contained New Haven—consistently had the highest Democratic support of any district in the state. The 70-year logjam was finally broken in 1912 when Connecticut gained a new seat in the federal apportionment and was finally motivated to redistrict.

At-Large Elections

Not all states that gained seats, however, opted to redistrict. Another tactic, after 1872, was to elect part of the congressional delegation in statewide, at-large elections. The decision to use at-large districts arose when a state gained new seats in the federal apportionment. Although Congress had outlawed statewide districts in 1842, they modified this policy in 1872 by allowing gaining states to temporarily elect their new members at-large. Typically a state would keep its old map intact and elect any newly gained seats at-large. Many states took advantage of this opportunity, not only in 1872, but also in every subsequent apportionment (until 1967, when Congress finally banned at-large elections). Between 1872 and 1940, 47 of the 121 states that gained seats elected their new members through at-large elections.

For some states, at-large elections arose because of the inability of factions within the state legislature to agree on a new set of districts (Martis 1982, 4–5). Typically, this happened when there was divided partisan control of state government. Since both parties could veto the other's preferred redistricting scheme, stalemate would lead to the use of at-large elections.

In other cases, strong political parties may have used at-large elections to preserve or extend their dominance. As Martis notes, "Another possible scenario is that the party in power with the allegiance of the majority of the state's electorate would be certain their at-large candidate would win the election. Re-dividing the state into several smaller districts could make some districts more vulnerable to defeat by creating a large opposition faction in each" (1982, 4).

Thus, we should expect to see an increased probability of at-large elections under two different conditions. The first is when there is divided partisan control of state government. The second, following the conjecture offered by Martis, is that unified governments would prefer at-large elections when it was confident of winning the statewide vote.

To test these predictions, I examined the choices states made when they gained seats and the use of at-large elections was an option (i.e., after 1870). Because the time frame from 1870 to 1900 provides so few observations, I extended the data collection up through 1940. This provides enough observations for us to make reasonable inferences from the data. The dependent variable is a dummy variable coded one if a state redistricted upon gaining new seats and zero otherwise. To test the prediction that at-large elections should be more likely during periods of divided government, I included a dummy variable for unified partisan control (*Unified Government*). I expect this coefficient to be positive. To test the possibility that strong parties would be more likely to use an at-large election the stronger they believed they could carry the state, I interacted *Unified Government* with the strong party's statewide vote in the most recent congressional election. Before polling, the vote tally from the past congressional election likely served as the most reliable indicator of a party's upcoming prospects (Kernell and McDonald 1999, 803). I expect the coefficient on this interaction to be negative, indicating less willingness to redistrict the larger their expected vote share. In addition, I included controls for the size of the state's delegation (*Delegation Size*) and years since last redistricting. As in the previous section, I estimate the model using a probit maximum-likelihood estimator.

The results are presented in table 4.5. The coefficient for *Unified Government* is, as expected, positive and significant. Redistricting became more

TABLE 4.5. Estimating the Probability of Redistricting when a State Gained New Seats, 1870–1940 (probit estimates; dependent variable = redistricting)

	Coefficients (robust standard errors)
Unified Government	1.732**
	(.661)
Strong Party's Vote Share in Last	−.014*
Election × Unified Government	(.008)
Delegation Size	−.018
	(.012)
Years since Last Redistricting	.029
	(.021)
Constant	−.535**
	(.163)
N	121
Log-Likelihood	−74.387

Note: Robust standard errors (clustering by state) in parentheses.
$**p < .05; *p < .10$.

likely during periods of unified partisan control. It also means that at-large elections were more likely during periods of divided control. Moreover, the interaction between unified government and strong parties statewide vote share was negative and significant (at .10).

To see the substantive effects of the variables more clearly, I converted these estimates into the probability of a state redistricting upon gaining a new seat (where the converse is an at-large election). When there was divided government, and the control variables are at their median values, the probability of a redistricting is .35. When there was unified government, and a statewide vote share of 55 percent, the probability of redistricting jumps to .71. Moreover, this probability increases with the size of the strong party's most recent vote share. Increasing a party's vote share from 50 percent to 70 percent boosts the probability of redistricting by 10 percent. Thus, as state parties became more confident they would carry the statewide vote, the more willing they were to keep the current districts dormant and elect new members at-large.

The strategic use of at-large elections could also aggregate into national, partisan ramifications. In fact, the impact of at-large elections on party ratios in Congress may have been the impetus behind the congressional decision in 1871 to allow at-large elections in the first place. First, consider that that 16 of the 19 elections held at-large in 1872 went to Republicans. Not coincidentally, Republicans held control of Congress and the presidency, and were the chief proponents of the at-large provision.

Further evidence of a partisan motivation behind the adoption of the at-large provision comes from floor debates in the House. Because the apportionment of 1872 boosted the size of the House by over 20 percent, a large proportion of states were slated to receive new seats. This worried many congressional Republicans who realized that without an at-large provision they risked losing many of these additional seats. For example, Indiana's Republican delegation expressed concern that they would lose their two additional seats because the state legislature had already adjourned for the year. The Republican John Shanks of Indiana reported that:

> In Indiana we have today no legislative body that can meet until an election shall take place under a proclamation of the Governor, and there will probably be no such election in time to have legislative provision for the election of additional members by districts . . . If we do not elect the additional member at-large then we shall not get our full quota. (*Congressional Globe*, 42nd Congress, 2nd Session, 63)

Confident they could carry the Indiana statewide vote, and knowing the Republican governor was averse to calling the Democratic-controlled legislature back into session, Congressional Republicans saw at-large elections as a way to pick up a few extra seats.

More explicit charges of partisanship emerged from the Democratic side of the aisle. Democrats recognized that a statewide minority would be shut out of any at-large representation, and in strong Republican states like Illinois, which was gaining four new seats, Democrats were potentially facing substantial losses. Samuel Marshall, a Democrat from Illinois, identified the looming pitfalls to a statewide minority party if the at-large provision were adopted:

> Suppose that in Kentucky, Missouri, or in the State of Illinois, there should be two, three, four, or five additional Representatives to be elected by the State at large, to allow the majority party in the State to elect all of those members, and to hold out a temptation to the Legislature to refuse to redistrict the State, thus depriving the minority of any representation through these additional members, would be an outrage which this Congress, I am sure, would not tolerate for one single moment. (*Congressional Globe*, 42nd Congress, 2nd Session, 63)

Unfortunately for Marshall, and his fellow Democrats, Congress did tolerate the at-large provision. Eleven states chose to use elect their new seats at-large. These states combined for a total of 19 at-large seats, 16 of which went to Republicans. As with the case of unprompted redistricting, the use of at-large elections quickly became another weapon in party battles.

General-Ticket Elections

Throughout most of the 19th century, states rarely had to deal with the thorny problem of redistricting after losing seats. Before 1880, if a state lost seats and failed to redistrict, then they lost their representation in Congress. In the 1880 Federal Apportionment Act, Congress added a provision allowing losing states to temporarily elect their entire congressional delegation on a statewide ballot—the general ticket. A party that was confident it could win the statewide vote could be empowered.

Although the number of states losing seats between 1880 and 1900 was minimal, two later cases, both following the 1930 census, illustrate how the strategic game between parties often played out. The elections following the census of 1930 were the first since 1840 in which a substantial number of states lost seats. Because the federal government had not apportioned the House in nearly 20 years, and the size of the House did not change, a number of states saw their representation in Congress decrease. The first case comes from Missouri. There the Democratic governor vetoed the Republican-controlled legislature's attempt at a partisan gerrymander, throwing the entire delegation into a general-ticket election. Confident that Democrats would win the statewide vote, the governor knew he could safely veto. Democrats went on to sweep all 13 of Missouri's seats with only 62 percent of the statewide vote. After this massive setback, Republicans relented and drew up a districting law benefiting Democrats (Mitchell 1968).

In Minnesota, the Republican legislature passed a partisan gerrymander, mistakenly believing—or hoping—that it could pass a redistricting law without the governors' signature.[8] Governor Floyd Olson, a member of the opposition Democratic-Farmer-Labor party, vetoed the bill, thereby forcing all the congressional seats onto a general-ticket ballot. Two years later, Republicans relented and grudgingly agreed to a plan favoring the Democratic-Farmer-Labor party. "The Republicans disliked the Farmer Labor version of congressional reapportionment," writes Olson's biographer, "but accepted it rather than face another election of representatives at large" (Mayer 1951, 139). Thus, at least in Missouri and Minnesota, the strategic deployment of a general-ticket election dramatically strengthened the hand of the party with the strongest electoral future.

The Past and Future of Mid-Decade Redistricting

Part of the impetus for studying the history of redistricting is that it can also provide insight into modern redistricting politics. As noted in chapter 1, many political observers worried that other states would follow the lead of the 2002 Texas remap and devise their own mid-cycle maps. The result would be a gerrymandering arms race. Indeed, both Colorado and Georgia attempted to redraw their districts mid-decade, although with less drastic consequences than the map in Texas.

As the results presented earlier indicate, just because a state can legally redistrict mid-decade, it does not follow that it will. The political conditions that would motivate a party to take the dramatic step of redistricting mid-decade also need to be present. Thus, the findings with respect to the timing of redistricting raise an interesting question: why hasn't there been more recent mid-cycle redistricting? How often have modern state legislatures found themselves in a position similar to that of the Texas Republicans in 2002 or Ohio Democrats in 1878? To answer this question, I collected data on the partisan composition of state legislatures and the party affiliation of governors for the time period 1972–2005. I combined this with data on the type of redistricting plan each state had enacted in the previous redistricting (Carson and Crespin 2004). Redistricting plans were classified as either non-legislative, meaning they were drawn by a commission or judicial officers; bipartisan, meaning they were enacted by non-unified state governments; or partisan, meaning they were enacted by either a unified Democratic or Republican government.

Eliminating the nonpartisan, unicameral Nebraska legislature, and states with only one congressional district, leaves us with 1,436 state-years to analyze. Table 4.6 presents the tabular results. Perhaps the most striking finding from these data is how few partisan redistricting plans have been enacted in the past 35 years. Only 10.3 percent of the state-years in the dataset have a unified partisan redistricting plan. The overwhelming majority of plans (79.9 percent) were drawn by divided state governments, with non-legislative plans making up the remaining 9.7 percent. The fact that so few plans have been enacted by unified party governments in the past three decades severely limits the motivation for a mid-cycle redistricting. The bipartisan compromise at the heart of these plans means that each party is invested, to some degree, in the plans. These plans are often drawn to protect congressional incumbents, which makes it even more difficult for state legislatures to enact new plans that would disrupt entrenched congressional incumbents.

Table 4.6 also displays the frequency with which unified or divided state governments faced plans drawn either by the other party, a non-legislative entity, or a bipartisan plan. By far, the most common occurrence in the data is a divided state government living under a bipartisan plan. In these cases, we would not expect there to be a majority sentiment to change to a more partisan plan in the state. In the instances in which we see a unified state government facing a partisan plan, in all but one case, the plan was drawn by the party in power. The one exception was Georgia in 2005, where much like Texas, the legislature convened with a newly unified Republican majority. This case did not stay out of equilibrium long as the Georgia legislature enacted a new plan, which is the only other mid-cycle legislative redistricting in the data set. All other unified state governments faced a plan they had drawn, a bipartisan plan, or a plan drawn by a non-legislative entity—all of which are more difficult to change.

The bottom portion of table 4.6 presents the comparable data for the period between 1870 and 1900. This was the period of most intense redistricting activity and therefore offers a useful baseline to compare with the modern period. The first thing to note is the infrequency of divided government. Reading the totals at the bottom of each column we see that only 93 state-years, or 17 percent, had divided party control of state government (compared to 53 percent for the modern era). This infrequency of divided government in the 19th century is also reflected in the paucity of bipartisan redistricting plans. During this period, only 6 of the 105 redistricting plans were passed during divided government (and all but one was prompted

TABLE 4.6. The Frequency of State Party Control and Redistricting Type

1970–2006		
Party Control of State Government		
Bipartisan	Democratic	Republican
Existing Plan		
Bipartisan		
643	386	119
(83.5)	(76.9)	(72.6)
Democratic		
15	82	1
(1.9)	(16.3)	(0.6)
Republican		
16	0	34
(2.1)	(0)	(20.7)
Non-Legislative		
96	34	10
(12.5)	(6.8)	(6.1)
Total		
770	502	164
1870–1900		
Party Control of State Government		
Bipartisan	Democratic	Republican
Existing Plan		
Bipartisan		
5	15	20
(5.3)	(6.6)	(6.9)
Democratic		
23	161	42
(24.7)	(71.2)	(14.6)
Republican		
65	50	226
(69.9)	(22.1)	(78.5)
Total		
93	226	228

Note: Numbers in parentheses are column percentages.

by a change in a state's apportionment of seats). Second, the number of years in which a party with unified control faced an existing plan drawn by the opposition was also much higher than in the modern era. There were 50 state-years where Democrats had a Republican-drawn plan, and 42 instances where Republicans faced a Democratic-drawn plan.

Overall, these results indicate that the conditions that prompt off-cycle redistricting were much more prevalent in the 19th century. Turnover of state government was more frequent, unified government was more frequent, and these new governments often found themselves with a distasteful redistricting plan currently in place.

Conclusion

Judicial entry into the redistricting process in the 1960s revolutionized the process of drawing district lines (Ansolabehere and Snyder 2008; Cox and Katz 2002). One consequence was to set a floor on the amount of redistricting that had to take place. States have to redistrict at least once a decade. This has created a regular 10-year redistricting cycle. At the same time, the courts have not created a ceiling on redistricting. The Supreme Court confirmed the legality of mid-decade gerrymanders in their decision to uphold the Texas remap. Unless there is an explicit prohibition in a state constitution, states can continue to redistrict more than once a decade.

In this chapter, I took a historical step back and examined an era before court-ordered redistricting. Freed from the constraints of the courts, state parties gerrymandered quite differently. Sometimes they would redistrict frequently; at other times, they would let their districts lay dormant for decades. Both outcomes were tied directly to the nature of party competition within a state. When a new party came into power, and found the districts recently drawn by the out party, the probability of redistricting shot up. On the other hand, once a strong party had designed districts favorable to their candidates, the probability of redistricting dropped practically to zero.

The variegated redistricting of the era interjected an often forgotten dynamic into 19th-century politics. Redistricting was much more variable. While a few states went long stretches without redistricting, many other states redistricted often. In the next three chapters, I examine the consequences of these redistricting decisions on party ratios, electoral competition, and the decisions of representatives to run for reelection.

FIVE

Stacking the States, Stacking the House

*The Partisan Consequences of
Congressional Redistricting*

In early 1890, the Ohio state legislature assembled for its new session. The state elections, held in 1889, had given the Democratic Party a slim majority in both the state assembly and state senate. With their newfound majority, the newly assembled Democratic caucus immediately turned to an issue of both local and national importance—redrawing congressional districts. Republicans held 16 of the 21 congressional seats. At the national level, Republicans held a razor-thin two-seat majority in the House of Representatives. Thus, with the November midterm elections looming, Democrats across the country looked to the new Democratic majority in Columbus for help. Seizing the opportunity, the Democratic caucus thoroughly reworked the states' 21 congressional districts. No district went untouched. Reflecting on the audacity of the pro-Democratic map, the *New York Times* wrote that, "The dose of gerrymandering, with which the Democratic legislature has repaid old wrongs of the same character, has made more changes in the map of Ohio than have occurred in African geography in recent years" (*New York Times*, July 25, 1890).

The gerrymander was astonishingly successful. In the November elections, Democrats won 14 seats, turning a 5- to 16-seat deficit into a 14 to 7 surplus. The 9-seat swing to Democrats was all the more remarkable considering that Republicans actually out-polled the Democrats, 49 percent to 47.5 percent. The impact of this gerrymander had far-reaching national implications as well. The swing of seats in Ohio, coupled with a strong pro-Democratic tide in other states, propelled Democrats into majority control of the House. With Republicans in control of the Senate and the presidency, capturing majority control of the House provided Democrats with an institutional beachhead to fight off the legislative initiatives of the opposition.

This highly partisan, and consequential, gerrymander was by no means an isolated incident. This chapter demonstrates that strategic redistricting had a profound impact on congressional election outcomes and the national balance of power throughout the 19th century. Throughout the 19th century, state political parties used gerrymandering to bias congressional election outcomes in their favor. Significantly, these state-level activities generated important ripples in the national balance of power. Majorities in the House during this period were often razor-thin, and timely shifts in a few seats could swing partisan control of the House. In fact, on at least two occasions—the elections of 1878 and 1888—strategic mid-decade gerrymanders altered partisan control of the House. Thus, fluctuations in party control of the House resulted not only from an evenly divided partisan nation, but also from the strategic manipulation of electoral districts.

Beyond deepening our understanding of 19th-century American politics, the results of this chapter speak directly to contemporary debates over the impact of redistricting. Almost everything that is known about the national consequences of gerrymandering comes from research conducted on the redistricting cycles that have occurred since the court-led reapportionment revolution of the 1960s. This research typically shows that each of the subsequent rounds of redistricting produced, at best, only a minimal impact on the partisan balance of power in Congress (e.g., Glazer, Grofman, and Robbins 1987; Seabrook 2010; Swain, Borrelli, and Reed 1998).

However, no consensus has emerged about why gerrymandering has had such little influence. Some scholars have argued that constraints on gerrymandering in the modern period, including court oversight; one-person, one-vote mandates; and demands by congressional incumbents for secure seats, have made it virtually impossible to engage in a full-blown partisan gerrymander (e.g., Glazer, Grofman, and Robbins 1987; Tufte 1973). Others contend that the partisan gains to be had from gerrymandering are limited, regardless of the institutional configuration under which redistricting takes place (e.g., Butler and Cain 1992, 8–10). By moving beyond the relatively fixed institutional and political context of modern redistricting, 19th-century elections provide a unique opportunity to assess these competing explanations.

The results presented in this chapter suggest that redistricting can indeed alter partisan control of Congress, but only when the conditions are right. In particular, a highly polarized party system and a close division between the two parties at the national level dramatically raised the incentives and payoffs from strategic partisan gerrymanders. As such, the findings presented in this chapter have direct implications for contemporary redistricting controversies. Looking back to the late 19th century—also an era of polarized politics—can shed new light on the question of whether the recent mid-decade gerrymander in Texas is unique or if there are general conditions under which strategic gerrymanders can reshape the national balance of power.

Partisan Balance and Strategic Redistricting in the Partisan Era

Between 1840 and 1900, competition for control of Congress—and the House of Representatives in particular—was fierce. Figure 5.1 displays the Democratic share of congressional votes and seats for this period. Between 1840 and 1858, Democrats held a slight edge over Whigs—and later Republicans. On occasion, Democrats had substantial majorities in the House, but these majorities could be fleeting. For example, Democrats were wiped out in the 1854 election—losing 74 seats—only to regain control of the House two years later. While seat shares fluctuated in the antebellum House, the national division of the vote remained close. For most of the period from 1840 until the Civil War, Democrats' share of the national vote hovered around the 50 percent mark. The onset of Southern secession and the Civil War ushered in a period of Republican dominance. But even during the Civil War, Democrats remained a viable opposition party (Silbey 1977). Congressional Democrats, for instance, gained seats in the 1862 midterm election, and actually came close to capturing the House (Carson, Jenkins, Rohde and Souva 2001).

But the most intense period of electoral competition during the 19th century—if not the entirety of American history—was between 1872 and 1894. The two parties were in virtual tie for most of these years. This can be seen in table 5.1 which presents information on party control of the House between 1870 and 1900. During this period, Democrats averaged 50.7 percent of the two-party congressional vote and a similarly razor-thin 49.7 percent of seats in the House. The dead-even balance between the

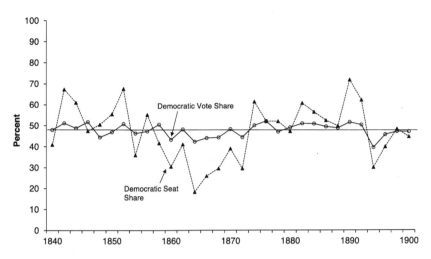

Fig. 5.1. Partisan competition in U.S. House elections, 1840–1900. Vote is the Democratic percentage of the total congressional vote. Seats are the total percentage of seats won by the Democrats on Election Day. (Data from Rusk 2002.)

TABLE 5.1. Party Control of the U.S. House in the Post-Bellum Era

Year (Congress)	Democratic Congressional Vote	Democratic House Seats	Party Control of the House
1870 (42)	48.91	38.93	R
1872 (43)	45.61	29.45	R
1874 (44)	52.39	61.30	D
1876 (45)	52.23	51.88	D
1878 (46)	53.65	51.88	D
1880 (47)	51.27	47.10	R
1882 (48)	54.91	60.62	D
1884 (49)	51.72	56.31	D
1886 (50)	52.01	52.31	D
1888 (51)	50.50	49.69	R
1890 (52)	54.42	71.69	D
1892 (53)	54.81	62.08	D
1894 (54)	44.87	29.97	R
1896 (55)	47.43	39.78	R
1898 (56)	48.90	48.18	R
1900 (57)	48.08	44.54	R
Average	50.73	49.73	

Source: Rusk 2001.
Note: The vote is the Democratic percentage of the two-party vote. The seats are the total percentage of seats won by the Democrats on Election Day.

national parties resulted from the combination of strong Democratic states in the South (following the end of Reconstruction), strong Republican states in the Northeast, and intense competition throughout the Midwest and border states.

This split within the national electorate was also reflected in the fragile partisan control of Washington, DC. The reappearance of Democratic southern delegations beginning in the early 1870s, coupled with the party's success nationally in the 1874 midterm election, reintroduced fierce competition for control of the House. And control of the House often meant the difference between unified and divided government. The strategic admittance of pro-Republican western territories into the Union gave Republicans a structural advantage that allowed them to control both the Senate and presidency for most of this period after the Civil War (Stewart and Weingast 1992). Thus, whether partisan control of the national government was unified or divided often pivoted on which party could capture the House of Representatives. Between 1870 and 1900, each party controlled the House in exactly half of the Congresses (eight times apiece).

With voter loyalties that were tough to change (Silbey 1991) and mobilization efforts near their maximum (Burnham 1982), parties searched out other opportunities for an extra source of advantage. The clever manipulation of congressional districts was one of those opportunities. Compared to their modern counterparts, 19th-century parties in control of state governments were afforded a large degree of discretion in choosing both the timing and nature of their redistricting events. As seen in the previous chapter, the state legislatures exercised wide discretion over when to redistrict. But in addition to deciding *when* to redraw district lines, state legislatures had broad discretion in determining *how* to draw district maps. Unlike modern state legislatures, they were not bound by the one-person, one-vote requirements. Although Congress occasionally added language to the decennial Apportionment Act requiring that districts contain equal numbers of people, there is little evidence that these provisions were ever enforced, much less achieved.

Once a party decided to gerrymander, its members typically pursued one of two strategies. As discussed in chapter 2, the first strategy was to pack supporters of the opposition into one or a few districts and distribute in-party loyalists evenly throughout the rest of the state in marginal, yet winnable, districts. A good example of this packing strategy comes from post-reconstruction Alabama, where the majority Democrats placed every possible Black Belt (i.e., Republican) county into one district (the Old Fourth Alabama), preferring "to lose one district rather than run the risk of a Republican triumph by a much smaller majority in several districts" (McMillan 1978, 222).

The second strategy was to create an efficient or dispersal gerrymander (Cain 1984, 1985; Owen and Grofman 1988). A party that was confident in its ability to win the statewide vote for the foreseeable future could maximize its seat share by having each district mirror this favorable statewide partisan distribution (Cain 1985; Cox and Katz 2002). By efficiently distributing its supporters in marginal but winnable districts, the controlling party could win every seat in the state. An illustration of this efficient strategy comes from Maine, where Republicans gerrymandered the state in 1884 and, for the next five elections, captured all four congressional districts despite an average district vote of only 54 percent.

These anecdotes suggest that state politicians recognized the payoffs in the currency of congressional delegation share from gerrymandering. The possibility that these state-level decisions might also shape the national balance of power was not lost on national party leaders. For example, Democrats' precarious hold on the House entering the midterm elections of 1878 led national Democratic leaders—including the Speaker of the House, Samuel Randall (D-PA)—to implore Democrats in the Ohio legislature to redraw its congressional districts. In May 1878, the *New York Times* gave the following report:

> Dispatches have poured in upon them [Democratic state legislators] from all parts of the country, and especially from the Democratic leaders at Washington, who have declared that the passage of this bill was the only way to save the next Congress from falling into Republican hands. (*New York Times*, May 14, 1878)

State party leaders in Ohio, along with Democrats in Missouri, did indeed redistrict—swinging nine seats to the Democrats—and, as we will see shortly, helped the Democrats retain their slim majority in the House. The re-redistricting of Ohio and Missouri provides further anecdotal evidence to suggest that gerrymandering may have played an important role in shaping the partisan composition of state delegations and, at times, the composition of the House.

Stacking the States

Were state parties using redistricting to stack their state congressional delegations and possibly alter the partisan composition of the House? As was done in chapter 2, the primary way to answer this question is to analyze the effect of districting partisanship on the translation of votes into seats. Following standard reasoning in the redistricting literature, one can think of districting plans as affecting two elements of the vote-seat translation: partisan bias and electoral responsiveness (e.g., Gelman and King 1994; Tufte 1973). Partisan bias is defined "as the difference between the expected seat share that the Democrats would get with an average vote share of 0.5 and their 'fair share' of 0.5 (half the seats for half the votes)" (Cox and Katz 1999, 820). A districting plan that packs Republican voters into a few safe districts and places Democrats in a number of marginal, yet winnable, districts would produce a pro-Democratic bias (i.e., they would win more than their "fair-share" of seats given their overall vote).

Responsiveness—or swing ratio—is the change in a party's aggregate seat share given a 1 percent change in their vote share. For example, a responsiveness value of three (i.e., the cube law) means that a shift in the statewide vote from 50 percent to 51 percent would produce a three-percentage-point seat shift. A districting plan with a number of marginal, highly competitive districts will have a high value of responsiveness (i.e., a small swing in the statewide vote will generate a large swing in seats). A plan with numerous safe seats will have a lower level of responsiveness because it will take a large swing in the statewide vote before seats start changing hands.

If parties used redistricting to tilt electoral outcomes in their favor, then plans passed when a single party controlled state government would lead to high levels of both responsiveness and partisan bias. A bias in favor of the controlling party is consistent with that party skewing the districts in their favor. What about plans during divided government? Although plans passed during divided state governments were rare in the 19th century, there were a few, and their dynamics differed from partisan plans. Since both parties could veto the other's schemes, bipartisan plans typically protected incumbents of both parties. We should, therefore, expect to see lower levels of bias and responsiveness under bipartisan plans (Cox and Katz 2002).

Consider the redistricting of North Carolina in 1852. Whigs controlled the lower house while Democrats controlled the state senate. Although Democrats had done well in the prior election and could expect to poll well in the future, Whig control of the lower house in the state legislature put them in a position to prevent total electoral disaster. The historian Marc Kruman writes that, "After interminable haggling over the redistricting, the parties approved compromise plans. Whigs, though, clearly felt they had gotten the best of the bargain since they voted more heavily in favor of the plans than did the Democrats. Whigs thus prevented Democrats from reapportioning them out of existence" (Kruman 1983, 154).

To measure the impact of different partisan regimes on electoral outcomes, I estimated the bias and responsiveness for redistricting plans passed between 1840 and 1900. I matched the precise date of each redistricting (Martis 1982) with the partisan composition of the state legislatures and governors at the time of passage (Burnham 1985). With this information, I then assigned each election, by state and year, to one of three plans: partisan Democratic, partisan Republican/Whig, and bipartisan (taking into account the various veto override provisions) (Cox and Katz 2002).

Similar to the empirical modeling strategy used in chapter 2, for the years between 1840 and 1900, I estimated the following vote-seat equation,

$$ln(s_{it}/(1 - s_{it})) = \lambda + \rho(ln(v_{it}/(1 - v_{it}))) \tag{1}$$

where s_{it} was the proportion of seats won by the Democrats, and v_{it} was their vote share in state i at time t.[1] The model includes a constant, λ, tapping partisan bias, and an independent variable, $ln(v_{it}/(1 - v_{it}))$, with the coefficient ρ measuring electoral responsiveness. The model allows λ and ρ to vary across the different districting plans (i.e. partisan Democrat, partisan Republican/Whig, bipartisan). To control for third-party movements, I also included the statewide minor-party vote.[2] In addition, anticipating that congressional elections within a state might affect one another, I estimated the model with an extended beta-binomial distribution (Cox and Katz 2002; King 1998).[3] This model is appropriate given that the dependent variable is a proportion and that there is potential correlation in the probability across districts (within a state) of a Democratic victory.

The estimates in table 5.2 show that the partisanship of districting plans directly affected the translation of votes into seats. Partisan Democratic plans produced a significant bias of 8.25 percent—in other words, for 50 percent of the vote, Democrats received 58.25 percent of the seats. Partisan Republican/Whig plans produced a significant bias of 5.7 percent. Bipartisan plans, however, failed to produce statistically significant levels of bias. Substantively, these results indicate that the partisanship of districting plans was systematically related to outcomes on Election Day. At 50 percent of the vote, a party could expect to win roughly between 58 percent and 44 percent of a state delegation, depending on which party drew the district lines.

Both types of partisan plans produced high levels of responsiveness—4.0

and 4.25 for Democratic and Republican/Whig plans, respectively. Bipartisan plans, as expected, produced a lower level of responsiveness (3.68) than the two partisan plans. These levels are substantially higher than any found in the 20th century (Brady and Grofman 1991; Engstrom and Kernell 2005).[4] They provide evidence that, in addition to biasing election outcomes, parties also tried to maximize their seat share by efficiently distributing their supporters across districts.

Efficient gerrymanders were, in part, made possible because incumbents were not in a strong position to push for safer districts. Though this was a period of emerging careerism (Price 1975), congressmen were still at the mercy of local political organizations for nomination and access to the ballot. Moreover, the importance of seniority in determining committee positions had yet to fully take root (Katz and Sala 1996). An intriguing implication is that the frequency and partisanship of redistricting may have contributed to this era's high retirement rates and helped slow the development of congressional careerism. If parties were more willing to pursue extra seats rather than protect sitting representatives, we should find incumbents more readily retiring when their district was altered. I take up this issue in chapter 6.

TABLE 5.2. Partisan Bias and Responsiveness under
Different Districting Plans, 1840–1900

	Coefficient	Standard Error
Bias		
Partisan Democrat	8.25*	1.96
Bipartisan	2.15	3.62
Partisan Republican/Whig	−5.70*	1.84
Responsiveness		
Partisan Democrat	4.00*	.27
Bipartisan	3.68*	.56
Partisan Republican/Whig	4.25*	.31
Minor Party Vote	.014*	.004
γ	.004*	.011
Log-Likelihood	−2,386.69	
N	531	

Note: Maximum likelihood estimates of the vote-seat equation following an extended beta binomial distribution. The γ parameter captures the correlation across districts within a state in the probability of a Democratic victory. There is no constant because the intercept was suppressed.
    *$p < .05$.

The Partisan Consequences of Redistricting

The results presented in the previous section are consistent with the hypothesis that parties drew electoral maps to bias outcomes in their favor. Here we consider the intent behind redistricting plans. In the 19th century, strategic state legislators took the most recent election results, broken down by county and ward, and combined these data to forecast the partisan effects of new district lines. Because counties were the building blocks of most districts, politicians could easily aggregate county vote returns and calculate the partisan consequences of new district lines. For example, Governor Joseph Foraker (R-OH), bragged to the *New York Times* that the Republican gerrymander in 1886 would allow his party to capture 14 of Ohio's 21 congressional seats (*New York Times*, May 18, 1886). Foraker's dead-on predictions were based on the aggregation of the 1884 presidential vote by county into the newly drawn district lines. These simple forecasting exercises, therefore, appeared to be standard practice for those redrawing district lines. With the use of historical election results and 19th-century congressional district maps, we can do the same.

To do this, I took the two-party congressional vote by county (Clubb, Flanigan, and Zingale 1987) from the most recent election before a new redistricting and then aggregated the county results into the new district lines (Martis 1982). When district lines crossed county boundaries or multiple districts were contained within a single county (e.g., New York, Philadelphia, Chicago), I tracked down the necessary ward- and town-level election data.[5] A district with an intended Democratic two-party vote share greater than 50 percent was assigned to the Democrats. Adding up the number of intended Democratic victories in a state allows for a comparison between the pre-redistricting election results and what would have happened had the new lines been in place.

To measure the effect of partisanship on the intent of district plans, I estimated an equation where the dependent variable is the intended change in the Democratic proportion of seats (i.e., the post-redistricting proportion minus the pre-redistricting proportion). The key independent variable is the partisanship of those responsible for drawing the new districts (Born 1985). This latter variable, *Partisanship*, is coded +1 for Democratic plans, 0 for bipartisan plans, and −1 for Republican or Whig plans. If parties reconstructed district lines to add to their congressional delegation, then this variable should be positive and significant. In addition, I also included the proportion of congressional seats Democrats held at the time of redistricting (*Lag Seat percent*) (see Born 1985) because it is harder for a party to add seats if they already hold most, or all, of the congressional delegation. A variable indicating whether a state lost or gained seats in the federal apportionment is also included as a control. This variable is scored 1 for a gain, 0 for no gain, and −1 if a state lost seats. Finally, the analysis is confined to states with more than two congressional seats.

The results are presented in the first column of table 5.3. The coefficient for *Partisanship* is indeed positive and significant ($p < .01$). The value of the coefficient is .15, indicating that going from a bipartisan plan to a Democratic plan increased the intended Democratic gain to 15 percent of the delegation, and going from a Republican to a Democratic plan meant a switch of 30 percent of the delegation. In a state with 20 congressional seats, we would expect that going from a Republican to a Democratic redistricting plan would produce, on average, an intended swing of roughly six seats to Democrats.

Ohio exemplifies the immense impact partisan redistricting could have on the party ratios of congressional delegations. To illustrate this, figure 5.2 plots the Democrats' percentage of the two-party vote in Ohio along with the intended number of seats the mapmakers were trying to manufacture. Next to each data point is a label (D or R) indicating which party drew

TABLE 5.3. Intended and Actual Seat Change for Redistricting Plans

	Intended Seat Change	Actual Seat Change
Partisanship	.15*	—
	(.02)	
Lag Seat %	−.43*	—
	(.06)	
Intended Seat Change (independent variable)	—	1.02*
		(.22)
Actual Vote Change	—	.01*
		(.001)
Gain/Loss in Seats	.01	−.03
	(.02)	(.03)
Constant	.21*	.03
	(.03)	(.03)
R^2	.31	.29
N	135	135

Note: The equation in column 1 was estimated using OLS. The second equation was estimated using two-stage least squares. A Breusch-Pagan test revealed no heteroskedasticity for either column. Standard errors in parentheses.
   *$p < .05$.

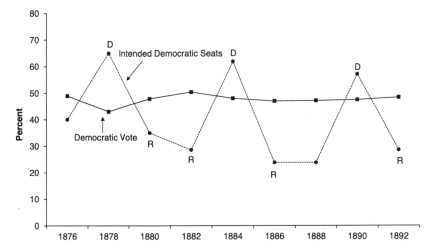

Fig. 5.2. Gerrymandering in Ohio, 1876–92. Solid line shows the Democratic share of the vote. Dashed line is the intended number of Democratic seats under the district maps. For the two years with no redistricting (1876 and 1888) the Democrats' actual share of seats was used. The symbols D and R indicate whether Democrats or Republicans redrew congressional districts.

the district maps. One can see striking partisan intent behind these gerrymanders. The intended seat shares flip back and forth depending on which party drew the maps. In 1886, for example, Republicans replaced the map drawn by Democrats two years earlier. The new map was intended to give Republicans 16 of Ohio's 21 seats—a boost of 6 new seats for Republicans. Democrats returned the favor in 1890 when they redrew the state map to give Democrats 12 of the 21 seats.

One can also see in this figure that each party adopted an efficient gerrymander strategy. The vote share during this period is flat, hovering near the 50 percent line. Yet seat shares fluctuated wildly as each party attempted to capture as many seats possible. Indeed, for most of this period, the vote in Ohio was dead even. But as these astute politicians understood, changing district lines could turn a narrow statewide vote margin into a supermajority of seats.

Of course, intent may not match reality on Election Day. The best-laid plans of strategic mapmakers may be undone by shifting partisan tides, changing migration patterns, or merely poor calculations. To investigate the correspondence between intent and the results, I borrowed the technique used by Born (1985) in his study of modern redistricting. This technique regresses the actual change in the Democratic delegation (*Actual Seat Change*) on the intended seat change. In addition, the change in the Democratic vote share (*Actual Vote Change*) and whether a state lost or gained seats are included as controls. Because the actual shift in seats is endogenous with the intended change, a standard Ordinary Least Squares (OLS) equation would be inappropriate. Instead, two stage least squares is employed. In the first stage, *Intended Seat Change* is regressed on the independent variables *Partisanship, Gain/Loss in Seats, Lag Seat percent*, and *Actual Vote Change*. The predicted values for *Intended Seat Change* from this first stage can then be used as an instrumental variable that is plugged into the second-stage equation. The coefficient of this instrumental variable will indicate to what extent the intentions of partisan mapmakers came to fruition.

The results are presented in the second column of table 5.3. The positive (1.02) and significant coefficient for intended vote change suggests a very tight correspondence between intent and Election Day outcomes.[6] On average, almost 100 percent of what was intended was actually realized on Election Day. Bear in mind that this model also controls for shifts in the vote across elections. So, it does not mean that every gerrymandering simply determined future outcomes, but that after controlling for changes in the vote, the correlation between intended seat gains and actual seat gains were nearly perfect. This is a striking testament to the ability of 19th-century politicians to skillfully draw electoral maps with precision.[7] It is even more remarkable considering mapmakers lacked modern polling technology and sophisticated computer software.

One might reasonably wonder how, despite technological limitations, mapmakers were able to accurately pull off these gerrymanders. Although sophisticated polling techniques had yet to exist, there is good reason to suspect that mapmakers had plenty of information about local electorates. State party leaders were kept abreast of local conditions by information networks that ran from local precincts up to the state capitol. The widespread use of the party strip ballot—listing candidates of only one party—made split-ticket voting cumbersome and rare (Engstrom and Kernell 2005). The lack of secret voting made it easy for party workers to monitor, and pay, voters at the ballot box (Bensel 2004; Cox and Kousser 1981). Altogether, these factors provided party leaders with sufficient information about the electorate to construct efficient partisan gerrymanders. The numbers in table 5.2 bear this out.

As the overall pattern of results indicates, 19th-century politicians were clearly adept at achieving the two necessary conditions for a successful partisan gerrymander: they systematically drew state electoral maps to bias elections in their favor, and these efforts were largely realized at election time. The next section examines the degree to which these state-level decisions cumulated to influence party ratios in the House of Representatives and the overall national balance of power.

Stacking the House

Since most of what was intended in redistricting plans came to fruition, one can take the state-by-state intended effects of redistricting for each year and simply add them to see how many national seats can be attributed to gerrymandering. So, for each year, I took the number of seats each party gained via gerrymandering and summed them to get a net redistricting effect. These numbers can then be used to develop counterfactuals for party ratios in the House. In other words, one can compare the effects of gerrymandering with what would have happened in the absence of gerrymandering.

The results of this simulation are presented in figure 5.3. The figure compares the simulation to the actual party ratios in the House. There are a number of instances in which the simulation differs from actual history. In 1882, for example, gerrymandering padded the Democratic majority by 14 seats. In 1890, Democratic efforts in Ohio wrested seven seats away from Republicans. In a couple of instances, pro-Democratic gerrymanders were counteracted by pro-Republican gerrymanders. For example, in 1880, Democrats picked up two seats from gerrymandering, and Republicans four, for a net of only two seats.

Perhaps more important are the elections of 1878 and 1888, in which gerrymandering actually helped determine party control of the House. In 1878, the nine seats Democrats picked up via Ohio's and Missouri's gerrymandering allowed Democrats to retain majority control. Without these nine seats, Democrats most likely would not have had a majority in the House. In addition, Democrats' capture of the House prevented Republicans from gaining unified control of the national government. In 1888, Republicans in Pennsylvania carved 21 pro-Republican districts out of 28 total despite only having 53 percent of the statewide two-party vote. This was just enough to put Republicans over the top in the House, and it also gave them unified party control of the national government. The consequences of these elections on the future trajectory of American history are hard to overstate.

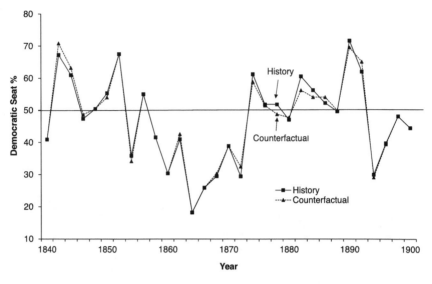

Fig. 5.3. Counterfactual composition of the U.S. House, 1840–1900

1878: Enforcement of Voting Rights in the South

For Democrats, the House of Representatives constituted *the* institutional beachhead to fight against the Republican policy hegemony of the era. In the years after the Civil War, Republicans held a virtual lock on the presidency and the Senate. Republicans had manufactured this advantage through the strategic admittance of sparsely populated, but strongly Republican, western states. These western "pocket" boroughs provided Republicans with a head start in the Electoral College, and an almost insurmountable lock on the Senate (Stewart and Weingast 1992). The Republican hegemony allowed them to pass, and protect, currency, tariff, and other legislation that fundamentally determined the politics and economy of the era.

The one place where Democrats held any hope of influencing national policy was in the House and, in particular, through the appropriations process (Stewart 1991). Notably, Democrats passed the Holman Rule in 1876. This rule allowed for riders to be attached to appropriations legislation. The two parties fought over the Holman Rule—and, by implication—national spending and policy priorities, for the next 50 years. The vote to pass the rule had Democrats favoring by 151–6, while Republicans opposed it 4–94.

The most dramatic instance of the Holman Rule was in its use by Democrats to roll back the appropriations funding U.S. Marshals to police elections in the South. Unlike existing policies which live from one congress to the next, appropriations bills must be passed every year; otherwise, spending reverts to zero. In cases of split control of Congress, this gives each party an institutional veto over funding decisions. So, even if Democrats had little chance of simultaneously capturing both chambers of Congress and the presidency in the post–Civil War years, they did have a chance at capturing the House. From here, they could influence national policy through their negative power in the appropriations process.

Nowhere was this more evident than in 1878. Given the Republican dominance of the presidency and the Senate, the House was the pivotal branch for the Democratic Party hoping to influence national policy on currency, tariffs, civil service, and perhaps most importantly, federal enforcement of Fifteenth Amendment in the South. No clearer example of the power of gerrymandering to shape party balances, and, hence, national policy, comes from 46th Congress. Recall this is the Congress in which timely pro-Democratic gerrymanders in Ohio and Missouri tipped the partisan balance and placed the Democrat Samuel Randall in the Speaker's Chair.

Chief among Democrats' aims was to restrict the supervisory power of the army at Southern polling stations. The implementation of suffrage, via the Fifteenth Amendment, in the South, depended upon its actual enforcement. In the years following the Civil War, the federal government had used its constitutional power to regulate federal elections to send U.S. Marshals to police federal polling stations and prevent restrictions of suffrage. With a Democratic House, the result of strategic gerrymandering in Ohio and Missouri, Democrats finally were able to restrict army policing of the polls. It now became open season on restricting the franchise.

This was achieved through a rider to the army bill. Federal marshals were now restrained from supervising polling places throughout the South. In effect, the federal government had conceded the South to the Democratic Party and its supporters. Congress eventually zeroed out funding for the marshals in the South (Stewart 1991; Wang 1997). The vote on the rider to the Army Bill passed in the House 117–96. Of the yea votes, 106 came from Democrats, while 93 of the no votes came from Republicans. Not a single Democrat voted against the rider. No Republican voted in favor. The other 11 yea votes came from 6 Independent Democrats and 5 Greenbackers, while the other 3 nay votes were cast by Greenbackers. Thus, setting aside the divided Greenbacker vote, the vote on the rider split straight down party lines. Given the partisanship of the roll-call vot-ing, it is safe to assume that if Republicans had a majority they would have handily defeated any restrictions on federal marshals.

President Hayes vetoed the rider, but Democrats had drawn their line in the sand. Thus, Democrats may not have been able to put the restric-tions on marshals directly into law—they were able to achieve restrictions in practice by denying funding to the marshals. Appropriations legislation requires the assent of both chambers otherwise funding reverts to zero (Kiewiet and McCubbins 1988; Stewart 1991). This put Democrats in a position of power; they could zero out appropriations in a policy area by simply refusing to pass a piece of legislation. In fact, Democrats ended up getting what they wanted. Because neither party could agree on a final version of the appropriations bill, funding for the marshals reverted to zero (Stewart 1991; Wang 1997). The defunding of the marshals came at a decisive juncture in Southern electoral politics. Here we have a clear case where had partisan gerrymanders in the North not taken place, the legacy of Southern, and national, politics would have been radically different.

1888: Reed's Rules, Tariffs, and Currency

The other election where gerrymandering determined majority control of the House was the election of 1888. For understanding modern Ameri-can politics, one cannot overestimate the transformative impact of Reed's actions as Speaker during this Congress. Scholars generally agree that Reed's Rules "permanently and significantly changed voting behavior and policy outcomes in the House. . . . After Reed's system of agenda control had been constructed, with its decisive advantage for the majority party, subsequent rules never pushed the playing field in the House back to any-thing close to what it had been" (Cox and McCubbins 2005, 50–51, 59). Indeed, many congressional scholars have argued that the history of Con-gress, and, consequently, the political history of America, can be divided into two periods: "Before Reed" and "After Reed" (see, for example, Valelly 2009).

As the analysis here reveals, there is an important part of the story miss-ing. Simply put, Reed and Republicans would not have been in power save for a timely gerrymander in Pennsylvania. The extra seats from the Penn-sylvania gerrymander gave Republicans, and Reed, majority control of the House. Also, it is worth noting that Reed was the beneficiary of an espe-cially devious efficient gerrymander in Maine, which gave Republicans all four of Maine's seats, despite a statewide Republican vote share of only 55 percent. At stake were more than inside-baseball issues of parliamentary procedure. Reed and Republicans needed stricter control over the agenda to achieve a vigorous policy agenda. Notably, Republicans sought to break Democratic obstruction in order to pass the Federal Elections Law and restructure "party competition in the South" (Valelly 2009, 115).

This Congress also featured the passage of a primary economic piece of legislation—the McKinley Tariff. Following the Civil War, the issue of tariffs had deeply split the parties. Republicans primarily were in favor of protective tariffs, while Democrats generally preferred lower tariffs and a more laissez-faire approach to trade. During the 1880s, the tariff system had worked so well in generating revenues that the federal government often operated with a budget surplus. Once tariffs were in place they were difficult to remove. Democrats, whose coalition included rural farmers, disliked domestic tariffs because they led to retaliatory tariffs for U.S. exports.

Thus, unwinding the protectionist scheme built up over decades of Republican rule became the rallying cry for Democrats. According to Stewart, "In one of the most crucial policy areas of the time, the protective tariff, years of split control helped entrench protection as a national policy. In those same years, however, Democrats were able to use their bargaining leverage to reduce federal spending" (Stewart 1991, 224). In effect, the era was one in which either Republicans were expanding or retrenching protectionist tariffs. Democrats, when it came to tariffs, were only in a position to block further expansion of the pro-Republican tariff policies. Once tariffs were written into law they were notoriously difficult to remove (Stewart 1991). Eliminating tariffs required a new statute. As long as Republicans held an institutional veto, they could protect their tariff regime.

Thus, during the 1880s and early 1890s, when Republicans were able to seize control of the House, it opened the door for further expansion of protectionist policies. In this vein, arguably the most dramatic extension of pro-Republican tariff policy occurred with the passage of the Tariff Act of 1890—more commonly known as the McKinley Tariff. The McKinley Tariff led to a "radical extension of the protective system" (Taussig 1931, 283). The House passed the McKinley Tariff by a vote of 164–142. The vote almost perfectly split along party lines. All but one Democrat voted against its passage, and all but two Republicans voted in favor. Again, the pro-Republican gerrymander in Pennsylvania provided the critical seats necessary for Republicans, and Thomas Reed, to lead the House. As seen in the next chapter, the subsequent electoral swing against Republicans in the following election helped set the stage for the dramatic electoral reversals of the 1890s.

Coupled with the McKinley Tariff was the passage of the Sherman Silver Purchase Act. This act placed the federal government front and center into the nation's currency markets. Farmers and western silver miners both pressed for the federal government to purchase silver. For farmers, saddled with debt, the purchase of silver, it was argued, would boost the economy and increase inflation, thus reducing the real debts of farmers. For miners, governmental purchase of silver, it was hoped, would prop up demand in the silver market. Because the price of silver had plummeted as a result of overmining and oversupply of silver, miners were eager for the government to step in and rescue their dwindling profits. The act, which required the government to purchase silver every month, passed along straight party lines. In the wake of the 1893 economic panic, the newly elected Democratic Congress, along with President Cleveland, repealed the purchase act.

So, here we see in these two Congresses that history would have proceeded quite differently in the absence of partisan gerrymandering. These legislative outcomes included transformative policy decisions that would cast a long shadow over the future of American politics and society. Who would wield political power in Congress (i.e., Reed's Rules), who would hold power in the South and the nation (i.e., enforcement of Reconstruction and the Reconstruction amendments), and fundamental decisions about economic winners and losers (i.e., tariffs and currency).

Conclusion

The image of politicians manipulating district lines for partisan gain suggests that the path to national power may run through the state legislatures. Yet, political-science research on congressional redistricting in the 1970s, 1980s, 1990s, and 2000s has found, at most, only minimal national partisan consequences (e.g., Campagna and Grofman 1990; Seabrook 2010; Swain, Borrelli, and Reed 1998). Taking a historical step back and examining the partisan consequences of redistricting in the late 19th century sheds new light on this debate. Between 1840 and 1900, redistricting systematically influenced state party delegations in ways that occasionally cumulated into substantial national effects.

First, the partisanship of districting plans systematically affected the translation of congressional votes into legislative seats. Parties in control of the districting process were able to engineer favorable vote-seat translations, which allowed them to magnify their share of state congressional delegations. The difference between Republican- or Democratic-drawn district lines meant a difference of roughly 14 percent of the congressional delegation. Second, county-, ward-, and town-level vote returns before and after redistricting, reveal that parties successfully used gerrymandering for partisan advantage. Third, these state-level effects, at times, produced important national-level consequences. On at least two occasions, it appears that gerrymandering helped determine party control of the House.

The reversals in party fortunes within the House also carried with it direct implications for national policy making. During this era, the House was often the pivotal branch that determined whether control of the federal government was unified or divided. This was especially the case between 1870 and 1894. Given the deep partisan polarization over issues such as federal policy in the South (Kousser 1992) and the tariff (Stewart 1991), control of the House was a key ingredient for parties seeking to shape the direction of federal policy. As such, gerrymandering served as a potent tool in the pursuit of state and national power.

From this perspective, it is not surprising that strategic politicians have again turned to partisan gerrymandering in the bid for national power. The relatively tight national balance between the two parties in the current period has once again raised the payoffs from the manipulation of electoral institutions. The similarities between 19th-century American politics and recent mid-decade redistricting events in Texas and Georgia indicate that congressional redistricting is not exempt from partisan politicians' efforts to stack the electoral deck in their favor.

SIX

Electoral Competition and Critical Elections

Few doubt that contemporary House of Representatives elections are, on the whole, uncompetitive. The average vote margin for winners in recent House elections hovers at 70 percent of the vote (Jacobson 2009). The vast majority of House races are blowouts. In 2004, for example, only 32 contests, out of 435, were decided by 5 percent or less of the vote. The striking absence of competition in modern House elections has prompted much scholarly concern. Indeed, one might frame the vast contemporary literature on congressional elections as a quest to uncover the causes of uncompetitive elections.

In this quest, scholars have examined a number of suspects. One that has occurred to many scholars is redistricting. The suspicion is that incumbents of both parties have colluded to draw lines that protect themselves (e.g., Hirsch 2003; McDonald 2006; Tufte 1973). As a result, seats are safe for members of both parties. For example, in an editorial published in the *Los Angeles Times*, constitutional scholar Mitchell Berman (2004) voiced a common belief stating that "Both Democrats and Republicans have sought to manipulate the system by drawing 'safe seats' for their own members. The result: fewer competitive elections."

A number of other scholars, however, have argued that redistricting has had little impact on declining competition. Indeed, the general thrust of the research literature appears to be that while redistricting may marginally depress competition here and there, it can only account for a small proportion of the overall decline in competition (e.g., Abramowitz, Alexander, and Gunning 2006; Friedman and Holden 2009).[1] But, much like the subject of the previous chapter, the debate about the impact of redistricting on competition revolves around research conducted almost entirely on post–1960s redistricting cycles. It is still an open question whether this minimal impact is inherent in gerrymandering, or reflects the institutional constraints of modern redistricting.

In this chapter, I explore the impact of redistricting on competition in 19th-century congressional elections. Examining district-level vote margins and statewide swing ratios, I find that parties in control of redistricting often manufactured competitive districts in the search for partisan advantage; redistricting in this era often *increased* district-level competition. Beyond establishing that gerrymandering can, at times, have pronounced effects on district-level competition, these findings also help explain one of the more striking features of 19th-century national elections—the sharp swings in partisan fortunes. Specifically, in this chapter, I provide a detailed examination of the impact of redistricting on congressional elections in three periods: 1850–54, 1870–74, and 1890–94. These three election periods constitute, by far, the largest seat swings in U.S. history. The reversals of fortune were startling. In 1854, Democrats lost 74 seats (in a chamber of 234). In 1874, Republicans lost 94 seats (in a chamber of 292). And in 1894, Democrats lost 114 seats (in a chamber of 357 seats). No elections before, or since, have approached the seat swings found in these three elections.

I argue that strategic redistricting played a fundamental role in creating a competitive environment and set the table for these huge swings in House seats. The logic of the argument is as follows. In all three periods, one party was in charge of redistricting for the vast majority of states: Democrats in 1852 and 1892, and Republicans in 1872. Following the standard partisan strategies of the day, they drew electoral maps with narrow, yet winnable, margins for fellow partisans. This produced an overabundance of marginal Democratic seats in 1852 and 1892, and an overabundance of marginal Republican seats in 1872. Thus, the relatively moderate anti-majority vote swing in the subsequent elections—1854, 1874, and 1894—produced a huge swing in seats. Previous research has demonstrated the presence of massive vote-seat distortions in 19th-century elections (Brady 1985; 1988), but no one has identified the critical aspect that strategic redistricting played in helping to construct these vote to seat ratios.

Competition in House Elections

Congressional elections throughout much of the 19th century were fiercely competitive. Certainly compared to modern standards, the margin between winners and losers was much closer. In the late 19th century, nearly 40 percent of House elections were decided by 5 percent or less (Brady and Grofman 1991). This threshold is a traditional way of classifying districts as either competitive or noncompetitive (Jacobson 2009; Mayhew 1974b). A steep drop off in the number of close contests occurred near the end of the 19th century. By 1920, only 25 percent of House races fell into this competitive range. This decline was followed by another drop off in the 1960s, where it has resided ever since. Competition reached its nadir in 2004, when only 7 percent of House contests were decided by less than 5 percent of the vote. A further inkling of the decline in competition can be seen by considering the 2010 election. This election, by many accounts, was one of the most competitive in recent memory. Nearly 25 percent of the contests fell into the marginal category. Yet, even though this number is high by modern standards, it still pales in comparison to levels of competition in the 19th century. In 1870, for example, half of all House races met the definition of a marginal district.

One consequence of the intense competition at the district level in the 19th century was that national elections, and House majorities, could turn on a dime. A landslide election in one direction could easily be followed two years later by a landslide in the other direction. No majority was seemingly safe. For instance, Republicans gained 64 seats in the 1872 election, only to surrender 94 seats in the following election of 1874. These whip-saw elections were common, especially in the Gilded Age. That sharp swings in national-party fortunes should correlate with competitive district elections is unsurprising; the two factors are intimately related. The more districts that are competitive the more districts that will shift with changes in the national vote (Mayhew 1974b). For instance, a district that is split 52–48 in favor of Democrats will more likely flip if there is a small shift in the vote to the opposition party; however, a district split 70–30 in favor of Democrats will be much less likely to flip even if there is a major national vote swing to the opposition party. In other words, the more districts that are evenly split the more districts that have the potential to change party hands. Thus, as individual districts become more competitive, the responsiveness of congressional membership to changes in the national vote surges.

Against the backdrop of this hypercompetitive system, 19th-century mapmakers weighed their strategic options. As we saw in the previous chapter, partisan mapmakers had two basic strategies they could pursue (e.g., Cain 1985; Cox and Katz 2002; Owen and Grofman 1988). One strategy was to pack out-party supporters into one or few districts while distributing in-party supporters evenly throughout the rest of the state. This packing strategy ensured a number of easy victories for the in party, yet conceded some districts to the opposition. The second strategy involved drawing districts that are a microcosm of the statewide vote—in other words, constructing as many marginal, yet winnable, seats as possible. A party that was confident of its ability to win the statewide vote over the foreseeable future could maximize its seat share by having each district mirror this favorable statewide partisan distribution (Cox and Katz 2002). Under such a strategy, "the dominant party magnifies its popular vote by creating many districts it can reliably but narrowly carry" (Argersinger 1992, 75). This strategy has been termed "efficient gerrymanders" (Cain 1985) or "dispersal gerrymanders" (Owen and Grofman 1988).

Throughout the 19th century, state political parties were notorious for pursuing the efficient strategy—crafting district plans with an eye toward winning as many seats as possible (Argersinger 1992). In Maine, for example, Republicans gerrymandered the state into a solid five Republican districts despite only having 55 percent of the statewide vote. In other words, with 55 percent of the vote, they were able to capture 100 percent of the seats. This map was a masterful example of an efficient gerrymander. No Republican vote was wasted, and no seat was conceded to Democrats. Indeed, from 1884 to 1892, Republicans completely shut out Democrats, winning every single congressional race over this eight-year period.

As the example from Maine demonstrates, the potential gains from efficient gerrymandering were immense. But the strategy also carried many risks. With so many districts on the knife-edge, a slight shift in the vote to the opposite party could spell electoral doom. So, why were parties more willing to pursue these efficient gerrymanders? First, on the legal side, they faced fewer constraints than their modern counterparts. In this era before one-person, one-vote, redistricting took place out of the watchful eye of the judiciary. Beyond adhering to the congressional mandate requiring single-member and contiguous districts (after 1842), states could redistrict whenever and however they wanted.

On the political side, many of the factors that constrain modern mapmakers from pursuing full-blown partisan gerrymanders were absent. The importance of careerism and seniority within the House had yet to fully take hold, creating less pressure by sitting congressmen for incumbent-friendly districts (Kernell 1977; Price 1975). Even if there was incumbent pressure for safer districts, local party managers had fewer reasons to heed their wishes. Partisan control over nominations and balloting gave party managers the incentives to pursue collective party interests at the expense of any individual candidate (Brady, Buckley, and Rivers 1999; Carson and

Roberts 2005). Individual politicians, therefore, owed their electoral fortunes to their local party organization, and had little opportunity or incentive to engage in the candidate-centered activities typical of modern House
members (e.g., Fenno 1978; Mayhew 1974a). If the party wanted to tinker
with congressional districts, incumbents might grouse, but there was little
else they could do.

Consider the 1886 redistricting in Ohio. Congressional incumbents of
both parties reacted with dread upon learning that the states districts would
be redrawn yet again. In 1886, Republicans controlled the state legislature
and sought to undo the gerrymander perpetrated by Democrats two years
earlier. While the new districts stood to advantage Ohio Republicans col-
lectively, sitting Republican incumbents were not thrilled. The *New York
Times* reported that "Many members of the [state] House opposed the
measure and it would have undoubtedly failed but for the very spirited
manner in which the Washington contingent opposed it and excited the
hostility of certain members in both branches here" (*New York Times*, May
18, 1886). Ultimately, the interests of incumbents were overridden by the
collective good of party success.

Similarly, the importance of seniority in allocating committee assignments had yet to fully take root in the House (Polsby, Gallaher, and
Rundquist 1969). The lower value placed on House seniority may have
led state parties to refrain from pro-incumbent gerrymandering. Seniority
puts a premium on holding existing seats and lessens the importance of
targeting opposition held seats. Cox and Katz note this possibility arguing,
"The more valuable seniority is, the more valuable it is to keep one's own
incumbents and the less valuable it is to knock off the other party's incumbents" (Cox and Katz 1999, 823). The converse naturally follows. The less
valuable seniority is, the less important it is to protect incumbents. Thus,
we might reasonably suspect partisan mapmakers to shy away from pure
incumbent-protection plans solely for the purpose of increasing their delegations seniority. Having more partisans in Congress also increased access
to federal patronage. Federal appointments were lubricants that helped
keep the local- and state-party machines running. Thus, state parties had a
vested interest in securing as many congressional seats as feasible.

Efficient gerrymandering was further aided by the structure of voting
in the 19th century. The party-ticket balloting system, in which voters cast
ballots listing the candidates of a single party, induced a high degree of
straight-ticket voting (Rusk 1970). The result was fairly predictable short-
term voter behavior that further allowed mapmakers to trim districts into
small, but winnable, margins.

All told then, gerrymandering in this era was less about protecting incumbents and more about maximizing the dominant parties' (or dominant factions') share of the congressional delegation. In many cases, these gerrymanders manufactured a surplus of seats despite relatively narrow statewide margins. As an example, consider the pro-Democratic redistricting of Indiana in 1852. Democratic mapmakers essentially fashioned the state into a winner-take-all system. With only 54 percent of the vote, in 1852, Democrats won a remarkable 91 percent of the seats (10 out of 11 seats).

Gerrymandering and Electoral Margins

If parties were pursuing efficient gerrymanders, then we should expect to see three things. First, at the district level we should expect that parties in control of drawing the maps will trim the margins of their uncompetitive districts (i.e., make them more competitive), and shore up the margins of their very close seats (Cain 1985). Moreover, they should pack their opponents districts with surplus supporters. Second, the variance of the vote should go down in districts of the controlling party. Third, at the state level, we should see redistricting plans with steep vote-to-seat translations. And, as a corollary, the vote-richer party should receive a substantial seat bonus.

Examining these claims requires a measure of the partisan intent of the mapmakers. Fortunately, following the behavior of 19th-century politicians offers a solution. In the 19th century, state legislators would take the most recent election results, broken down by counties, wards, and towns, and combine this data to forecast the partisan effects of changes to district lines. Because counties were most often the building blocks of congressional districts, politicians could readily aggregate county-vote returns and calculate the likely electoral consequences of new district lines. With the aid of 19th-century electoral-returns and historical-district maps, the contemporary researcher can do the same and, in essence, look over the shoulder of these mapmakers.

The procedure was to take the two-party congressional vote by county from the most recent election before a new redistricting, and then aggregate these votes into the newly drawn district boundaries. County-level electoral returns for the House come from Clubb, Flanigan, and Zingale (1987). Data on congressional district boundaries comes from Kenneth Martis's *Historical Atlas of U.S. Congressional Districts* (1982). In those instances where a county contained more than one district (i.e., urban areas such as Philadelphia or New York City) or congressional district lines cut across county boundaries, where available, I turned to historical newspapers and state legislative manuals for ward- and town-level results.

District Vote Margins

The first test examines the vote margins in districts before and after a redistricting. If states were constructing efficient gerrymanders, parties in control of the districting process would draw maps such that the seats they control have, on average, narrower margins than in the previous election. The construction of an efficient gerrymander implies that, under pro-Democratic plans, Democratic districts will be trimmed (i.e., those with large margins in the previous election), while those with very narrow margins will be shored up (Cain 1985). Under pro-Republican plans, the few Democratic districts not converted into Republican districts should be packed with more pro-Democratic voters.

To test this, I constructed a dependent variable that takes the projected margin of victory in the newly redrawn district *minus* the margin of victory in the election just prior to redistricting. The margin of victory is measured as the value of the winners' two-party vote minus 50 percent. Critical to constructing this dependent variable is correctly matching up districts across a redistricting. In essence, one needs to identify the old, or parent, district for each new district. This was done by identifying the old district that contributed the largest share of population to the new boundaries. The dependent variable, then, is the projected margin of victory in the newly drawn district minus the margin of victory in the parent district. A negative value indicates a district was made more competitive; a positive value, less competitive.

The key independent variables are whether or not the district was intended to be a Democratic district (i.e., a projected post-redistricting vote above 50 percent) and a series of dummy variables for each type of redistricting plan (i.e., Partisan Democrat, Bipartisan, Partisan Whig/Republican). To measure how Democrats are treated under different redistricting plans, the *Democratic District* variable is interacted with each of the plan-type dummy variables. If Democratic mapmakers, on average, trimmed the margins of Democratic districts, then the coefficient on the stand alone *Democratic District* variable will be negative. Moreover, the interactive variable between *Democratic District* and *Whig/Republican Plan* should be positive, indicating that under pro-Republican plans Democratic districts had their margins increased (i.e., more likely to be packed).

The model is estimated using Ordinary Least Squares (OLS). Because states differ in their mean level of competition, separate state intercepts are included (α_j). Moreover, because changes in district-level margins within states are likely not independent of each other, the analysis is clustered by state-year and estimated with robust standard errors.

The results are presented in table 6.1. Consistent with expectations, Democratic-controlled districts that were drawn by Democratic state parties had their margins reduced by an average of 1.8 percentage points. The interactive variable between Republican/Whig-drawn plans and Democratic districts is positive and significant. The value of the coefficient is 3.09. This result indicates that under a Whig plan, Democratic districts were made less competitive. The net effect was to increase the average margin in Democratic districts by 1.3 percentage points. Thus, districts were treated very differently depending on which party controlled the mapmaking process.

Overall, these results support the argument that throughout the 19th century, mapmakers helped strategically manufacture competitive congressional districts for their fellow partisans. This provides strong evidence that parties were following an efficient gerrymander strategy; making districts they controlled more competitive and making the opposition less competitive.

TABLE 6.1. The Impact of Partisan Gerrymandering on District-Level Vote Margins, 1840–1900 (dependent variable = district level difference in margin before and after redistricting; OLS, clustered by state with robust standard errors)

	Coefficient
Democratic District	−1.80*
	(.72)
Democratic District × Whig/Republican Plan	3.09*
	(.88)
Democratic District × Bipartisan Plan	.07
	(1.95)
Whig/Republican Plan	−.64
	(.54)
Bipartisan Plan	1.39
	(1.04)
Constant	.50
	(.52)
Adjusted R^2	.15
Number of Observations	1,189

Note: Robust standard errors, clustered by state-year, are in parentheses. State fixed effects were also estimated but not reported.

*$p < .05$.

A second implication of the efficient-gerrymander thesis is that plans should reduce the variance of the vote in districts for the controlling party. Because uncompetitive districts will be trimmed and very marginal districts shored up, there should be a reduction in the variance around the mean vote in Democratic districts. Each Democratic district should come to resemble every other Democratic district in the state. Consider the pro-Democratic gerrymander of New York in 1884. The map, devised by Democrats, carved the state into 23 Democratic districts and 11 Republican districts. This was all the more remarkable given that Democrats and Republicans had exactly half of the statewide vote. The standard deviation of the Democratic vote in districts controlled by Democrats was 6.6. In Republican districts, the standard deviation of the vote was 18.2.

To examine this visually, figure 6.1 shows the standard deviation of the vote across districts, within a state, before and after redistricting. The x-axis displays the standard deviation of the two-party vote in districts before redistricting; the y-axis is the standard deviation after redistricting. Note that I only include districts controlled by the redistricting party in calculating these standard deviations. So, for example, in states where Democrats redrew districts, the "before" standard deviation is the variance of the vote for districts won by Democrats prior to redistricting. The "after" standard deviation is the variance of the vote across districts where the majority of the projected two-party vote, under the new maps, favored Democrats. I then did the same for Whig/Republican plans. This produces the two panels displayed in figure 6.1. The 45-degree line indicates no change. States above the line had an increase in the variance of the vote; states below the line had a decrease. If parties were implementing efficient gerrymanders, then we should expect to see the observations fall below the 45-degree line.

In figure 6.1, this is largely what we see. In both panels, the bulk of observations fall below the 45-degree line. This is strong evidence that states were distributing their voters in a more efficient manner. In other words, districts for the controlling party came to resemble a microcosm of the statewide vote. Of course, not every state hewed to this strategy—a few observations do fall above the 45-degree line. But almost all of these were in states where the variance of the vote was small to begin with. Here the votes were already roughly allocated in an efficient manner.

One can further demonstrate this pattern by performing an F-test on the difference in the standard deviations before and after redistricting. For Democratic states, the average standard deviation before redistricting was 10.6, and after, it declined to 6.6. This difference of four was statistically significant ($p < .01$). In Republican states, the standard deviation before and

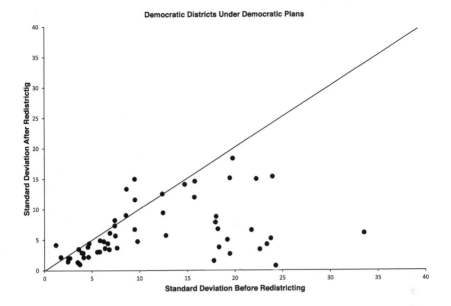

Democratic Districts Under Democratic Plans

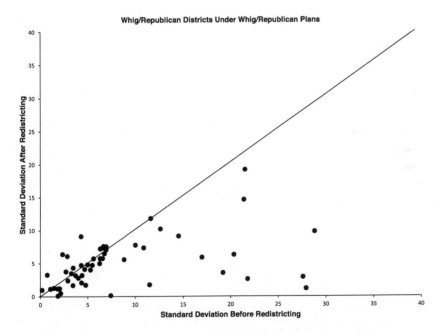

Whig/Republican Districts Under Whig/Republican Plans

Fig. 6.1. Variance of the vote before and after redistricting. The figure displays the standard deviation of the two-party vote in districts held by the dominant party before and after redistricting. The top panel displays Democratic-controlled districts in states controlled by the Democrats. The bottom panel shows Whig/Republican-controlled districts in states controlled by Whigs/Republicans. The x-axis is the standard deviation before and the y-axis is the standard deviation after. The solid line is drawn at 45 degrees. Dots falling below the 45 degree line indicate a reduction in the variance of the vote across districts.

after was 8.3 and 5.1, respectively. This difference of 3.2 was also significant ($p < .01$).

Overall, the results show that parties in command of redistricting made the seats they controlled, on average, more competitive. This stands in contrast to most research on modern redistricting, which finds that it either reduces competition or has no effect. The results here suggest that redistricting can amplify electoral competition. When parties are motivated to maximize seats rather than protect incumbents, redistricting can increase competition and accelerate seat swings. The next section considers how these district-by-district decisions added up to hyperresponsive state electoral systems.

Votes and Seats

If state parties used redistricting to manufacture extra seat shares, via competitive elections, then one should expect that state governments with unified party control constructed vote-seat translations with steep swing ratios. This would be further evidence of efficient gerrymandering. Districting plans where the districts have very narrow margins will exhibit high swing ratios. Moreover, the swing ratio also indicates the size of the "seat bonus" that accrues to the party winning the statewide vote. The larger this number, the larger the size of the dominant party's seat bonus.

Increasing the swing ratio increases the seat bonus that accrues to the dominant party. To see this, consider holding the vote share constant at 55 percent and then varying the swing ratio. To see this, figure 6.2 presents an example of how increasing the swing ratio can increase a party's seat bonus. A party's vote percentage is placed on the x-axis. The party's resulting seat percentage, at different values of the swing ratio, is presented on the y-axis. In the example, the party's vote percent is 55 percent. With a swing ratio of three, the dominant party can expect to receive 65 percent of the state's seats with 55 percent of the vote. But increasing the swing ratio to a value of five raises the expected seat share to 75 percent. Thus, manipulating district lines and efficiently distributing votes across districts can greatly enhance a party's seat bonus. However, as the graphic also reveals, this strategy comes with increased risk. A shift in the vote leftward on the x-axis (i.e., against the dominant party) will be magnified in a highly competitive system. Not only are seats on the razor-edge when drawn competitively, but there are also more of them total. Thus, a large swing ratio also can portend large losses.

To test how redistricting changed the translation of votes into seats, I

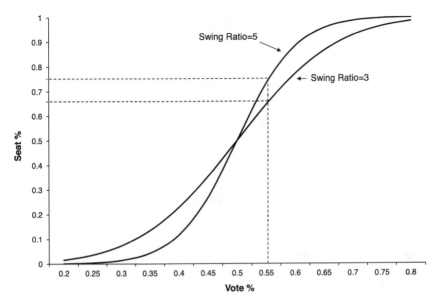

Fig. 6.2. Example of seat bonus at different values of the swing ratio

estimate the average state-level swing ratios before and after redistricting. Building on standard practice in the electoral systems literature (e.g., Cox and Katz 2002; Grofman 1983; King and Browning 1987; Tufte 1973), the following vote-seat equation is estimated.

$$\ln(s_{it}/(1 - s_{it})) = \lambda_1(Pre) + \lambda_2(Post) + \rho_1[Pre \times (\ln(v_{it}/(1 - v_{it})))]$$
$$+ \rho_2[Post \times (\ln(v_{it}/(1 - v_{it})))] \tag{2}$$

where s_{it} is the statewide proportion of seats won by Democrats, and v_{it} is their statewide vote share in state i at time t (the constant is suppressed to avoid perfect collinearity). The rho coefficients (ρ_1 and ρ_2) measure the swing ratio for pre- and post-redistricting plans, respectively. The focus here will be on those states with partisan redistricting plans. Those few plans passed under divided government are excluded.[2] The critical test is whether the swing ratios are significantly higher after redistricting. If parties were ratcheting up the swing ratio in search of partisan advantage, then the forecasted election under the newly drawn maps should have higher swing ratios than the election just prior to redistricting.[3]

The lambda coefficients (λ_1 and λ_2) on the stand-alone *Pre* and *Post* variables measure partisan bias for pre- and post-redistricting plans, respectively. Partisan bias is defined "as the difference between the expected seat share that the Democrats would get with an average vote share of 0.5 and their 'fair share' of 0.5 (half the seats for half the votes)" (Cox and Katz 1999, 820). So, if a party wins 60 percent of a state's House seats when its candidates receive 50 percent of the statewide vote, we say there is a 10 percent bias. It is standard to transform the raw estimated lambda coefficient and calibrate it to what would have happened if the vote were split 50–50. This is done by passing the lambda coefficient through the following equation: $\exp[\lambda]/(\exp[\lambda] + 1) - 0.5$.

Because the dependent variable is based on a proportion—the proportion of seats going to Democrats—the model is estimated using maximum likelihood with an extended beta binomial distribution. Using this distribution also accounts for any potential correlation in the probability across districts (within a state) of a Democratic victory.[4]

The results are presented in table 6.2. If state parties were ramping up the swing ratio in attempt to secure more seats for their side, then the swing ratio in the newly drawn districts should be higher than those just prior to redistricting. In table 6.2, this is what we see. The average swing ratio in the states during the election just prior to redistricting was 3.46. Under the newly drawn maps, the average expected swing ratio jumped to 4.96. The difference of 1.5 is statistically significant ($p = .02$). These

TABLE 6.2. The Conversion of Votes into Seats before and after Redistricting

	Coefficient
Swing Ratio Before	3.46*
	(.38)
Swing Ratio After	4.96*
	(.50)
Partisan Bias Before	2.33
	(2.35)
Partisan Bias After	4.28
	(2.48)
γ	.12*
	(.02)
N	262
Log-Likelihood	−1,423.59

Note: The cell entries are maximum likelihood estimates that follow an extended beta binomial distribution. Standard errors are in parentheses. The difference between the swing ratio coefficients was significant at .05 ($p = .02$).
*$p < .05$.

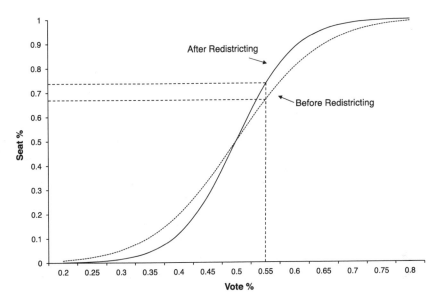

Fig. 6.3. Estimated vote to seat translations before and after redistricting

results suggest that the new maps pushed the states towards winner-take-all systems.

To better visualize the impact of these changes, figure 6.3 traces out the vote-seat curves associated with these swing ratios. Dashed lines indicate the estimated pre-redistricting swing ratio and solid lines the expected post-redistricting swing ratio. First, one can see the increased seat bonus that accrues with steeper swing ratios under the new redistricting plans. For example, at 55 percent of the vote, a dominant party could expect to win 66 percent of a state congressional delegation before redistricting. After redistricting, the percentage of seats they could expect to win, with 55 percent of the vote, jumps to 73 percent.

Thus, there were clear benefits to gerrymandering efficiently. But figure 6.3 also illustrates the potential risks. Ratcheting up the swing ratio magnified a party's seat share, but it also meant that the dominant party now had more to lose. Moreover, steeper swing ratios meant that changes in the vote produced larger changes in seats. An unexpected vote swing could parties on the wrong side of these steep slopes. Even a relatively small shift in the vote could produce an avalanche of losses. Consider a party whose vote share drops from 55 percent to 45 percent. Under the pre-redistricting swing ratio of 3.45, their percentage of seats would go from 66 percent to 33 percent. Under the post-redistricting swing ratio of 4.95, the percentage of seats would plummet from 73 percent to 27 percent.

The Promise and Perils of Hyper-Responsive Gerrymanders

Thus, the redistricting strategies of the 19th century took an already competitive system and made it even more competitive. While in the short term the strategy of efficient gerrymandering produced big partisan gains, it also set the parties up for big losses. Some inkling of this possibility can be seen by noting that the three largest seat swings in congressional history occurred soon after major redistricting happened across the country: the elections of 1854, 1874, and 1894.

The seat losses in the congressional elections of 1854, 1874, and 1894 were astounding. In 1854, voter reaction to the Democratic-led passage of the Kansas-Nebraska Act, combined with rising nativism in many Northern states (Holt 1978), led to widespread defeat for Democrats.[5] In House elections, they lost a startling 74 seats in a chamber of 234. The bulk of those losses were concentrated throughout the Midwest and Mid-Atlantic. In Ohio, for example, Democrats suffered a crushing defeat. In 1852, they won 12 of the states' 21 districts. In 1854, they won none. The consequence was a dramatic reshuffling of party coalitions and sectional alliances that placed the nation on a path eventually ending in civil war (Aldrich 1995; Gienapp 1987; Holt 1999).

In the midterm election of 1874, Republicans were on the losing end of the seat swing. Republicans lost 94 seats (in a House of 292 total members). The shift in fortunes handed Democrats control of the House of Representatives for the first time since 1856. The precipitating event was the economic panic of 1873. With Republicans controlling both the White House and Congress, voters punished the party in power. Moreover, Democratic resurgence in a number of southern states put Democrats back in control of congressional delegations throughout the South (Perman 1984). But even after taking these important events into account, the seat swing in this election was dramatic; especially when placed against the vote swing. Democrats' share of the vote only increased by 5 percent, yet their seat share rose by 32 percent.

The midterm election of 1894 was another massive reversal of fortune for Democrats. The Panic of 1893—the second-worst depression in American history—propelled the opposition Republicans into majority status in the House for the next 16 years (Glad 1964). Democrats lost a staggering 114 seats. In the Northeast, Democratic representation plummeted from 44 seats to 7 (McSeveney 1972). In New York, for example, Democrats surrendered 14 seats—their state delegation dropping from 19 to 5. Democratic losses were also devastating in the Midwest. In 1892, the midwestern states had sent 44 Democrats to Washington. Two years later, they sent 4.

When placed within the historical time-series of congressional elections, these three elections stand head and shoulders above the rest. The top panel of figure 6.4 displays the absolute value of the swings in Democratic House seats from 1840 through 2006. The seat swings in 1854, 1874, and 1894 clearly stand out. Indeed, the swings in more recent, but no less famous, elections pale in comparison (e.g., the Watergate election of 1974; the Republican revolution of 1994; the Democratic resurgence of 2006).

Placed against the seismic shifts in legislative seats, however, the vote swings in these two elections were comparatively tame. The bottom panel of figure 6.4 shows the absolute value of national Democratic vote swings from 1840 to 2006. The elections in 1854, 1874, or 1894 do not stand out. The Democratic percentage of the national two-party vote dropped 7.6 percent and 7.4 percent in 1854 and 1894, respectively (Rusk 2001, 217–18). In 1874, Democrats increased their vote share by 6.8 percent. Of course, one should not downplay the size of these vote swings—they are indeed substantial. However, within the time-series of congressional elections, they are not outliers. Thus, we are presented with a puzzle: what was present in these elections that caused small vote swings to translate into massive seat swings?

Past research has not entirely ignored these abnormal seat swings. In a series of important works, David Brady (1985; 1988) found that the electoral transformations of the 1850s and 1890s were not the product of overwhelming shifts in partisan loyalties. Instead, razor-thin margins in numerous congressional districts led to big seat swings. Because so many districts were near the tipping point, it only took a moderate anti-Democratic national vote swing to produce an avalanche of seat losses. Although Brady did not focus on the 1874 election, his logic would almost certainly apply there as well.

Brady's argument and evidence are certainly compelling. Yet his findings raise important questions: Why were these districts so competitive to begin with? Why did modest vote swings produce massive seat swings in these particular elections and not others? There are several reasons to suspect that redistricting helped set the table for the massive seat swings in 1854, 1874, and 1894. First, in the redistricting cycles that began these

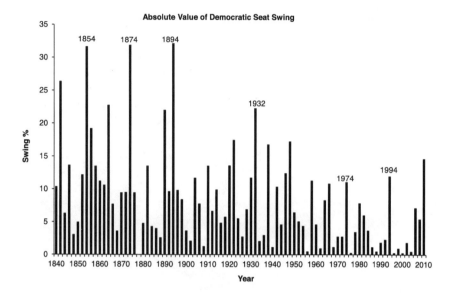

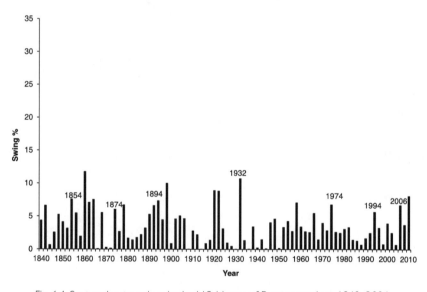

Fig. 6.4. Seat and vote swings in the U.S. House of Representatives, 1840–2006

decades, Democrats found themselves in the position of controlling the state legislature and the governorship in a disproportionate number of states. The numbers in table 6.3 illustrate the imbalance of partisan control of redistricting in these cycles. In the 1850s, Democrats were the majority

TABLE 6.3. Partisan Control of Redistricting in 1852, 1872, and 1892

1852–54		
Partisan Democrat	Bipartisan	Partisan Whig
ME (6)	PA (25)	VT (3)
MA (11)	LA (4)	NY (33)
NH (3)	MD (6)	GA (8)
NJ (5)	NC (8)	TN (10)
IL (9)		
IN (11)		
MI (4)		
OH (21)		
VA (13)		
AR (2)		
SC (6)		
MO (7)[a]		
AL (7)[a]		
MS (5)[a]		
Total Districts: 110	43	54
1872–74		
Partisan Democrat	Bipartisan	Partisan Republican
MO (13)	CA (4)	MA (11)
VA (9)		RI (2)
NC (8)		NJ (7)
KY (10)		IL (19)
MD (6)		MI (9)
AR (4)[b]		OH (20)
GA (9)[b]		WI (8)
TX (6)[b]		IA (9)
TN (10)[b]		MN (3)
MS (6)		
PA (27)[b]		
IN (13)[b]		
KS (3)[b]		
FL (2)[b]		
LA (6)[b]		
SC (5)[b]		
Total Districts: 75	4	150

TABLE 6.3.—*Continued*

	1892–94	
Partisan Democrat	Bipartisan	Partisan Republican
NY (34)	MN (7)	OH (21)
MI (12)	NE (6)	CO (2)
WI (10)	MA (13)	CA (7)
MO (15)		OR (2)
AL (9)		NJ (8)[c]
AR (6)		
GA (11)		
NC (9)		
TX (13)		
IL (22)[c]		
SC (7)[c]		
Total		
Districts: 148	26	40

Note: The number of districts in each state is indicated in parentheses. In 1852–54 there were 234 total representatives in the House. In 1872–74 there were 292 total representatives in the House. Tennessee also redistricted in 1872 but that is not listed here. In 1892–94 there were 356 total representatives in the House. New Jersey redistricted in 1892 (partisan Democrat) and again in 1894 (partisan Republican). Only the latter is included in this table.

[a]Redistricting conducted prior to 1854 election.
[b]Redistricting conducted prior to 1874 election.
[c]Redistricting conducted prior to 1894 election.

party in 14 out of the 22 redistricting states. They controlled the drawing of 110 districts, while Whigs were responsible for drawing only 54 districts. A similar pattern emerged in the 1870s. Republicans controlled redistricting in 16 states, compared to Democrats' 9. Republicans were, therefore, in charge of drawing 150 districts, compared to Democrats' drawing 75 districts. The same thing happened in the 1890s—when Democrats controlled 11 of the 19 redistricting states. This included the populous Midwestern and Mid-Atlantic states, giving them a district-level advantage in drawing new lines of 148 to Republicans' 40 districts. Thus, in each period, one party had a disproportionate opportunity to redraw vast swaths of the country's political map.

If parties were constructing efficient gerrymanders, and the bulk of plans were pro-Democratic, then the national distribution of seats should display a surplus of marginal Democratic seats with a lesser number of marginal Whig/Republican seats. In figure 6.5, one can see exactly this pattern playing out. The x-axis plots the winners vote share based on the

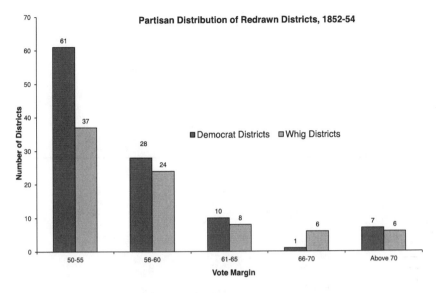

Partisan Distribution of Redrawn Districts, 1852-54

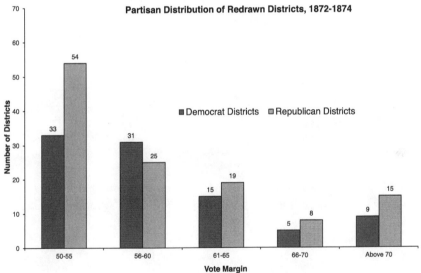

Partisan Distribution of Redrawn Districts, 1872-1874

Fig. 6.5. The distribution of redrawn districts

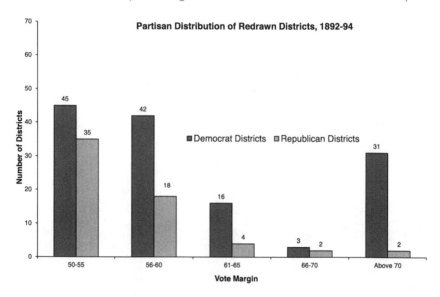

Fig. 6.5. *(cont.)*. The distribution of redrawn districts

expected vote in the newly drawn districts. In the 1852–54 round of redistricting, Democrats emerged with 89 districts between 50 percent and 60 percent of the vote. By comparison, Whigs had only 61 districts in this range. After redistricting in 1872–74, Republicans had 54 districts in the marginal range, while Democrats had only 33. Turning to 1892, we again see a stark asymmetry in the distribution of districts. Democrats had 87 districts between 50 percent and 60 percent of the vote, while Republicans only had 53.[6]

This figure provides a proximal answer for the sudden reversal of political fortunes. First, because Democrats controlled a disproportionate number of seats they had more to lose. This surplus of seats was well above Democrats' equilibrium level of seats for those particular eras (Oppenheimer, Stimson, and Waterman 1986). Second, the bulk of their redrawn districts were in a range where it would only take a modest national swing to turn over a great number of seats. Thus, when voters reacted in response to the Kansas-Nebraska Act, the Panic of 1873, and the Panic of 1893, they each produced a deluge of losses.

A couple of examples further illustrate the point. In Indiana, heading into the 1854 election, Democrats controlled 10 of the state's 11 congressional seats. This was all the more astonishing considering Democrats only captured 54 percent of the statewide vote in 1852. Thus, as long as partisan tides stayed in Democrats' favor, they stood to reap huge rewards. But it also set them up for big losses if national tides turned against them, as it did in 1854. In 1854, Democrats won only two seats, although their vote share had only fallen to 46 percent.

In 1892, Democrats in Missouri fashioned 13 Democratic districts out of 15 total. This was especially remarkable given their statewide vote share was only 50.1 percent. In 1894, Democrats' vote share dropped by six points to 44 percent. Despite this somewhat modest drop in their vote share, they lost a stunning eight seats. In other words, with a six-point swing in the vote, Democrats' share of the congressional delegation dropped from 87 percent to 33 percent.

What If the Swing Ratios Had Not Been So Large?

Overall, how much did redistricting contribute to these seat swings? One way to gauge the impact of gerrymandering is to examine a counterfactual. Perhaps, the most appropriate counterfactual is to assess what the seat swing would have been had a "neutral" vote-seat translation been in place. The baseline typically used in the literature to characterize and assess single-member district systems is a swing ratio of three (i.e., the cube law) (Tufte 1973). This is also the baseline that Brady uses, and will be the one used here as the counterfactual.

The strategy is to run the 1852 (or 1872 or 1892) vote, for each state, through a vote-seat translation of three, and then do this again for 1854 (or 1874 or 1894). Specifically, I ran the statewide vote through the following formula: $\ln(Seats/(1 - Seats)) = 3 \times (\ln(Vote/(1 - Vote)))$. This produces an expected number of statewide seats. Note that this model sets partisan bias to zero in order to focus the attention on the comparative impact of different swing ratios. Taking the difference between the predicted number of seats between the two adjacent elections (e.g., 1854 minus 1852) will tell us how many seats would have swung had a neutral set of district lines been in place. As an example, consider New York between 1892 and 1894. In 1892, the Democratic statewide vote was 48.8 percent. Passing this vote share through the above formula leads us to expect Democrats to win 16 of New York's 34 seats. In 1894, Democrats' vote share dropped to 41.4 percent. At this value of the vote, the expected number of seats would have been 9 seats. Thus, the simulated swing in seats for New York was 7 seats ($16 - 9 = 7$). In actuality, Democrats' swing in seats in New York was 15 seats (from 20 to 5).

Table 6.4 reports the results of this simulation and the actual seat swings. These numbers reveal a substantial discrepancy between the actual and counterfactual seat swings. In 1854, under a neutral-districting system, Democrats would have lost only 21 seats compared to the 74 they actually lost. The biggest difference is located in states with partisan Democratic redistricting plans. In 1874, the simulation indicates that Republicans would have lost 37 seats under neutral-districting plans. This is much lower than the 94 seats they actually lost. The largest share of losses occurred in states drawn by Republicans. A similar pattern emerges in 1894. Again, Democrats suffered much greater losses than they would have under neutral districts. The counterfactual is 59 seats compared to the actual 114. The greatest contributors to this difference were Democratic-controlled Northern states.

TABLE 6.4. Counterfactual Seat Swings

1854–55 Election		
Type of Redistricting Plan	Seat Swing in Neutral Districts	Seat Swing in Actual Districts
Partisan Democrat	16	41
Partisan Whig	10	18
Bipartisan	2	11
Did Not Redistrict	2	7
Total	21	74
1874 Election		
Type of Redistricting Plan	Seat Swing in Neutral Districts	Seat Swing in Actual Districts
Partisan Democrat	15	25
Partisan Republican	13	42
Bipartisan	2	11
Did Not Redistrict	7	16
Total	37	94
1894 Election		
Type of Redistricting Plan	Seat Swing in Neutral Districts	Seat Swing in Actual Districts
Partisan Democrat	29	69
Partisan Republican	3	6
Bipartisan	2	11
Did Not Redistrict	25	28
Total	59	114

This does not mean that Democrats would not have found themselves in a deep hole or would not have been the minority party in the House. Losing 21 or 59 seats is nothing to dismiss. This counterfactual does illustrate, however, that Democrats would not have had an overabundance of seats in 1852 and 1892. The national seat swings in 1854 and 1894 would have been substantially dampened. And for scholars looking backwards, and subsequently constructing an elaborate political theory of change and stability, they would not stand out.

The Policy Consequences of Hyper-Responsive Elections

1854: The Kansas-Nebraska Act

As this chapter has shown, Democratic representation in the House just prior to the 1854 election was well above its historical average and well above what its vote share might indicate. Nationally, Democrats won 50.7 percent of the vote in the 1852 election (or 53.7 percent of the two-party vote), yet they ended up controlling a whopping 67.5 percent of House seats. A huge fraction of these seats came from states gerrymandered in favor of Democrats.

We can trace this extreme boost in seat shares back to the wave of pro-Democratic gerrymandering following the 1852 reapportionment. The lopsided Democratic margins in the House had enormous short-term policy consequences and long-term political reverberations; in fact, the reverberations can still be felt to this day. Notably, these manufactured seat shares provided Democrats with enough congressional votes to pass the infamous Kansas-Nebraska Act. The act was a pivotal juncture in the ongoing political battle over the extension of slavery into the American West.

Notably, the act repealed the Missouri Compromise of 1820 and allowed for popular sovereignty in determining whether slavery would be allowed in the territories of Kansas and Nebraska (and future territories). By repealing the Missouri Compromise, the Kansas-Nebraska Act undid the fragile armistice over the issue of westward expansion of slavery that had lasted 30 years. The act passed the House on May 22, 1854, by a margin of 113–100 (Holt 1999, 821). The bulk of support for the bill came from Democrats who voted in favor by a margin of 100–44. Northern Democrats voted in favor 55–43, while Southern Democrats voted in favor 45–1. Northern Whigs voted 7–44, while Southern Whigs voted 6–7. Four Free Soilers and one Independent also voted against the bill.

We can see the pivotal role of gerrymandering on this transformative policy decision by examining how many seats Democrats would have had under a set of neutral redistricting plans. Passing the state vote through a neutral districting plan—one with no bias and a swing ratio of three—produces an estimate in which Democrats would have had 121 seats (or 51.7 percent of the House seats). In actuality, however, with the same vote share, they ended up with 158 seats (or 67.5 percent). Given the split within the Northern wing of the Democratic Party, it is more than reasonable to assume that Democrats would have fallen short of enough votes to pass the Kansas-Nebraska Act.

To see this, we can consider the outcome of the vote on the Kansas-Nebraska Act had the House been elected through neutral state-electoral systems. As an approximation, consider that an individual Democratic representative had a .7 chance of supporting the bill, while a Whig representative had a .2 chance. Using these proportional propensities to support the bill, we can make some rough counterfactual estimates of the outcomes of a Kansas-Nebraska vote under this set of neutral redistricting plans. With 121 seats multiplied by .7 we get an estimated 85 Democratic votes in favor, and 36 against. Whig support was at .2, thus under the counterfactual, we get an estimate of 23 votes in favor, and 90 votes against. (Under the counterfactual estimates, Whigs would have had 113 seats total). Hence, after further counting the four Free Soilers and one Independent as opposed to the act, there would have been an estimated 108 total votes in favor, and 126 votes against. In other words, the Kansas-Nebraska Act would have failed.

Although one should be cautious when forecasting alternative historical trajectories, there is little disagreement about the massive consequences of the Kansas-Nebraska Act. As seen in this chapter, the passage of the act interacted with a highly responsive electoral system to produce the massive swing against Democrats in the subsequent 1854–55 election. The trajectory of American history was fundamentally altered. The termination of the Whig Party, the emergence of the Republican Party, and the fractious split within the Democratic Party placed the country on a collision course that ended in the Civil War. The war still may have happened when it did. However, had Democrats not passed the Kansas-Nebraska Act, there is ample reason to suspect that the course of the next decade would have been different.

These electoral ramifications directly fed into the policy course of the government over the next five years. In the years preceding the Kansas-Nebraska Act, the North and South had operated under a tacit contract.

Every admission of a free state would be accompanied by the admission of a slave state. This so-called balance rule gave the South equal representation in the Senate, from which they could maintain and protect the institution of slavery. But, as Barry Weingast (1998) has powerfully argued, the breakdown produced by the Kansas-Nebraska Act and the resulting election threw the commitment of the North to the balance rule into question. Without explicit Northern commitment to the balance rule, Southern states no longer viewed Northern statements to protect slavery as credible. Once a Northern Republican was elected president, the South decided to secede. It is critical, however, to remember that this unraveling of the Northern and Southern détente over the slavery question can be traced back directly to the Kansas-Nebraska Act and the resulting election of 1854–55.

Gerrymandering further contributed to the political tumult by producing the massive swing in party fortunes in the following elections. As seen in this chapter, although the national vote swing against Democrats in 1854–55 was modest, it nevertheless resulted in a massive swing in seats. The highly responsive gerrymanders drawn by pro-Democratic state legislatures directly fostered these seat swings.

The results of the election threw the subsequent Congress into tumult. For example, the House spent eight weeks fighting over who would be the Speaker (Jenkins and Stewart 2001). Had Democrats not been wiped out, the fight over the Speaker likely would have been shortened, and Democrats would have wielded more influence. The implications went well beyond the narrow confines of Capitol Hill politics. The fight over the speakership shaped policy over the next Congress and determined policy toward the westward extension of slavery. Indeed, the political battles fought within the halls of Congress over slavery in the early 1850s would eventually erupt into civil war, and engulf the whole nation, only a few years later (Holt 1999).

1874: Reconstruction and Suffrage Rights

A similarly dramatic policy consequence of gerrymandering can be seen in the policy outcomes following the 1874 election. As seen in this chapter, Democrats captured the House of Representatives for the first time since the Civil War. The new Democratic majority spelled doom for Reconstruction policy in the South. Because the Republican Ulysses S. Grant still occupied the White House, Democrats could not outright repeal Reconstruction or the enforcement acts that had been passed in the years prior to 1874. However, Democrats were in a position to radically affect appropriations and spending decisions. In other words, they could halt the enforcement of Reconstruction policies through budget starvation.

Democrats' position of power stemmed from the asymmetric bargaining power that can arise in the federal appropriations process. In particular, if an appropriation bill fails to pass, then spending in that policy area reverts to zero. Thus, a legislative party that wants to reduce spending, even if it only controls one branch of government, can be granted a position of real leverage (Kiewiet and McCubbins 1988; Stewart 1991). Democrats used this leverage to their advantage to reduce spending on enforcement in the South whenever they gained control of the House.

In effect, Democrats' sweeping victory in the election of 1874 began the death knell of Reconstruction. The federal government ceded the South to local elites. The dramatic consequences of federal abandonment of the South could most readily be seen in Mississippi, where the Democratic state government passed a radical plan to disenfranchise African Americans. Thus, even before the national government formally pulled federal troops out following the presidential election of 1876, the commitment of the federal government to protection of voting rights had been severely undermined. As the historian Kenneth Stampp has argued, "After the Democrats gained a majority in the House, there was no chance that additional federal protection would be given to southern Negroes. Instead the House Democrats, in 1876, refused to pass an army appropriation bill in order to force the President to withdraw federal troops from the South. . . . Under these circumstances the absence of federal intervention when the Mississippi Plan went into operation is understandable" (Stampp 1965, 209).

The rapidly diminished role of the federal government in Southern elections can also be seen in federal prosecutions of electoral fraud in Southern congressional districts. In the early 1870s, Republicans passed a sweeping set of laws which empowered the federal government to challenge and prosecute violations of the Fifteenth Amendment. The purpose was to prevent violations of African-American voting rights in the South (and voting rights in the North). Before 1874, the Justice Department investigated 1,973 cases of electoral fraud in the South. Following Democrats' takeover of the House, and the reduction in appropriations for federal marshals, the number of prosecutions declined almost to zero (Wang 1997, 300–301). Between 1871 and 1874, the Justice Department successfully prosecuted 1,022 cases of fraud and vote suppression in the South. Between 1875 and 1880, after Democrats took control of the House—and control of the Justice Department budget—the number of prosecutions plummeted to 38 total cases (Gillette 1979, 43; Wang 1997, 300). In effect, the guarantee of federal enforcement and protection of African Americans' Fifteenth Amendment suffrage rights vanished following Democrats' sweeping capture of the House in the 1874 election.

1892–94:The Repeal of Federal Enforcement and the One-Party South

The fight over enforcement of Fifteenth Amendment and the suffrage rights of African Americans continued, after 1874, for the next 20 years. As party power shifted back and forth in Washington, the fortunes of African Americans in the South shifted as well. The tenuous battle over enfranchisement finally came to end in 1894. The boost to Democrats' majority in the 1892 election, which, as we have seen, owed much to gerrymandering, gave Democrats a sufficient majority to enact one of their longstanding policy goals—repeal of the Federal Enforcement Act. Thus, in 1894, before surrendering majority control, Democrats enacted legislation that pulled the plug on the Federal Enforcement Act (Wang 1997).

As seen in the previous chapter, a centerpiece of Republican-policy agenda following the passage of the Fifteenth Amendment was the creation of the Federal Enforcement Act. As the title of the act telegraphed, its purpose was to provide a statutory basis for the federal government to enforce the suffrage rights of African Americans laid out in the Fifteenth Amendment. The act had originally passed in the early 1870s; over the next 20 years, the two parties fought over the support of the act. When Democrats controlled the House, they sought to starve the enforcement bureau of appropriations. But with firm control of Congress following the 1892 election, and a Democrat in the White House, Democrats were finally in a position to pass legislation repealing the Federal Enforcement Act.

Absent highly responsive gerrymanders, Democrats' majority would have been much more modest. Using our counterfactual baseline of a swing ratio of 3 and no partisan bias, we would predict that the vote share in the 1892 election would result in 182 Democratic seats (or 51 percent). Democrats still may have had the necessary votes to repeal the Federal Enforcement Act, but the vote would have been much tighter. Or Republicans may have found it possible to amend the bill and save parts of the repeal act. The vote split right along party lines. 194 Democrats voted in favor, and 102 voted against. No Republican voted in favor, and no Democrat voted against (Wang 1997, 256). The long-term consequences of this act for the trajectory of subsequent American political and social history were, obviously, enormous. It would be another 60 years before the federal government intervened in the Southern electoral process. The legacy of these decisions continues to shake American politics.

Conclusion

Starting with Edward Tufte's (1973) pioneering article, which suggested a link between gerrymandering and the declining swing ratio of 20th-century congressional elections, there has been considerable debate in the political-science literature over the impact of redistricting on competition in congressional elections. The current status of the debate is that redistricting either reduces, or has no effect, on competition. In this chapter, though, I have found that redistricting in the 19th century often *increased* competition. These results suggest that the impact of redistricting on electoral competition is conditional upon the broader institutional environment affecting the strategies of partisan mapmakers.

The findings in this chapter also cast a new perspective on electoral change in American political history. A traditional, organizing perspective of American politics is that periods of realignment produce large-scale transformations in public policy and political institutions. Critical elections are the manifestation of pent-up public demand for changing the status quo, currently frustrated by the regime in power. But what if the elections typically considered critical were, if only unintentionally, manufactured by politicians via institutional design? What if instead of large shifts in mass opinion, the swings in party fortunes were the unintended byproduct of strategic politicians manipulating electoral districts?

The elections of 1854, 1874, and 1894 brought together a rare confluence of events: manufactured competitiveness, an overabundance of marginal districts for one party created by redistricting, and a vote swing against that current dominant party. High vote-seat ratios were a necessary, but not sufficient, condition for a huge seat swing toward one party. It also required that the party on the losing end of the vote swing had an overabundance of marginal seats. One can see this by considering what would have happened had there been an equivalent five-point swing the other way, in favor of the dominant party. Even in this extremely competitive party system, such a swing would have generated comparatively modest gains for Democrats in 1854 and 1894, and Republicans in 1874. In this regard, 1854, 1874, and 1894 would have looked more like the elections of 1958 or 1964—a majority party adding to its already substantial advantage—than the "critical elections" they have since been christened by historians and political scientists.

This argument is not meant to deny the historical and political importance attached to events such as the Kansas-Nebraska Act, the Panic of 1873, or the Panic of 1893. The majority party at the time, in all three instances, would have suffered at the polls, regardless of district design. Yet, the magnitudes of the seat swings were directly influenced by the particular redistricting strategies pursued by state political parties. These results remind us that that in interpreting change in political representation it is critical to recognize how the strategic design of electoral districts channels political events to accelerate or decelerate changes in public preferences.

SEVEN

A Congress of Strangers

Gerrymandering and Legislative Turnover

The contemporary Congress is a highly professionalized organization with a relatively stable membership. In any given election year, few incumbents retire, and even fewer are defeated. Most run for reelection, and most win. In 2008, for example, 93 percent of incumbents ran for reelection, and 94 percent of those won. At the beginning of the 110th Congress, which followed the 2008 election, only 12 percent of House members were serving in their first term. The average length of service for members of this Congress was 10 years (or five terms). Thus even a fairly nationalized election, such as the 2008 election, produced comparatively modest turnover.

By contrast, turnover in the 19th century was immense. The start of a typical mid-19th-century Congress closely resembled a body of neophytes. For example, at the opening of the 42nd Congress, following the 1870 election, nearly 45 percent of the House members were serving in their first term. Even the "veterans" were recent arrivals; the average House member at the beginning of the 42nd Congress had only served four years (two terms). Nor was the 42nd Congress atypical. Indeed, most politicians of the 19th century did not view service in the House of Representatives as the pinnacle of the political-career ladder until very late in the century (Kernell 1977; Polsby 1968; Price 1971). Instead, politicians tended to rotate among offices. A typical 19th-century political career might have involved serving in local office, moving onto the state legislature, serving in Congress for a few terms, and then returning to state or local office (Kernell 2003).

130

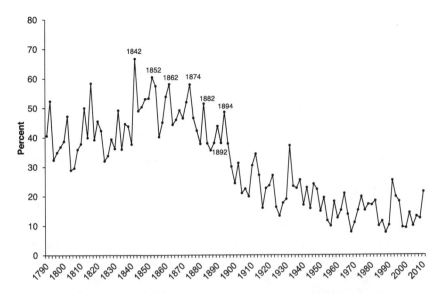

Fig. 7.1. Percentage of House members serving their first term, 1790–2010. (Data compiled by the author from Inter-University Consortium for Political and Social Research and McKibbin 1997; and Ornstein, Mann, and Malbin 2008.)

To get a visual idea of turnover patterns in the 19th century, figure 7.1 plots the number of first termers at the opening of each Congress—from 1790 to 2010. As this figure reveals, turnover in the 19th century was enormous. The average number of first-termers over this period was an astonishing 46 percent. Nearly half of the membership of a mid-century Congress, for example, would have been serving their first term. In some Congresses, the numbers soared even higher. The record was set by the 28th Congress (1842) in which 67 percent of the membership was serving their first term in the House. One can also see in the figure the oft-noted decrease in turnover over the course of the century. But even after taking this general decrease into account, the amount of turnover in the 19th century still dominates the modern Congress, where the average number of first-termers hovers around 13 percent.

Given the importance of legislative turnover, there is little surprise that the evolution of turnover has attracted much scholarly attention. Students of the U.S. Congress generally agree that the primary determinant of 19th-century turnover can be found in the decisions of members to run for reelection. In particular, voluntary retirement, rather than electoral defeat, was by far the leading reason for turnover (Brady, Buckley, and Rivers 1999;

Kernell 1977; Price 1975). Scholars disagree, however, in their explanations for this era's high rate of voluntary retirements. Some have identified the changing benefit, or value, of holding a seat in Washington, DC. As governing and administrative capacities gradually shifted from the state capitals to Washington, DC, the value of holding onto a seat in the House became increasingly attractive. Other scholars have argued that the intense party competition of the era soured members on the idea of holding onto a congressional seat for long stretches (Price 1975). As districts became safer following the landslide elections of 1894 and 1896, members found their electoral environments more hospitable for longer stays in Congress. Others have pointed to norms of "rotation" that operated in some districts where the party nomination would be rotated among local factions.

Likely, all of the just-mentioned factors played a role (see Kernell 2003). Yet, few have looked to redistricting as another potential factor contributing to this era's high levels of voluntary departures. Given the rampant partisan gerrymandering of the era, one may reasonably have expected redistricting to have entered into the strategic calculus of 19th-century incumbents. As seen in the previous chapter, bipartisan pro-incumbent gerrymanders were rare. States instead gerrymandered to the bone, pushing partisan advantage as far is it would go. Even incumbents of the party drawing the districts were rarely given safer seats. Instead, many of these incumbents had their districts trimmed as partisan mapmaker's reallocated voters to maximize their overall seat share. Moreover, redistricting was an ever-present threat hanging over many incumbents. As seen in chapter 2, states did not hesitate to redraw districts mid-decade. Thus, unlike modern incumbents who typically can count on a 10-year window of district stability, 19th-century incumbents could find themselves having their district carved up at any point during a decade.

Some prima facie evidence for a link between redistricting and turnover can be discerned in figure 7.1. In the figure, I have labeled particular years where redistricting was pervasive. Strikingly, the peaks of House turnover occur simultaneously with these peaks in redistricting. Indeed, the all-time record for first-termers (setting aside the first Congress) was the Congress following the election of 1842–43. In this Congress, a stunning 67 percent of House members were serving their first term. This massive turnover of legislative personnel, of course, came on the heels of the massive wave of redistricting prompted by the 1842 Apportionment Act. Running a simple regression with the total percentage of incumbents seeking reelection as the dependent variable and the percentage of districts redrawn nationwide as an independent variable, one finds a positive and significant relationship.

The value of the coefficient on the percentage of redrawn districts is 15.5, indicating that if every district were redrawn one would expect turnover to rise by 15.5 percent.

Although this evidence is suggestive of a link, one potential counterargument is that the high percent of first-termers in reapportionment years may have resulted from changes in the size of the House (Fiorina, Rohde, and Wissel 1975). Since 1911, the size of the House has been fixed at 435 members, but throughout the 19th century, Congress regularly added new seats and expanded the size of the House. For example, the 1882 Apportionment Act increased the membership of the House from 293 to 325. One source prompting the addition of seats was the admission of new states. To accommodate newly admitted states, the House typically would tack on new seats to the overall membership. A second cause was the spectacular growth of the American population. As population swelled and expanded westward, rather than make the unpopular decision to take seats away from older states, Congress often opted to simply add new seats to the House. From the perspective of analyzing first-termers in Congress, therefore, one needs to take into account these new seats. Otherwise, we may overstate the connection between reapportionment and turnover (Fiorina, Rohde, and Wissel 1975).

To account for the possibility that new seats inflated the relationship between first-termers and redistricting, figure 7.2 presents the percentage of members who were replaced by someone else. In effect, this is a turnover measure purged of any members elected in newly gained seats (see Fiorina, Rohde, and Wissel 1975). As figure 7.2 shows, purging new seats from the time-series does not alter the overall picture. There is again a very visible link between reapportionment years and replacement members. Regressing the percentage of replacements on the total percentage of districts redrawn yields a coefficient of 16.3 ($p < .01$). If every district was redrawn, we would expect the percentage of replacements to increase by 16.3 percent. So, controlling for growth in the House actually accentuates the effect of redistricting.

These aggregate patterns also find support in various pieces of anecdotal evidence. For example, following the North Carolina mid-decade redistricting in 1847, the Whig Alfred Dockery found himself placed into a district with fellow Whig incumbent, Daniel M. Barringer. According to historian Marc Kruman, "After considering a run for reelection Dockery decided against it and gave his support to Barringer" (1983, 39). In Ohio, in 1890, a pro-Democratic gerrymander abruptly ended the burgeoning careers of a number of Republican incumbents. For example, Robert P.

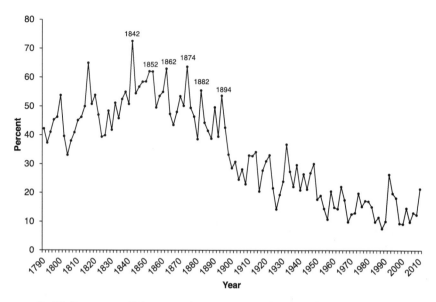

Fig. 7.2. Percentage of House members replaced, 1790–2010. (Data for 1790 to 1970 compiled by the author from data presented in Fiorina, Rohde, and Wisell 1975, 29–31. Data for 1972 to 2010 constructed by the author.)

Kennedy was one of those Republican incumbents. Having only just begun his service in the House, the new district maps cut his fledgling congressional career short. The *New York Times* wrote, "Kennedy was elected to Congress two years ago from the Logan district, and hoped that his career would be continuous as a national lawmaker. The dream was short-lived, and has had a gloomy ending. His county has been bunched with Allen, Putnam, and Auglaize, all heavily Democratic with Hardin and Van Wert, both close thrown in. Nearly four thousand majority stare him in the face" (*New York Times*, July 25, 1890). Unsurprisingly, Kennedy did not stand for reelection.

In sum, there is good reason to suspect that incumbents responded strategically to changes in their district boundaries—often opting to retire rather than run for reelection. Indeed, some of the early research on the evolution of congressional careerism raised this possibility. Kernell (1977), for example, noted that "Nineteenth century reapportionment may have had a disruptive effect on congressional careers. With a growing population necessitating periodic redistricting and highly partisan state legislatures redrawing district boundaries, some congressmen may have had their careers abruptly ended when redistricting carved up their formerly secure seats" (679). Similarly, Fiorina, Rohde, and Wissel (1975), in the appendix to their study of replacements, noted an aggregate relationship between reapportionment years (i.e., years ending in 2) and the total number of new members in a given Congress.

Neither of these articles, however, examined the district-level decisions of members to seek reelection. Nor did they take into account mid-decade redistricting. Thus, it remains an open question whether or not redistricting curbed political ambition, increased turnover, and stunted the growth of careerism.

Redistricting and Strategic Entry

Whether or not an incumbent returns to Congress is primarily the joint product of two factors: seeking reelection and winning reelection. Other causes may intervene to prevent an incumbent from returning—death or expulsion—but the failure to seek reelection or losing reelection conditional on seeking it are by far the greatest factors contributing to turnover. In this section, I focus on the decision to seek reelection.

Data on the individual decisions to seek reelection comes from the *Roster of United States Congressional Officeholders and Biographical Characteristics of Members of the United States Congress, 1789–1996: Merged Data* (ICPSR Study Number 7803). This dataset provides detailed biographical information on everyone who has ever served in Congress. For my interests here, the key is that this dataset includes information on whether or not each member sought reelection. If a person stood for reelection they were obviously coded as "seeking reelection." For those who did not seek reelection, the dataset includes information denoting the reason why. I coded anyone who retired from office, sought higher office, or was appointed to some other office, as "not seeking reelection." I excluded from the analysis anyone who died in office or was expelled from Congress; the logic being that they had no choice about whether to seek reelection.

Less obvious was how to code those listed in the directory as "not receiving the nomination." Because the records of 19th-party-nominating conventions are notoriously thin, one must make a choice about how to treat these cases. One interpretation is that these incumbents sought the nomination but were denied it, which would suggest treating them as "seeking reelection." Another interpretation is that they did not seek renomination at all, and therefore should be coded as "*not* seeking reelec-

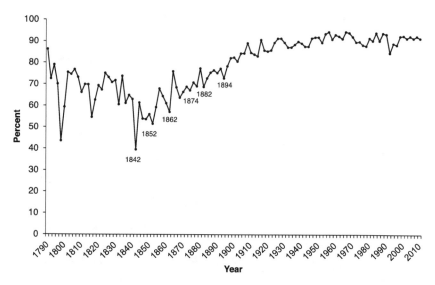

Fig. 7.3. Percentage of House members seeking reelection, 1790–2010. (Data compiled by the author from Inter-University Consortium for Political and Social Research and McKibbin 1997; and Ornstein, Mann, and Malbin 2008.)

tion." I opted to code this category as "seeking reelection." The rationale is that given our best guess these individuals stood for reelection, but failed to gain the nomination; in other words, their departure was involuntary. This coding is also consistent with previous research on 19th-century turnover (i.e., Brady, Buckley and Rivers 1999). Fortunately, only a handful fell into this grey area. Coding them the other way (i.e., as "not seeking reelection") had no impact on the overall results.

Figure 7.3 displays the percentage of members seeking reelection. The average between 1840 and 1900 was 67 percent. This is substantially lower than contemporary rates. Between 1980 and 2010, for instance, the average number of incumbents seeking reelection was 94 percent. One can also see a distinct upward trend over the past two centuries. But the trend is not a straight upward journey. As with the figure on total turnover percentages, the figure clearly shows that fewer incumbents ran following major periods of redistricting. Running a simple regression with the number of members seeking reelection as the dependent variable and the percentage of districts redrawn nationwide as an independent variable, one finds a significant negative relationship (see table 7.1, column 1). If every district were redrawn, one would expect the percentage of representatives seeking reelection to drop by 17 percent.

The next part of the analysis moves to the individual-level decisions of incumbents. If incumbents were making strategic decisions about when to leave Congress, we should see a district-level connection between redistricting and incumbent retirements. To evaluate this relationship, I created a dependent variable taking a value of one if the incumbent sought reelection and zero otherwise.

The key independent variable is whether a district was redrawn or not prior to the election. The model also controlled for factors past research has found to contribute to the decision to run for reelection. These included the incumbent's prior margin of victory, their age (logged), and the number of terms they had served in the House. To control for the upward growth in careerism over this period, I included a time trend variable that takes a value of one in 1840 and grows linearly through 1900 (i.e., 1840 = 1, 1842 = 2, 1844 = 3, and so on).[1] I also included a variable denoting whether it was a midterm election. The midterm election variable was then interacted with a variable denoting whether or not the incumbent was a member of the same party as the president. This should control for any strategic retirement in anticipation of a midterm decline.[2] Because the dependent variable is binary (i.e., 1 = Sought Reelection, 0 = Did Not Seek Reelection) the model was estimated via logit. The model also included robust standard errors clustered by member.

The results, in table 7.2, column 1, support the hypothesis that redistricting influenced incumbent decisions to retire. The coefficient on redistricting is negative and significant. Incumbents were less likely to run for reelection, all else being equal, following a redistricting. Setting all the other variables at their median value, the baseline rate of running when

TABLE 7.1. Redrawn Districts and Turnover, 1840–1900

	Percentage of Incumbents Seeking Reelection	Percentage of Seeking Incumbents Who Won
Percentage of Districts Redrawn	−.17*	−.09*
	(.06)	(.04)
Constant	.70*	.81*
	(.02)	(.01)
Adjusted R^2	.17	.09
Number of Observations	31	31

Note: Entries are OLS coefficients with standard errors in parentheses.
*$p < .05$.

there was no redistricting was .72. With a redistricting the probability dropped to .66. Thus, redistricting reduced the probability of running for reelection by 6 percent.

It is also worth noting the pattern for results for the control variables. Increases in both an incumbents' age and their length of service reduced the likelihood of running for reelection. Moreover, electoral marginality reduced the likelihood of running for reelection. Finally, in midterm elections, members who were of the same party as the sitting president were less likely to run for reelection. All of this provides evidence that incumbents of the 19th century, or the parties nominating them, were keenly strategic in deciding when to run for reelection. Indeed, these incumbents appear to be much more like their modern counterparts than is often assumed.

Winning Election

Although declining to seek reelection was the primary cause of departures in the 19th century (Kernell 1977), it was not the only source of turnover.

TABLE 7.2. The District-Level Impact of Redistricting on Seeking and Winning Reelection, 1840–1900

	Seeking Reelection	Winning Reelection
District Redrawn	−.25*	−.24*
	(.06)	(.09)
Age (logged)	−1.28*	−.25
	(.14)	(.21)
Terms Served	−.03	.10*
	(.02)	(.03)
Previous Margin	.007*	.05*
	(.001)	(.001)
Midterm Election	−.01	.64*
	(.07)	(.10)
Same Party as President	−.003	.72*
	(.07)	(.11)
Midterm Election × Same	−.21*	−1.77*
Party as President	(.10)	(.15)
Time Trend	.02*	.005*
	(.001)	(.002)
Constant	4.79*	1.19
	(.53)	(.77)
Number of Observations	8,041	5,248
Log-Likelihood	−4,787.20	−2,343.45

Note: Entries are maximum likelihood estimates from a logit model. Robust standard errors are in parentheses.

*p < .05.

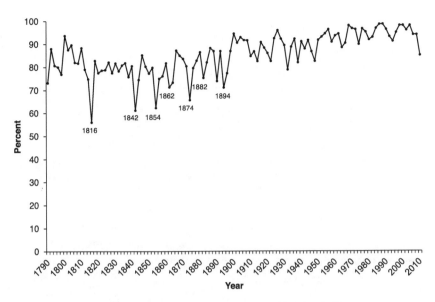

Fig. 7.4. Percentage of running incumbents reelected, 1790–2010. (Data compiled by the author from Inter-University Consortium for Political and Social Research and McKibbin 1997; and Ornstein, Mann, and Malbin 2008.)

The other source was the failure to win election conditional on seeking it (Brady, Buckley, and Rivers 1999). Given that redistricting and incumbent entry appear to be strongly related, one might also suspect redistricting to affect the ability of incumbents to secure reelection, even after seeking it. Gerrymandering can change the partisan composition of the district in a more favorable direction for the opponent. Moreover, incumbents who have built up a personal vote may see their vote share decline among constituents newly added to their district who know little or nothing about the incumbent (Ansolabehere, Snyder, and Stewart 2000; Carson, Engstrom, and Roberts 2007).

Looking first at the overall patterns of electoral defeats, figure 7.4 presents the percentage of running incumbents who were reelected. As the figure shows, reelection rates were surprisingly high during the partisan era. Most incumbents who ran for reelection won. The average reelection rate for running incumbents during this period was nearly 80 percent. Nevertheless, there does appear to be a link between redistricting and the percentage of seeking incumbents reelected. As the figure shows, periods with substantial redistricting had somewhat lower reelection rates. We can be more precise about the relationship by examining a simple regression.

Using the values of this series as a dependent variable, and the percentage of districts redrawn as an independent variable, we find a negative and significant relationship (in table 7.1, column 2). If every district were redrawn, the percentage of running incumbents winning reelection would drop by 9 percent.

We can further test this relationship by analyzing the individual probability that an incumbent won reelection following a redistricting. Here the dependent variable is equal to one if the incumbent won reelection and zero if they lost. The independent variables are the same as those in the model that estimated the decision to seek reelection. Table 7.2, column 2, presents the results. The coefficient on the redistricting variable is negative and significant. This indicates that redistricting reduced the likelihood that an incumbent would win reelection in a redrawn district. Without redistricting, and setting the other variables at their median value, the probability of incumbent reelection was .87. When there was a redistricting, this probability dropped to .83. Thus, redistricting reduced the probability of reelection by 4 percent. The magnitude, of the effect, however is not especially large indicating that the more substantive impact of redistricting came at the initial decision to seek reelection.

One point to bear in mind is that the impact of redistricting on winning reelection is likely understated. As the previous analysis indicted, incumbents who anticipated losing—or at least anticipated facing a difficult campaign—as a result of redistricting were probably more inclined to shy away from running again. Thus, the coefficient on the redistricting variable possibly underestimates the overall impact of redistricting. Nevertheless, putting the results for seeking and winning reelection together indicates that redistricting had a substantial impact on the career prospects of 19th-century incumbents.

One obvious question these findings raise is why parties would put their own incumbents at risk via redistricting. One possibility, and the one suggested by earlier chapters, is that state political parties were simply trying to maximize their collective share of seats. This goal often required trimming the district margins of their own congressional incumbents. There was clearly a trade-off here. Maximizing seat shares also made incumbents, on the margin, more vulnerable. Another related possibility is that districts were redrawn to bolster the aspirations of incumbent state legislators. One can find a few anecdotes in the historical literature supporting this notion, but there is not enough detailed evidence to offer more than speculation. Without more data on the career aspirations of state legislators it is difficult to say how much of this was taking place.

The Overall Impact of Redistricting on Turnover

The previous two sections have shown that redistricting profoundly influenced both who ran for reelection and who won. Having established that redrawing district boundaries influenced the individual components of turnover, the question now becomes: how much did these components affect overall levels of turnover? One way to assess the impact of redistricting on the individual, and joint, components of turnover is to examine a counterfactual. We can begin by first considering the extent to which redistricting influenced the aggregate number of congressmen seeking reelection.

Recall that the estimated aggregate impact of redistricting on the percentage of incumbents who sought reelection was −.09 (see table 7.1, column 1). Multiplying this coefficient by the percentage of districts redrawn in a given year provides an estimate of how many incumbents retired due to redistricting. For example, in 1872, the number of congressional districts redrawn was 50.2 percent. Multiplying this value by −.16 provides an estimated effect of redistricting on retirement rates of 8 percent. In other words, if there were no redistricting, we would have expected an additional 8 percent of incumbents to run for reelection. Adding this estimated number to the actual total of incumbents who retired provides a counterfactual estimate of how many incumbents would have retired if no redistricting had taken place. So, in the 1872 example, we would have expected 76.9 percent of incumbents to run for reelection if there was no redistricting, as opposed to the 68.9 percent who did in reality. Calculating this value for every election provides a counterfactual time-series where we can then compare to the actual percentage of incumbent retirements.

The results of this simulation, along with the actual rates of reelection seeking, are displayed in figure 7.5. The figure illustrates that redistricting sharply decreased the overall percentage of incumbents seeking reelection. The simulated trend line differs from the actual line substantially at a number of points. In 1852, for example, 52 percent of incumbents sought reelection, while the simulation indicates that 65 percent would have sought had there been no redistricting. Noteworthy is the Gilded Age. From 1870 through 1894, there is a consistent discrepancy between the simulated and actual number of Congressmen seeking reelection. The heightened redistricting of this period appears to have acted as a drag on reelection seeking.

Figure 7.6 presents a similar counterfactual estimating the impact of redistricting on the proportion of "seeking incumbents" winning reelec-

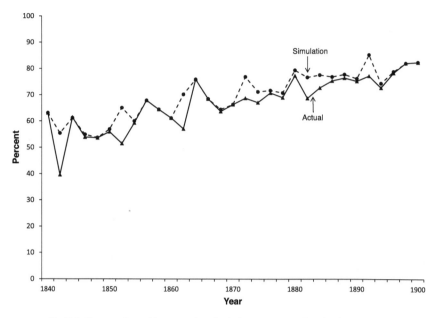

Fig. 7.5. Counterfactual impact of redistricting on rates of reelection seeking

tion. Here I have multiplied the percentage of redrawn districts by the coefficient in table 7.1, column 2 (i.e., −.09). Adding this number to the actual number who won reelection provides a simulated time-series of the percentage of seeking incumbents who would have won reelection, absent redistricting. The numbers again reveal discrepancies between the simulation and the actual percentage of incumbent winners, but the magnitude of the differences is modest. In 1872, for example, the simulated number of incumbents winning reelection was 81 percent as opposed to the 77 percent in actuality. The relatively smaller effect of redistricting on winning reelection meshes with previous research that has found voluntary exits to be the primary determinant of turnover. Nevertheless, there is an appreciable effect of redistricting on the aggregate number of incumbents winning reelection.

We can now put these two sets of results together to produce a measure of the overall impact of redistricting on turnover. Because the coefficients in table 7.1 are based on different sets of incumbents, one first needs to estimate the number of incumbents who voluntarily retired due to redistricting. I did this by first calculating the estimated number of incumbents who would have run had there been no redistricting. For example, in 1872,

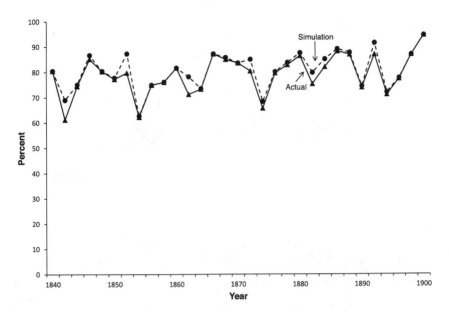

Fig. 7.6. Counterfactual impact of redistricting on incumbent winning percentage

168 of the potential 244 incumbents ran for reelection. In the simulation, 188 incumbents would have run. Then we can calculate how many of those who sought reelection would have won given the baseline rates of incumbent victory in the absence of redistricting. So, continuing with the 1872 example, we would expect the number of seeking incumbents winning reelection absent redistricting to be 153. The result is an estimate of the proportion of incumbents who would have sought election and won. We can then compare this proportion to the actual proportion of incumbents who returned.

Figure 7.7 displays the results of this exercise. Again, we see a number of differences between the simulation and the actual series. Not surprisingly, the largest differences are found in elections following a federal reapportionment. In 1842, the simulation predicts that 44 percent of incumbents would have returned, whereas in reality only 28 percent returned. In 1872, the simulation predicts that 63 percent of incumbents would have returned as opposed to the 53 percent who actually did. But the effect was not felt just in reapportionment years. For instance, in every year between 1872 and 1894, one finds a substantial discrepancy. Overall, at both the individual and aggregate level, redistricting increased legislative turnover.

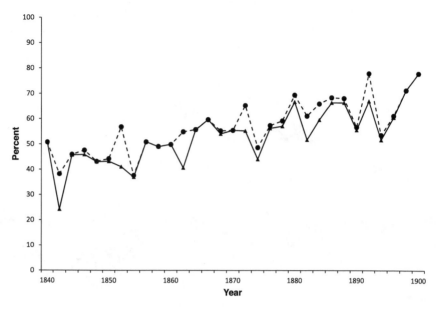

Fig. 7.7. The total impact of redistricting on the percentage of returning members

By no means was it the only cause of turnover during this era. But the frequency and partisanship of redistricting clearly acted as a drag on the development of careerism.

A Note on Challengers

This chapter has primarily been concerned with the decisions of incumbents. But incumbents were not the only actors making strategic calculations about when to run for office. Challengers represent the other side of the electoral coin. One might reasonably suspect that when a district was redrawn to make an incumbent vulnerable, one or more experienced candidates lined up for a chance at the nomination. Consider the Ohio redistricting of 1890. Following this very pro-Democratic gerrymander, a number of Republican incumbents found themselves in hostile territory. Democratic challengers throughout the state were more than ready to jump into the race against these newly vulnerable incumbents. The *New York Times* reported that for Republicans:

In some of the newly made districts there will woe and heaviness of spirit between the time of nomination and election day. No one will more keenly realize this than [Republican] Hon. T.E. Burton of the Cleveland district. He is in a gerrymandered district where a Democratic majority is almost a certainty; he is sure to be pitted against the strongest man the Democrats can name. (*New York Times*, July 25, 1890)

In research conducted with my colleagues Jamie Carson and Jason Roberts (2006), we examined whether redistricting affected the decisions of experienced challengers to run for Congress. In that project, we gathered background information on every major party candidate who ran for the House between 1872 and 1896. Following the standard definition in the contemporary literature (e.g., Jacobson 2009), we defined anyone who had held prior elected office as an experienced challenger. We then examined what impact redistricting had on the likelihood of an experienced challenger taking on an incumbent. We found that challengers with prior office-holding experience were more likely to run in districts that had been favorably altered in the redistricting process.

Table 7.3 presents the rates of collisions between incumbents and experienced challengers between 1872 and 1896. When districts were untouched, the probability of an experienced challenger taking on an incumbent was only 32.6 percent. When districts were redrawn, the probability of an experienced challenger entering increased to 38.4 percent. The data for that project only covered a portion of the 19th century, but the results lend further support to the larger story of this chapter. The decisions of challengers were just as strategic as those of challengers now. It also suggests a degree of electoral coordination among candidates, and the parties that nominated them, that many might suspect would not be pres-

TABLE 7.3. The Entry of Experienced Challengers against Incumbents, 1872–96

	Amateur Challenger	Experienced Challenger
District Untouched	67.4%	32.6%
	(1,479)	(716)
District Redrawn	61.6%	38.4%
	(241)	(150)

Note: The percentages are row percentages. Raw numbers are in parentheses. An "experienced challenger" is defined as anyone who has held prior elective office.

$\chi^2 = 4.92; p < .03$.

ent in the 19th century. Moreover, this strategic coordination enhanced the competitiveness of districts. Where incumbents faced off against strong challengers, races were more closely contested (Carson, Engstrom, and Roberts 2006). Thus, rather than inhibiting competition, redistricting in the 19th century enhanced it.

Conclusion

The framers of the U.S. Constitution sought to harness the self-interested ambitions of office holders, and would-be office holders, by designing a constitutional structure that would channel these ambitions toward the common good. Notably, frequent elections for the House were designed to keep representatives accountable and attuned to the wishes of their constituencies. If representatives are unconcerned about reelection, or have scant interest in seeking reelection, then the salutary benefits of frequent elections may be lost.

For this normative reason, many pundits and scholars have expressed concern about the lack of turnover in contemporary congressional elections. In the modern House, most members seek reelection and win reelection. This muted turnover has led to a vast literature searching for its causes. One suspect that has prompted much scrutiny is redistricting. In the wake of the 1960s reapportionment revolution, scholars such as Edward Tufte (1973) argued that the resulting wave of redistricting made seats safe for incumbents of both parties. Although many political scientists were quick to challenge Tufte's argument (e.g., Ferejohn 1977), his claim about the dampening effect of redistricting on competition continues to echo in popular commentary. One of the oft-heard refrains among journalists, editorial writers, and good-government groups is that redistricting depresses legislative turnover. Democrats and Republicans have colluded, so the argument goes, to secure safe districts for incumbents of both parties.

This argument, however, runs into the stubborn fact that even in the modern era redistricting, rather than inhibiting turnover, often induces incumbents to depart office. For example, Cox and Katz (2002, 166) found that since the 1960s, incumbents have been less likely to run for reelection following redistricting. In an analysis of the decisions of modern House incumbents to retire or run for higher office, Kiewiet and Zeng (1993) discovered that incumbent decisions to retire spiked when their district was substantially redrawn. More recently, Yoshinaka and Murphy (2009) found that the 2002 redistricting cycle increased incumbent retirements, particularly for incumbents whose districts were drawn by the opposition party.

An important question is whether these findings are confined to the modern era or whether they are a pattern found more generally throughout American history. In this chapter, I examined the impact of redistricting on the entry and exit decisions of 19th-century representatives. When districts were carved up, incumbents were less likely to seek reelection. As a result, members of Congress often faced a highly uncertain electoral environment. Redistricting could come at any time. When it happened, more often than not, it was intensely partisan. Rather than risk defeat, many members simply opted to retire. For those who did run for reelection, redistricting increased the probability of defeat. The net result was to amplify legislative turnover and hinder congressional careerism.

These findings lead to a profoundly ironic implication. If one truly wants more legislative turnover, then a solution might be more partisan gerrymandering—not less. Partisan redistricting, rather than restrain turnover, can raise it. Indeed, the peaks of legislative turnover were reached precisely in those years when there was vigorous partisan gerrymandering. Whether such immense turnover is a good thing, however, is another question. As historian J. Morgan Kousser has written, "The prospect of repeated interaction in the future gives careerist twentieth century members more reason to compromise and to develop policy incrementally. Congressmen in the nineteenth century, who could not expect to sit long enough to benefit from a 'tit-for-tat' strategy, had less reason to compromise and less stake in the incremental development of policy" (Kousser 1992, 153). The waves of turnover found in the 19th century often produced a Congress of strangers. Congressmen arrived in Washington, DC, with little political experience at the national level and little incentive to forge longterm political relationships with their fellow legislators. The future career opportunities of legislators resided back home, not on Capitol Hill.

EIGHT

The Partisan Impact of Malapportionment

In the federal reapportionment that followed the 2000 census, Pennsylvania was allocated 18 congressional seats. This was two less than Pennsylvania's previous allotment and therefore necessitated a thorough redrawing of their congressional district boundaries. The Republican Party held sizable majorities in the state legislature and controlled the governorship, and therefore had solid control of the redistricting process. Republicans took full advantage of their fortuitous situation by pursuing an aggressive partisan gerrymander. Their efforts were supported and cheered on by national party operatives including White House senior advisor Karl Rove (Barone and Cohen 2003, 1351). The resulting map eliminated four Democratic districts and created two new Republican-leaning districts.

Unsurprisingly, the plan was immediately challenged by Democrats, who filed lawsuits in both state and federal courts. In April 2002, a three-member federal court struck down the plan. The basis of the ruling, however, was not that the plan was an illegal partisan gerrymander. Instead, the federal court ruled that the map violated the one-person, one-vote doctrine. In particular, the judges found that district populations deviated by 19 persons. And according to the ruling, the maximum acceptable population deviation across congressional districts was *one person*.[1]

This episode highlights one of the striking differences between past and present redistricting. Contemporary mapmakers operate under strict population constraints. A deviation of more than a single person across congressional districts violates current legal doctrine. By contrast, 19th-century mapmakers had ample freedom to draw districts of unequal size. Although Congress attached provisions to the decennial apportionment acts, between 1872 and 1912, stating that districts should be as "equal as practicable," there is no evidence that this provision was ever enforced.

Many states responded to the absence of constraints by drawing districts that varied widely in size. In 1882, for example, New York's 12th District (comprised of Westchester County) contained 108,988 people, while the 3rd District (a subset of Brooklyn) contained 222,718 people: over double in size. Nor were these disparities confined to states with large urban populations. In 1872, for instance, Wisconsin's 8th District had only half as many people (82,217) as the nearby 5th District (158,421).

These anecdotes suggest that districts *could* vary greatly in size throughout the 19th century. Yet we know surprisingly little about how widespread malapportionment was during this era and its impact on the national partisan balance of power. While the political and policy consequences of district apportionment in the years immediately before and after the Supreme Court's reapportionment decisions of the 1960s has received substantial scrutiny (e.g., Ansolabehere and Snyder 2008; Cox and Katz 2002; Erikson 1972; Lax and McCubbins 2006; McCubbins and Schwartz 1988), there is almost no research on the partisan impact of malapportionment during the 19th century.[2] With the notable exception of an article by Altman (1998), which provides an overview of historical variations in district size and the nature of district contiguity, almost all of our current understanding of this subject is conjectural. How unequal in size were congressional districts in the 19th century? Did political parties in control of the districting process create different sized districts to rig the electoral system in their favor? If so, did these electoral biases cumulate across states to alter the partisan composition of the House of Representatives?

To see the relevance of considering unequal district sizes as a distinct source of partisan bias, consider the following example.[3] Consider a hypothetical state with five congressional districts. Assume each district has an identical voting population of 70,000 voters. In the first two districts, Democrats win by a margin of 60,000-10,000. In the other three districts, Republicans win by a margin of 40,000-30,000. This districting arrangement produces a sizable pro-Republican bias—Republicans win 60 percent of the seats with only 44 percent of the statewide vote—yet the bias emerges entirely from the partisan distribution of voters across districts. Unequal district sizes, by construction, contribute nothing to the resulting bias.

Now consider what happens if we allow for malapportionment in these districts. Imagine that Republicans still win their three districts with 57 percent of the vote (40,000-30,000) and Democrats now also win their districts with 57 percent of the vote. Except that the Democratic districts are twice as big—such that the vote share in Democratic districts is 80,000-60,000. Here both the parties win their districts by the same percentage, yet the overall map is again biased against Democrats. Republicans win 60 percent of the seats. Yet, the statewide vote share is almost evenly split between the parties—Republicans have 240,000 votes, while Democrats have 250,000. In this example, therefore, the bias arises from malapportioned districts. The larger Democratic districts lead to more wasted Democratic votes.

In the rest of this chapter, I analyze the extent and partisan impact of malapportionment in House districts from 1840 to 1900. First, I examine when and how much districts varied in size. Second, I determine if these variations led to partisan biases both within state congressional delegations and, cumulatively, in the House of Representatives. To do this, I decompose the bias of 19th-century congressional elections into its constituent parts (i.e., bias from malapportionment and bias from the distribution of partisan voters via gerrymandering). The results show that partisan bias arising from malapportionment directly correlated with state party control of the districting process, but the net effect was modest. The most important source of bias was the distribution of voters into districts from gerrymandering, and less from malapportionment.

How Unequal Were 19th-Century House Districts?

In the modern era, the one-person, one-vote standard, and its elaboration in subsequent case law, necessitates that states create congressional districts of equal population. Because population naturally shifts over the course of 10 years, states are compelled every decade to bring the equality of their districts back into equality. By contrast, politicians of the 19th century enjoyed much wider latitude in deciding both when and how to construct congressional districts. Although Congress attached provisions to the decennial apportionment acts between 1872 and 1912 stating that districts should contain "as nearly as practicable an equal number of inhabitants," there is no indication that this standard was imposed.

How pervasive was malapportionment during the 19th century? There are a number of different approaches to measuring inequality in district sizes.[4] One simple approach is to compare the smallest and largest districts within a state. To get a baseline idea of how much district populations varied, table 8.1 displays a few examples of how populations differed between the smallest and largest districts within states. In 1842, for instance, the largest district in Ohio had 82,791 people, while the smallest had 61,572. In 1892, Pennsylvania's largest district contained 309,986 people; the smallest contained 129,764.

A more systematic view of these population inequalities can be seen by considering the average difference between the smallest and largest district within states. Specifically, for each state, I calculated the difference in population between the largest and smallest district. Averaging across the states in each year provides a measure of the overall levels of district inequality—the results are displayed in figure 8.1. During the 1860s, the average difference within states was roughly 30,000 people. By 1900, this number had climbed to 70,000 people.[5] To help contextualize the 19th-century numbers, figure 8.1 also shows the average differences in district populations for the decades before and after the reapportionment revolution of the 1960s. One can see the growth in population differences that carried on throughout the 20th century and its abrupt reversal following the abolition of malapportionment.

Certainly some, if not most, of the growth in these differences can be attributed to the explosive growth of population in the United States. In 1840, the United States had roughly 17 million people. By 1900, the total population had risen to 76 million people. Even though the size of the House also grew during this period—primarily to accommodate the expanding country—the addition of new House seats failed to keep pace with population growth. One way to account for the increased size of House districts is to examine the ratio between the least and most populous districts. This metric, known as the "ratio of inequality," helps to normalize the levels of inequality over time. To get an idea of how the metric works, table 8.1, column 4, presents some examples of the ratio of inequality. For example, in 1882, the ratio of inequality in New York, was 2.04 (the largest district had 222,718 people, while the smallest had 108,988).

To visualize how extensive these inequalities were in total, figure 8.2 displays the average ratio of inequality for all states with more than one district. Specifically, I generated this figure by calculating the ratio of inequality for every state—with more than one district—and then averaged across the states to produce a national average. For the sake of comparison the figure also shows the average ratio of inequality for the 20th century. Throughout the 19th century, the average ratio hovered above 1.4, indicating that within states the largest district was on average 1.4 times bigger than the smallest district.[6] We do not see, however, a substantial increase in

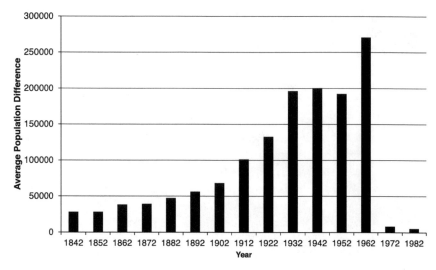

Fig. 8.1. Average differences in population between smallest and largest congressional districts within a state, 1842–1982. The figure shows the average difference between the smallest and largest populated districts following reapportionment years (years in ending in "2"). (Data for the period between 1842 and 1902 compiled by the author from data presented in Parsons, Beach, and Dubin 1986; and Parsons, Dubin, and Parsons 1990. Data from 1912 to 1982 was collected from various issues of the Congressional Directory.)

TABLE 8.1. Representative Examples of District Inequalities

State	Year	Population in Smallest District	Population in Largest District	Ratio of Inequality
Ohio	1842	61,572	82,791	1.34
Ohio	1852	78,255	110,697	1.41
Illinois	1862	98,334	144,954	1.47
Indiana	1872	125,729	172,241	1.37
New York	1882	108,988	222,718	2.04
Pennsylvania	1892	129,764	309,986	2.38

Source: Compiled by the author from data presented in Parsons, Beach, and Dubin 1986 and Parsons, Dubin, and Parsons 1990.

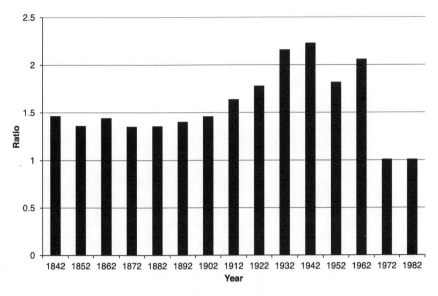

Fig. 8.2. The average ratio of inequality, 1842–1982. (Data for the period between 1842 and 1902 was compiled by the author from data presented in Parsons, Beach, and Dubin 1986; and Parsons, Dubin, and Parsons 1990. Data from 1912 to 1982 was collected from various issues of the Congressional Directory.)

the ratio of inequality during the 19th century. Although absolute population differences increased steadily over this time, the ratio of these differences largely held firm. If anything, the ratio of inequality dipped slightly between 1850 and 1900. In the 20th century, however, one sees a surge in inequality and its eradication following the 1960s reapportionment revolution. The rise of malapportionment in the 20th century is explored more closely in chapter 9.

While the ratio of inequality effectively detects large discrepancies in district size within states, it can be a misleading indicator of the overall distribution of population differences—by definition it tracks outliers. Another commonly used metric of malapportionment is to examine the extent to which districts deviate from the state average. This measure, known as "population deviation," is widely used by the courts to evaluate modern redistricting plans. It is calculated by determining how much each district deviates from the state mean and then averaging across those deviations.[7] Specifically, it is measured as follows:

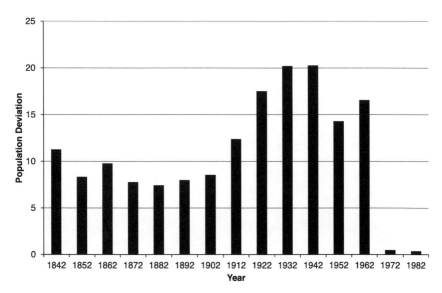

Fig. 8.3. Average population deviation, 1842–1982. (Data for the period between 1842 and 1902 was compiled by the author from data presented in Parsons, Beach, and Dubin 1986; and Parsons, Dubin, and Parsons 1990. Data from 1912 to 1982 was collected from various issues of the Congressional Directory.)

$$Population\ Deviation = |\,[(District\ Population - Population\ in\ State)/$$
$$(Population\ in\ State)] \times 100\,|$$

A state with equal population across districts, for instance, would have a population deviation of zero. To produce a national measure of population deviation, I calculate the average of these state-level averages (weighting by the size of each state).

Figure 8.3 displays the nationwide average population deviation by decade between 1842 and 1982 (excluding at-large districts and single-seat states). For the period between 1842 and 1902, the average deviation was at its highest in the 1860s when it was just under 10 percent. The average deviation dipped to around 7 percent between 1872 and 1900 and then picked back up beginning with the apportionment of 1902.[8] Again, we also see that malapportionment gained steam during the early to mid-20th century. Thus, whether measured by differences between largest and smallest districts, or population deviations, congressional districts in the 19th century were by no means equal. The question now becomes whether or not these population inequalities correlated with partisan outcomes.

Even though districts may have differed in size, this does not necessarily mean that one party (or faction) was gaining at the expense of the other. In the next section, I examine the extent to which partisan mapmakers used malapportionment as a tool for partisan advantage.

Malapportionment as a Partisan Strategy

For malapportionment to have partisan consequences, two conditions have to be met. First, there must be some inequality in population between districts. The previous section has established that population inequalities were present throughout the 19th century. Second, these inequalities must be correlated with the partisan distribution of voters across districts. For instance, malapportionment benefiting Republicans would occur when the districts won by Republicans were, on average, smaller than districts won by Democrats. As a consequence, in this example, Republicans would pay less in votes for the seats they won relative to how much Democrats had to pay for their seats.[9]

In the era before one-person one-vote, partisan biases from malapportionment generally arose under two scenarios. The first was the conscious manipulation of districts by strategic mapmakers. A standard strategic use of malapportionment was for the dominant party to create districts of small size that it won while stacking their opponents in districts of much greater size. This forced the opposition to waste a greater proportion of its votes, hence producing a bias in favor of the party that controlled the smaller constituencies. Two well-known examples of this strategy are Great Britain's rotten boroughs before the Reform Act of 1832 and, in the United States, Republicans' strategic admission of sparsely populated, yet staunchly Republican, western states after the Civil War to stack the Senate (Stewart and Weingast 1992).

A second, complimentary, way in which malapportionment produced partisan biases arose when states failed to readjust their district boundaries to account for population changes and instead allowed population disparities to accumulate over time. If a state did not gain or lose seats in the decennial apportionment, there was no requirement that they redraw district boundaries. Even if a state gained seats they sometimes chose not to redistrict and instead placed their newly gained seats into statewide at-large districts. As a consequence, some states went decades without redrawing district boundaries. Following the reapportionment of 1892, for example, 17 of the 38 states with more than one House seat failed to redistrict.

Gross population inequalities often resulted from this deliberate neglect. And when the changes in district sizes correlated with the partisanship of the district, partisan biases emerged.

Consider the case of Connecticut. With a constant four congressional seats between 1842 and 1912, there was no outside prod for Connecticut to reconfigure its districts. Consequently, Connecticut did not redraw its district boundaries during this 70-year period. The result was a districting arrangement that, over time, produced dramatic population—and ultimately pro-Republican—disparities. Connecticut's 2nd District, containing New Haven, consistently had a larger population than the other districts. By 1900, the rural 3rd District had a population of only 130,000, whereas the 2nd District had over 300,000 people. This discrepancy worked quite well for Republicans. Between 1842 and 1912, not a single Democrat was *ever* elected from the small 3rd District, while Democratic strength in the state was heavily concentrated, and inefficiently wasted, in the much larger 2nd District. Because Whigs and then Republicans dominated the lower house of the state legislature (itself egregiously malapportioned), they effectively blocked any changes to the status quo.[10]

This example suggests that at least some politicians were well aware of the possible partisan gains from strategic malapportionment. To address whether the use of malapportionment for partisan gain was a more widely used strategy, I tested whether or not deviations in district size correlated with party control of the mapmaking process. If parties were using malapportionment for partisan gain, then we should expect that in states where Democrats created the districting plans, Democratic districts will on average be smaller than districts won by Republicans, and vice versa. To test the above expectation, I estimated the following equation:

$$Population\ Deviation_{ijt} = \alpha_j + \beta_1 Democratic\ District_{ijt} + \beta_2 Republican/Whig$$
$$Plan_{jt} + \beta_3 Bipartisan\ Plan_{jt} + \beta_4 Democratic\ Plan_{jt} + \beta_5 Democratic\ District_{ijt}$$
$$\times\ Republican/Whig\ Plan_{jt} + \beta_6 Democratic\ District_{ijt} \times Bipartisan\ Plan_{jt} + \varepsilon_{ijt}$$

The dependent variable (*Population Deviation$_{ijt}$*) is the percentage deviation of congressional district i in state j at time t. Negative values indicate the district is smaller than the state average and positive values indicate the district is larger average districts. The key independent variables are whether the district was won by Democrats, and a series of dummy variables indicating which party was responsible for drawing the district lines. The *Democratic District* variable takes a value of 1 if Democrats won district i in state j at time t and zero if Republicans (or Whigs) won. *Republican/Whig Plan*, *Bipartisan Plan*, and *Democratic Plan* indicate which type of plan existed in state j at time t. The coefficient β_1 measures the size of Democratic-held districts operating under a redistricting plan created by Democrats. The expectation is that this coefficient will be negative, indicating that Democratic districts are, on average, smaller than Republican/Whig districts operating under a Democratic plan. Likewise, a positive coefficient (β_5) for the interaction between Democratic districts and Republican/Whig redistricting plans would indicate that Democrats received larger districts when drawn by a Republican/Whig regime.

I estimated the above equation using Ordinary Least Squares. Because districts within a state are not independent, I clustered the standard errors by state. In addition, state fixed effects (the α_j coefficients) are included. I excluded states with only one seat and any at-large districts.

The results presented in table 8.2 provide clear evidence of partisanship guiding district sizes. The first column displays the results for every year between 1840 and 1900. Here we find that deviations in district population varied directly with party control of the districting process. The coefficient for the *Democratic District* variable is negative and significant (−1.11). Thus, under Democratic plans, districts won by Democrats were smaller, on average, than Republican/Whig districts. Moreover, under Republican/Whig plans, Democratic districts were significantly larger, as indicated by the positive and significant coefficient on the *Republican/Whig Plan* × *Democratic District* interaction. In other words, under Republican/

TABLE 8.2. The Impact of Party Control of Districting on Congressional District Size, 1840–1900 (dependent variable = population deviation [%] of district from statewide average; OLS, clustered by state with robust standard errors)

	All Years	Redistricting Years
Democratic District	−1.11**	−.92*
	(.55)	(.53)
Democratic District × Republican/Whig Plan	3.01**	2.06**
	(1.38)	(.99)
Democratic District x Bipartisan Plan	1.22	1.97
	(1.40)	(1.89)
Republican/Whig Plan	−1.33**	−.98**
	(.52)	(.46)
Bipartisan Plan	−.69	−1.07
	(.72)	(1.02)
Constant	.46	.22
	(.28)	(.33)
Number of Observations	7,741	1,550
R^2	.003	.002

Note: State fixed effects were also estimated but not reported. Robust standard errors clustered by state are in parentheses.

**$p < .05$; *$p < .10$.

Whig plans, Democratic districts increased in size. The overall difference between these two scenarios meant a deviation of 4.14 percent. In 1872, for example, a population deviation of this size would have translated into a difference in district population of about 10,000 people (where the average district size was roughly 138,000).

The second column of table 8.2 presents the results for just those state-years immediately following a redistricting. Here again the pattern of results is the same, although the size of the key coefficients decreased slightly.[11] Again, under Democratic plans, districts won by Democrats were, on average, smaller than when drawn by Republicans (or Whigs). Here the difference in size between Democratic and Republican/Whig districts was 2.98 percent. This slightly smaller value for years immediately following a redistricting suggests two things. First, redistricting parties deliberately used malapportionment to stack the deck in their favor. Second, the initial biases from malapportionment engineered at the time of a redistricting persisted into the future and likely continued to grow with time.

Overall, both sets of results are consistent with the hypothesis that the apportionment of congressional districts correlated with party control of the districting process. When Democrats controlled the maps, they created smaller districts for themselves. When Republicans/Whigs drew the maps, Democratic districts grew. In the next section, I examine whether these discrepancies in size led to electoral biases favoring one party over another at the national level.

Malapportionment, Gerrymandering, and Partisan Bias

Did malapportionment affect the partisan composition of state congressional delegations and possibly influence the national party balance in the House? To answer this question, in this section I analyze the impact of malapportionment on the translation of votes into seats. Malapportionment will produce partisan bias when one party dominates smaller constituencies while the other party's voters are concentrated in larger constituencies. In this case, partisan bias would favor the party winning the smaller constituencies. They would pay less for "their" districts than the opposition.

One way to examine this empirically is to look at the difference between the average vote proportion a party receives when all districts are treated equally and the vote proportion they receive when districts are weighted by population. To see how this works, table 8.3 presents a hypothetical state with three congressional districts. The rows display the raw numbers of votes for each party along with their district level percentages. So, Democrats win the first two districts with 57 percent of the vote and lose the final with 33 percent of the vote. The simple average of these district percentages is 49 percent. But this averaging treats each district equally. In other words, it assumes that each district contains 33.3 percent of the overall state population. But as the table indicates, the number of persons differs considerably across districts. In districts won by Democrats there are 70,000 voters, and in the lone district won by Republicans there are 150,000 voters. Each pro-Democratic district accounts for 24 percent of state population, while the lone Republican district accounts for 52 percent.

To account for these differences in population size, one can weight each of the district vote percentages by its proportion of overall state population. This calculation yields a malapportionment adjusted measure of voting strength. In the example just presented, this weighted vote share yields a Democratic value of 45 percent (i.e., $(57 \times .24) + (57 \times .24) + (33 \times .52)$ = 44.25). The difference between the unweighted and weighted averages tells us the size and direction of vote distortion attributable to malapportionment. A positive value indicates that Democrats were overrepresented, while negative values mean that Democrats were underrepresented. Thus, in this example, malapportionment accounts for a vote distortion of 4 percent in favor of Democrats.

To assess the partisan impact of malapportionment, I calculated the vote distortion state by state. I then regressed this measure on an independent variable indicating the partisanship of those responsible for drawing the new districts. This variable, *Partisanship*, takes a value of +1 for Democratic plans, 0 for Bipartisan plans, and −1 for Republican/Whig plans. If parties were apportioning populations to stack their congressional delegation, then this variable should be positive. In addition, the number of congressional seats in the state is included as a control variable. The regressions were run using weighted least squares, with the number of districts in the state serving as the weight.

The results, presented in table 8.4, indicate that party control of dis-

TABLE 8.3. An Example of Malapportionment Bias

	Democrats	Republicans
District 1	40,000 (57%)	30,000 (43%)
District 2	40,000 (57%)	30,000 (43%)
District 3	50,000 (33%)	100,000 (67%)
Total Votes	130,000	160,000
Unweighted Average	49%	51%
Weighted Average	45%	55%

tricting did indeed correlate with malapportionment bias. The first column presents the results for all years between 1842 and 1900. The coefficient for *Partisanship* is positive and significant. The value of the coefficient, .48, indicates that going from a Republican/Whig plan to a Democratic plan increased the intended pro-Democratic distortion by .96 percentage points. Column 2 presents results solely for elections immediately following a redistricting. The *Partisanship* variable is again positive and significant with a value of .39. Thus, moving from a Republican/Whig to Democratic plan increased pro-Democratic distortion by .78 percentage points. Overall, these results provide further evidence that political parties used malapportionment to stack the electoral deck in their favor.

The next question is how much this affected overall levels of national bias. It would not matter much of these vote distortions had little effect on the number of seats a party wins. One approach might be to look at the number of seats a party could expect to win with various vote share metrics (i.e., weighted versus unweighted) and compare those with reality. In the earlier example, for instance, Democrats won 66 percent of the seats. With 49 percent of the vote, one would say that the state had a 17 percent pro-Democratic bias based on the distribution of partisan voting strength across districts. With 45 percent of the vote (i.e., the weighted average vote), bias was, therefore, 21 percent. The difference between these two values—here 4 percent—would tell us how much bias was the result of malapportionment. This approach would be straightforward. But as seen in previous chapters, the slope of the vote-seat relationship in most states was far from linear. Parties that received more than 50 percent of the vote often have their seat shares rise nonlinearly. This is a regular feature of single-member plurality systems, and was certainly true in the 19th century. Thus,

TABLE 8.4. Vote Distortion from Malapportionment

	All Years	Redistricting Years
Partisanship	.48*	.39*
	(.10)	(.22)
Total Districts	−.01	−.04
	(.01)	(.15)
Constant	.68*	−.12
	(.17)	(40)
N	770	149
R^2	.02	.03

Note: Standard errors in parentheses.
*$p < .10$.

we also need to control for the nonlinear slopes of these vote-seat translations. In other words, we need to find an estimate of partisan bias from
malapportionment that also takes into account the nonlinear swing ratios
of 19th-century elections.

Recall that in earlier chapters, we estimated the relationship between
votes and seats using the following equation:

$$ln(s_{it}/(1 - s_{it})) = \lambda + \rho(ln(v_{it}/(1 - v_{it})))$$

We can get a handle on the impact of malapportionment by estimating the
this equation twice. First, for each state-year, we can insert the unweighted
average of the vote received by Democrats for v_{it}. Estimating a vote-seat
equation with the unweighted Democratic proportion of the vote provides
a measure of partisan bias after purging any bias due to malapportionment.
In the second equation, we substitute in the population-weighted average of the Democratic vote for v_{it}. Estimating a vote-seat equation with a
population-weighted Democratic vote proportion provides a measure of
partisan bias that includes malapportionment. Examining the different values of partisan bias across these two equations will provide an idea of how
much malapportionment contributed to any overall bias in the electoral
system.

The results are presented in table 8.5. Using the unweighted average
produces an overall pro-Republican/Whig bias of 3.24 percent. Recall that
this coefficient captures the size of partisan bias after purging malapportionment considerations. Thus, at an even 50–50 split of the vote, Republicans (or Whigs) could expect to win 53.24 percent of the seats. The
weighted average results, presented in column 2, show a pro-Republican/

TABLE 8.5. Vote-Seat Relationship Using the Two Different Vote Metrics,
1842–1900

	Unweighted Vote Average	Weighted Vote Average
Partisan Bias	−3.24*	−4.12*
	(.51)	(.89)
Swing Ratio	3.89*	3.28*
	(.14)	(.13)
γ	.04*	.05*
	(.001)	(.01)
N	770	770
Log-Likelihood	−3,574.88	−3,616.19

Note: Standard errors in parentheses.
*$p < .10$.

Whig bias of 4.12 percent. With 50 percent of the vote, Republicans could expect 54.12 percent of seats. Thus, taking malapportionment into account slightly increased the estimate of partisan bias. Malapportionment provided Republicans/Whigs, in the aggregate, with a small extra bump. The differences between these two values, however, are not overly pronounced. Although with two separate equations we cannot test the statistical significance of the difference between the estimates, the substantive differences remain slight. Thus, it would appear that most of the bias in this era arose from the allocation of partisan-voting strength across districts. This is consistent with findings for more recent eras in American politics which, for example, demonstrate that gerrymandering, and not malapportionment, was the main source of bias in the years leading up to the reapportionment revolution (Erikson 1972; Sickels 1966).

Conclusion

The Supreme Court decisions of the 1960s forbade the malapportionment of legislative districts. Not only did these decisions prompt a radical redrawing of state and congressional districts throughout the country, they have shaped the line-drawing process ever since. In congressional districting, for instance, the current standard implemented by the courts is nearly zero-population deviation. Because the courts have, for the most part, eliminated variation in district sizes, it can be difficult to determine how much the one-person, one-vote rule hampers the ability of modern mapmakers to gerrymander.

One way to discern the impact of one-person, one-vote is to examine a period in which states were free to ignore population equality. In this chapter, I have examined the causes and consequences of malapportionment during the 19th century. Did mapmakers use malapportionment for party advantage? If so, how much did malapportionment contribute to the partisan bias of the electoral system? In this chapter, I have explored the extent and impact of malapportioned districts on the 19th-century House of Representatives. Equal population between congressional districts was never enforced, nor achieved. Whether one compares the largest and smallest districts in a state, or examines population deviations, 19th- and early 20th-century House districts varied considerably in size. Second, these deviations directly correlated in a predictable, partisan fashion. Parties in control of the districting process created smaller constituencies for themselves, and larger districts for the opposition. Third, these variations in district size led to partisan biases that, along with gerrymandering, aggregated across states, leading to biases in the House of Representatives.

These finding serve as an important lesson for contemporary political and legal attempts to remedy "unfair" districting schemes. When it comes to drawing district lines, the judiciary has directed its ire almost entirely at malapportionment. The current preoccupation of the courts with strict population equality ignores other—potentially just as harmful—forms of electoral manipulation. Looking back to the 19th century informs us that malapportionment was not the most important source of partisan bias— gerrymandering was. Malapportionment made partisan bias worse, but bias would have existed without it.

PART III

Redistricting in the Candidate-Centered Era, 1900–Present

NINE

From Turbulence to Stasis, 1900–1964

As previous chapters have shown, the U.S. Congress of the 19th century was highly turbulent. Careers were short. Partisan majorities rarely lasted long. Small shifts in the national vote produced immense changes in party ratios. By the early 20th century, however, things had changed radically and permanently. Congressional careers extended into decades. Partisan majorities tended to remain steady. Indeed, the difference between the Congress of the 1880s and the Congress of the 1920s was arguably further than the gap between the 1920s and the present. Out of this transformation emerged the structure of modern American politics.

Central to this transformation was a drastic decline in both partisan swings and legislative turnover. Between 1900 and 1960, for example, majority control of the House turned over seven times. Of these, four episodes were concentrated between 1946 and 1952 when Republicans briefly gained control of the House only to lose it back two years later (the 80th and 83rd Congresses). Aside from these brief Republican interregnums, Democratic control of the House after the 1930 election was incredibly stable. Notably, the 40-year period from 1954 to 1994 constituted an uninterrupted stretch of Democratic dominance in the House. By contrast, between 1840 and 1900, majority control of the House flipped 11 times. And the longest any party held continuous control of the House was the 16-year period of Republican rule between the elections of 1858 and 1874. The decline of partisan turnover was also matched by a decline in individual-level turnover. By the end of the 20th century, the percentage of members seeking and winning reelection to the House had reached upwards of 90 percent.

Out of these changes in electoral politics emerged the foundations of modern congressional politics. To take one example, stable partisan regimes and stable legislative careers fostered the development of seniority norms in assigning the all-important committee chairmanships. Members pursuing constituent interests and crafting long-term relationships with their colleagues characterized a fundamentally different type of Congress than the frenzied, party-driven Congress of the 19th century. The professionalization of the House radiated throughout the rest of the political system. Presidents, judges, and federal bureaucrats each had to condition and adjust their behavior to the changing environment of this modernized House. The professionalized Congress became the "keystone" of the new Washington system (Fiorina 1989).

Indeed, one can view the enormous scholarly literature on modern congressional politics as a search to explain the causes and consequences of this candidate-centered system. The vast literatures on incumbency advantage, campaign finance, the policy pork barrel, and electoral accountability can all be placed under this scholarly umbrella. Thus, while the basic pillars of the modern Congress were forged in the early to mid-20th century, a number of essential questions remained unanswered. Why did partisan and individual turnover diminish in the early 20th century? And why did turnover remain so low thereafter?

Scholars have searched widely to explain the differences between 19th- and 20th-century politics. The most prominent narrative has followed in the footsteps of Burnham's highly influential research. Burnham, and his many followers, argued the presidential election of 1896 fundamentally altered voter behavior and partisan alignments. Citizens became less attached to the parties. The widespread victories of Republicans in the North and Democrats in the South turned these regions into the political preserves of one party. The result was to create a favorable climate for incumbents to run and win reelection at rapidly increasing rates. Safe districts facilitate easy election. But as seen in previous chapters, there is ample reason to be skeptical of claims about the 1894 or 1896 election as representing a fundamental shift in voter sentiments.

A second narrative emphasizes a gradual modernization of Congress. This narrative follows in the influential footsteps of Nelson Polsby (1969). The growth of federal-government power and more potent policy instruments enhanced the attractiveness of Washington to politicians. Where once political power resided in the state capitals, integration of the national economy and the vastly greater role of the federal government in regulating the economy turned Washington from a relative backwater into the seat of power. The gravitational pull of Washington impelled members of Congress to desire election. The increasing scope of the federal government also gave members of Congress access to policy instruments—such as the pork barrel and casework—that, strategically deployed, secured their continual reelection (e.g., Katz and Sala 1996).

We see in this chapter that gerrymandering played a foundational role in shaping the 20th-century professionalization of Congress. First, redistricting happened less often. Second, when redistricting happened it was less radical in its consequences. Just as the potent gerrymandering of the 19th century fomented a tumultuous House of Representatives, the decline of partisan gerrymandering in the early to mid-20th century set down the building blocks for the stability and modernization that took over the 20th-century House. Applying the tools of the prior chapters we can explore how changes in redistricting strategies shaped political behavior and ideological coalitions after 1900. These changes profoundly altered the structural basis of congressional elections and, in turn, the politics and policy of the House.

The transformation of gerrymandering also had enormous consequences for federal policy making. To take one example, the bias stemming from malapportionment gave extra voting weight to rural interests at the expense of metropolitan interests. In terms of legislative policy making, this electoral bias fed a policy making bias toward rural and agricultural interests and away from policies favored by metropolitan areas (Ansolabehere and Snyder 2008; McCubbins and Schwarz 1988). For instance, federal dollars were steered toward farm supports and agricultural subsidies at the expense of school-lunch programs and urban transportation (McCubbins and Schwarz 1988). As more citizens moved into metropolitan areas, the failure of state legislatures to readjust congressional district boundaries meant that federal spending lagged behind where citizens actually lived. This is but one example of how the electoral system shaped political and economic life in the 20th century.

Internally, the absence of partisan turnover combined with the decline of legislative turnover—both a consequence of the slowdown in redistricting—transformed the distribution of power within the House. For example, one can see the powerful effect that non-redistricting had by looking at the chairmen of the three prestige committees during the 1950s and 1960s: Ways and Means, Appropriations, and Rules. Consider, for example, the House Committee on Ways and Means. During the 1950s,

1960s, and 1970s the chairmanship of this powerful committee was held by the Democrat Wilbur Mills. Mills was from Arkansas, which had redistricted in 1902 and then only again in 1952. Having entered the House in 1937, the stable district boundaries fostered Mills' legislative ascent.

The chair of the House Committee on Appropriations during the mid-20th century was Clarence Cannon (D-MO). Cannon served either as the chair or ranking minority member of the Appropriations Committee from 1941 to 1964. A Democrat from Missouri, the state redistricted only four times between 1900 and 1960; and every one of those remaps was a solid pro-Democratic plan. Cannon, therefore, was never in jeopardy of losing his district to a hostile remap. Or consider the powerful Democratic chair of the House Committee on Rules—Howard W. Smith from Virginia. Smith served as the Rules chair from 1955 to 1967, from which he famously worked to bottle up civil rights legislation. Smith was originally elected in 1930 and accrued the necessary seniority to assume the chairmanship of this all-important committee. Critical to accumulating such seniority were the incredibly stable district boundaries of Virginia—the state redrew its district boundaries only three times between 1900 and 1960.

Thus, all of these powerbrokers had one thing in common—they came from states where they were rarely, if ever, in jeopardy of losing their district to a hostile remap. To understand the differences between the House of the 19th and 20th centuries, therefore, one must understand the differences between redistricting past and present.

The Changing Nature of Gerrymandering

Our comparison begins with the frequency of redistricting. As seen in previous chapters, the timing of redistricting shaped electoral and policy outcomes throughout the 19th century. States could redistrict whenever they wanted, and, in many cases, states redistricted often. In chapter 3, we found that gerrymandering throughout the 19th century was frequent in many states (e.g., Ohio, Indiana). Between 1840 and 1900, there were only two years in which at least one state did not redistrict. The strategic timing of redistricting altered party ratios in the House, changed ideological alignments, and shaped individual political-career decisions. Strategically timed mid-decade remaps, for example, altered majority control of the House during the Gilded Age, and, hence, the historical policy trajectory of the United States. The frequency and variability of redistricting also rendered

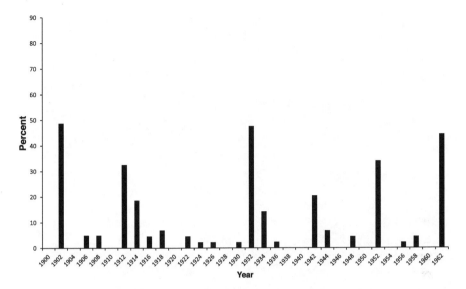

Fig. 9.1. The declining frequency of redistricting, 1900–1962. (Data compiled by the author from information contained in Martis 1982.)

it very difficult for individual representatives to fashion a long career in the House. Redistricting could come at any time.

But if the issue in the 19th century was too much redistricting, in the 20th century it became too little redistricting. As seen in chapter 4 (see fig. 4.1), the 20th century witnessed a precipitous decline in the frequency of redistricting. To get a sense of the 20th-century drop-off in redistricting, figure 9.1 reproduces part of the data previously presented in figure 4.1, but here just focusing on the years between 1902 and 1962. The figure shows that in most reapportionment years, less than half of the states redrew congressional district boundaries. Moreover, the number of mid-decade redistricting events significantly declined.

But even this figure masks, to some degree, the calcification of district lines. There are numerous examples of states essentially opting out of the redistricting process. Wisconsin redistricted in 1932, and not again until 1962. Illinois redrew in 1902, and then only again in 1948. Indiana went from 1942 to 1964 with the same district map. Connecticut redrew its boundaries in 1912, and not again until 1962.[1] Perhaps no state was more striking in this regard than Ohio. As seen in earlier chapters, Ohio redrew district boundaries on an almost biannual basis in the 1870s and 1880s. These gerrymanders tilted the balance of political power in Ohio, and, as a consequence, tilted the balance of political power in Washington, DC. During the 20th century, by contrast, this former hotbed of gerrymandering nearly dropped out of the redistricting game altogether. Notably, the state went 40 years between redistricting events (1914–52).

The slowdown of redistricting had profound consequences for the development of Congress, and continues to cast a long shadow on contemporary politics. To take one example, congressional careerism became fully entrenched in the years between 1900 and 1960. By 1960, over 90 percent of incumbents were running for reelection and winning. Gerrymandering—or, more accurately, the decline of gerrymandering—provides one of the keys to explaining this puzzling development. Because district lines remained static, incumbents found it much easier to plan and build a career in the House. They had some probability of actually controlling their district for long stretches. The uncertainty of when a redistricting might occur had largely been removed. The emergence of careerism has long been considered the primary factor behind the modernization of the House. Thus, to understand the evolution of modern American politics, one needs to answer a basic, but rarely asked, question: why did the frequency of redistricting decline so sharply?

A number of reasons suggest themselves. But perhaps the most important factor was the dramatic decline of party competition in the state legislatures. Following the landslide elections of the mid-1890s, many state legislatures became the political preserves of a single party (Schattschneider 1960). Where one party dominated a state legislature the incentives to gerrymander dissipated. There is little reason to tinker with a district map that is already producing numerous party victories. This logic was most obvious in the South, where Republicans ceased to exist as a meaningful party organization. In Louisiana, for example, Democrats occupied *every single seat* in the state legislature from 1900 to 1964. It should therefore come as no surprise that Louisiana went over 50 years with the same congressional-district boundaries (1912–66).

The demise of vigorous party competition, however, was not confined to the South. Party ratios in many Northern state legislatures, for significant chunks of the early 20th century, were just as out of balance. In Michigan, Republicans controlled every single seat in the state senate between 1918 and 1928. In Pennsylvania, Republicans controlled, on average, 83 percent of the seats in the Pennsylvania state assembly between 1910 and 1932.

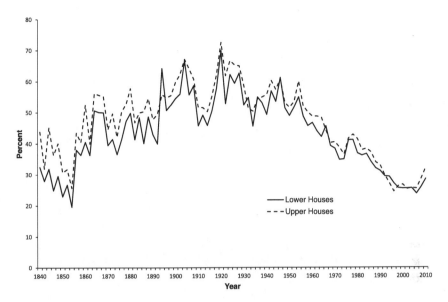

Fig. 9.2. Competition in U.S. state legislatures, 1840–2010. The figure displays the average absolute difference between Democrats and Republicans (or Whigs) in state legislatures between 1840 and 2010. (Data compiled by the author from Burnham 1985 for 1840–1940 and the *Book of the States* for 1942–2010.)

Without the prod of a federal reapportionment, the incentives to redistrict where one party dominated state government were essentially nonexistent. The sharp decline of competition within state legislatures can be seen in figure 9.2 which displays the average absolute difference in state legislative seat shares between Democrats and Republicans (or Whigs). The top and bottom panels present the data for lower and upper chambers, respectively. As one can see, there is a noticeable uptick in the seat differences over the course of late 19th and early 20th centuries.

As seen in chapter 3, absent a change in seat share from the decadal federal reapportionment, the key factor triggering a redistricting was a switch in party control of state government. When a new party came into control of state government, and the prior congressional-district map was drawn by the opposition party, the probability of redrawn congressional districts grew. Thus, the frequency with which partisan turnover of state government happened in the 19th century goes a long way toward explaining the frequency and partisanship of congressional redistricting in that era.

In the 20th century, these transitions of state party control substantially diminished.

The one outside prod, therefore, to redistricting, was a change in a states House delegation size resulting from a federal reapportionment. But even here the changing demographics of the country worked toward minimizing the frequency of redistricting. The growing movement of people into urban areas, both through external and internal migration, fostered a burgeoning split between rural and urban districts. This cleavage became the focal point around which many redistricting battles turned. The influx of immigration, coupled with the Industrial Revolution, spurred tremendous growth in America's cities. In 1840, 10.8 percent of the population lived in urban areas. By 1910, this number had jumped to 46.3 percent. Entrenched rural interests within state legislatures were naturally reluctant to relinquish power. As a result, many states avoided redistricting.

The split between rural and urban interests came to a head in Congress following the 1920 census. This census confirmed the growth of cities relative to rural areas of the country. It was the first census in which urban populations outstripped rural populations. This population shift also portended a profound shift of representation from states with large rural populations to states with urban centers. When it came time to reapportion, many members of Congress objected. Members from states that were bound to lose seats—mostly from rural-dominated states—headed this opposition (Eagles 1990). Holding sufficient votes in both the House and Senate, this coalition blocked the Apportionment Act's passage. Thus, for the only time in American history, the country skipped a new apportionment.

While some may see the failure to reapportion in 1920 as a historical curiosity, it had enormous consequences for the development of Congress. Without the spur of a federal reapportionment, almost every state went 20 years with the same district boundaries. Only two states—Pennsylvania and Colorado—redrew in 1922. Congress eventually reached an agreement for a new apportionment in 1929, although the actual reapportionment and redistricting would then take place following the 1930 census. In effect, the structural basis of the House stayed the same for two decades.

Even in those cases where a state gained new seats from federal reapportionment and might therefore be compelled into redistricting, the reluctance to redraw was abetted by the federal provision that allowed states to elect any newly gained seats in statewide at-large districts rather than reconfigure the entire state map. For example, from 1912 to 1946, rather than redraw their district boundaries, Illinois elected two members in at-large elections.

The upshot of these decisions, or nondecisions, can clearly be seen in

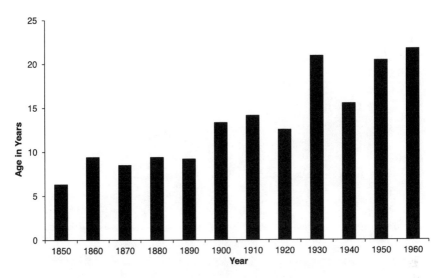

Fig. 9.3. The increasing age of redistricting plans. The figure displays the average age, in years, of redistricting plans at the beginning of each decade. For example, in 1960 the average age of congressional district maps was 22 years.

figure 9.3. This figure plots the average age of redistricting plans at the beginning of each decade. In 1850, the average age of redistricting maps was 6 years. By 1930, the average age of redistricting maps was 21 years. This pattern continued throughout the next decades. Indeed, in 1960, on the eve of the reapportionment revolution, the average age of state-district maps remained inched up to 22 years. In this slowdown lie the roots of modern congressional politics. The decline of vigorous redistricting had profound consequences on the partisan impact of gerrymandering, the evolution of candidate-centered politics, and the evolution of congressional policy making. The rest of this chapter highlights three major consequences of the redistricting slow down: the decline of partisan turnover, the emergence of careerism, and the growth of malapportionment. These structural features of the electoral system would only be refashioned with the entry of the federal judiciary into the political thicket.

The Partisan Impact of Redistricting

A central consequence of the decline of state legislative turnover, hence, was a change not just in the frequency of redistricting but also in the magnitude of its impact. Gerrymandering became much less virulent than it had in the 19th century. In particular, instances where one party replaced the map of another party happened much less often. One way to see the diminished virulence of redistricting is to look at the partisan transitions between redistricting plans. How often was a pro-Democratic plan replaced by a pro-Republican plan, and vice versa?

These transitions are where maps have the most transformative partisan impact. For example, in 1886, Republicans in Ohio turned a 10–11 congressional delegation deficit into a 16–5 majority by replacing a Democratic-drawn map with one of their own. As the numbers in table 9.1 indicate, these types of transformative gerrymanders sharply declined in the 20th century. Between 1840 and 1900 there were 45 wholesale partisan transitions—cases where one party had a map replaced by a map drawn by the opposite party. This type of transition accounted for 34 percent of the redistricting plans in the 19th century. By contrast, between 1900 and 1962 there were only 16 such transitions, accounting for 13 percent of the redistricting plans between 1900 and 1962.

We can also see the decline of transformative gerrymanders in the number of redistricting maps that simply maintained the status quo. In other words, how many redistricting plans were cases where the party that drew the prior map also created the new map? The numbers to answer this question are also presented in table 9.1. Before 1900, 52 percent of the plans either maintained or enhanced the status quo. After 1900, 65 percent of the plans maintained the partisan status quo. Further evidence of changes in the types of gerrymanders can be seen in the slight uptick of bipartisan maps (i.e., maps drawn under divided party control of state government). In the 19th century, bipartisan plans made up 9 percent of all redistricting, while in the 20th they made up 14 percent.

Thus, redistricting was less frequent and less transformative, in the short term, than it had been in the 19th century. The preservation of existing gains became more important than knocking off opponents. This is

TABLE 9.1. Types of Redistricting Transitions

Years	D to R	R to D	Bip. to R	Bip. to D	R to Bip.	D to Bip.	D to D	R to R	Bip. to Bip.	Total
1840–1898	23	22	4	4	5	2	36	34	3	134
1900–1962	8	8	10	1	12	2	48	32	3	124

Note: This table lists the prior plan and the newly drawn redistricting plan. For example, "D to R" stands for a plan previously drawn by a Unified Democratic state government that was replaced by a plan drawn by a Unified Republican (or Whig) state government. Cell numbers are the number of plans that fall into each category.

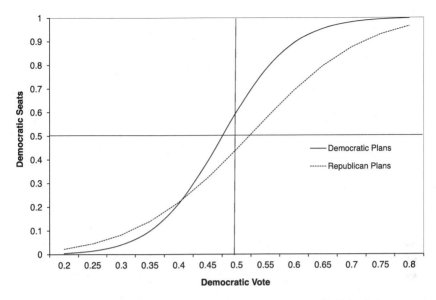

Fig. 9.4. Vote to seat translation by type of redistricting plan, 1900–1962

not to say that gerrymandering stopped having partisan consequences; far from it. The parties that drew district maps continued to profit from carefully crafted district lines. Instead, the stable district lines of the 20th century became silent gerrymanders. District lines entrenched existing political power within states and across the nation.

We can see this in figure 9.4, which plots estimates of the vote-seat relationship for different types of congressional maps during the early and mid-20th century. In particular, the figure shows estimates of partisan bias and electoral responsiveness for partisan Democratic plans, partisan Republican plans, and bipartisan plans. As was done in earlier chapters, the unit of analysis is the state. Using data from Martis on the timing of redistricting and data from Burnham on the partisanship of state legislatures, I identified the partisanship of the state government at the time in which each district map was drawn from 1900 to 1962. I stopped in 1962 because this year represented the last round of redistricting before the federal judiciary entered the process and changed the rules of the game.

The results in figure 9.4 show that district lines clearly biased electoral outcomes in favor of the party that drew the maps. For Democratic-drawn maps, one finds a partisan bias of 9.6 percent. In other words, at 50 percent of the vote, Democrats could expect to win 59.6 percent of seats when they had drawn the maps. Republican plans, on the other hand, produced a pro-Republican bias of 5.8 percent. At 50 percent of the vote, Republicans won, on average, 55.8 percent of the statewide seats. Overall, then, we see that partisan maps continued to generate significant amounts of electoral bias.

Of course one might worry that the strong bias found in Democratic plans was a result of the near-zero levels of competition in Southern states. We can examine this possibility by examining the vote-seat estimates with the southern states excluded. The results of this model were largely the same. Although the electoral responsiveness increased for Democratic plans, as one would expect given the low levels of competition in the South, there was still a positive and significant amount of bias in favor of Democrats in the non-southern states. The bias for Democratic plans in non-southern states was 10.1 percent, which is comparable to the results when all the states are included in the sample.

All told then, even though parties refrained from constantly tinkering with district boundaries, the maps of the 20th century still had substantial partisan consequences at the state level. Because state legislatures chose not to redraw boundaries nearly as often, this bias persisted for long stretches of time. The next question is to what extent these state level biases aggregated into national political power. One way to assess this is to examine the partisan balance of districts maps across the century.

Figure 9.5 plots the percentage of House districts under the different types of districting plan. For example, in 1912, 47 percent of House districts had been drawn by Democrats and 43 percent by Republicans, with the remaining districts either drawn by a divided government or a single-district state. This advantage at the state level then translated into pro-Democratic effects nationally. Even during the 1920s, when Democrats found themselves in the minority, their seat shares still tended to be larger than their vote shares warranted. The real payoff, however, from the Democratic district-level advantage came in the 1930s. The results of figure 9.5 along with the results on partisan bias, suggest that the New Deal majorities in the 1930s owed much favorable district lines. Democrats very likely would have been in the majority regardless, given their sizable vote shares, but their seat shares were even larger than their vote share warranted.

Beginning in the 1940s and continuing up to the 1960s, one sees a shift toward Republicans (Figure 9.5). Republican gains in the North and Midwest put them in position to reverse the Democratic advantage in district maps. The result was a closer correspondence between actuality and an unbiased system nationally. Strong pro-Democratic bias in the South and border states was matched with pro-Republican bias in the North and Midwest. This result meshes with previous studies such as Cox and Katz

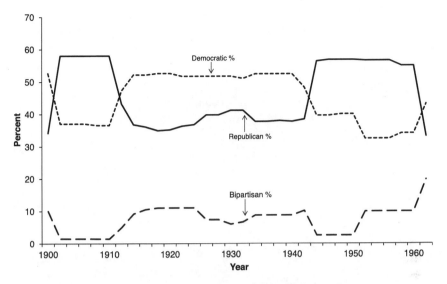

Fig. 9.5. The percentage of house districts under different partisan maps, 1900–1962. The figure presents the percentage of House districts in states with Democratic drawn maps, Republican drawn maps, and maps drawn during periods of divided party control (Bipartisan). States with only one district constitute the remainder but are not plotted in this figure.

(2001) and Erikson (1972) which also uncovered a strong pro-Republican bias outside of the South from 1942 through 1962. Much of this bias can be attributed to the Republican advantage in district maps. Throughout the North, Republicans held a substantial edge in the number of districts that were drawn by Republican redistricting regimes after 1940.

Of course, one natural question is: if there was a pro-Republican bias, why did Democrats control the House for most of the 20th century? The answer is that where there were Democratic plans, they fully maximized the number of seats they won. Obviously, this was the case in the South. But even in the border states, and in various western states, Democrats dominated congressional election outcomes. Thus, as long as Democrats put up a decent showing in the Midwest and Northeast, they would control the House (Ware 2006).

The Age of Malapportionment

Coupled with the rise of silent gerrymanders in the early and mid-20th century was a substantial rise in malapportionment. Rather than tinker with districts in the search for an electoral advantage, partisan state legislators could let demographics do the work for them. In other words, they could put districts on autopilot. In the 1960s, the U.S. Supreme Court put an end to malapportionment as a political strategy when it ruled unequal districts unconstitutional. In *Baker v. Carr* (1962), which outlawed malapportionment in state legislatures, the court ruled that malapportionment violated the voting rights of citizens by giving some citizens more weight in the electoral process than others. The legal doctrine of *Baker* was extended two years later to cover House districts in *Wesberry v. Sanders* (1964). By the end of the 1960s, with the oversight of the courts, newly drawn legislative maps essentially eradicated malapportionment.

In many ways, one can frame the electoral basis of congressional politics from 1900 to 1964 as the Age of Malapportionment. Although it is fairly well known that malapportionment existed, and the aftermath of the court-led reapportionment revolution is well documented, the magnitude and impact of malapportionment in shaping the history early to mid-20th century American politics are still underestimated. We can begin to get some idea of the magnitude of malapportionment this by examining the size and deviations of redistricting plans. Table 9.2 presents information on district size at the beginning of each decade from 1902 to 1982. The information on district size in the 20th century comes from the *Congressional Directory*, from the congresses following the decennial reapportionment. To start, we can first look at the average difference between the largest and smallest congressional districts within states. This metric provides initial insight into the raw magnitude of differences in district populations.

The data in the first column of the table clearly show that the discrepancies between House districts rapidly grew throughout the mid-20th century. In 1912, the average distance between the largest and smallest

TABLE 9.2. The Rise and Decline of Malapportionment in the Twentieth Century

Year	Average Difference between Largest and Smallest Districts	Ratio of Inequality	Population Deviation
1912	101,385	1.64	12.04
1922	132,875	1.78	17.53
1932	196,444	2.16	20.21
1942	200,532	2.23	20.27
1952	192,801	1.82	14.29
1962	270,748	2.06	16.67
1972	8,420	1.01	.51
1982	5,420	1.01	.37

districts was 101,385 people. By the eve of the reapportionment revolution, this average difference had grown to 270,748. In Tennessee, the district map of which was eventually overturned in *Wesberry v. Sanders*, the largest House district contained 627,019 people, while the smallest contained only 223,387—a difference of 403,632 people.

Of course, some of the growth in these differences can be chalked up to an overall growth in the nation's population. To adjust for overall population growth in making comparisons across time, table 9.2, column 2, presents the average ratio between the largest and smallest districts—or the "ratio of inequality." The numbers again show that malapportionment remained consistent throughout the 20th century. By 1962 the average ratio was 2.06 (s.d. = .83). In other words, on the eve of the reapportionment revolution, within states, the largest district was, on average, twice as large as the smallest district. In some states, the discrepancies were enormous. In Michigan, for example, the ratio of inequality had reached 4.5. The 16th District contained 802,994 people; the 12th contained only 177,341.

The ratio of inequality only incorporates the largest and smallest districts, and, therefore, provides one perspective on district inequalities. But because the ratio of inequality tracks outliers it provides only a partial picture of malapportionment. Recall from chapter 8 that another commonly used metric of malapportionment is to consider the average population deviation of districts from the average district population within a state. In 1912, the average district deviated from the mean population in a state by 12 percent. In 1922, following the failed reapportionment, the average deviation spiked to 17.5 percent. It stayed roughly at this level up until the 1960s. In 1962, districts deviated on average by 16.7 percent. Thus, by every metric, the malapportionment of congressional districts in the 20th century grew enormously compared to the 19th century.

The next question is who won and lost, in partisan terms, from malapportionment. Previous research has shown that on the eve of the reapportionment revolution, Democrats were the primary beneficiaries of unequal districts. Outside the South, Democratic districts were, on average, smaller than Republican-held districts (Cox and Katz 2002, 14–15). The advantage Democrats gained from malapportionment was also recognized by partisans at the time of the 1960s Supreme Court decisions. In an internal memo commissioned by the Republican Party, the memo's authors found that Republican candidates performed best in oversized districts, while Democratic strongholds tended to be smaller districts (Cox and Katz 2002, 13).

But Cox's and Katz's analysis, and the Republicans' internal memo, only takes into account the electoral situation following the 1962 election.

One might reasonably wonder whether Democrats' advantage held true for other parts of the mid-20th century. Especially given the Republican advantage in district maps following the 1942 election, there might be reason to suspect that Republicans benefited from malapportionment at times during the postwar years. Table 9.3 presents the results of a model in which the dependent variable is the population deviation of congressional districts from their respective statewide averages. The independent variable denotes whether Democrats won the district or not.

The results reveal that before 1962, Democratic-controlled districts actually tended to be *larger* than Republican districts. This result becomes even stronger in column 2, which excludes southern states. Column 3 shows that following the 1962 reapportionment, Democrats did turn the tables. The coefficient now flips signs, indicating that in the 1962 maps Democratic districts, on average, now became smaller. Thus, even though Republicans may have been right to call foul in 1962, they had gained from malapportionment over the previous 20 years. This also meshes with previous findings in the scholarly literature which has shown a pro-Republican bias in congressional elections outside of the South. Here we can see that malapportionment contributed to this bias (see Erikson 1972).

The profound impact of unequal districts extended beyond competition between the parties. Malapportionment also shaped the policy priorities and ideological alignment of the House throughout the mid-20th century. Malapportionment fostered a House that was more conservative and biased toward rural interests than would have been the case had districts been equalized. Malapportionment biased policy toward rural interests, and in particular, farmers. One way that analysts have shown the powerful

TABLE 9.3. Population Deviation and Partisanship of Districts

	All States, 1942–60	Non-Southern States, 1942–60	All States, 1962	Non-Southern States, 1962
Democratic District	2.94*	4.46*	−8.36*	−5.71*
	(1.04)	(1.11)	(2.89)	(2.79)
Constant	−1.02	−1.72	4.08	2.79
	(1.40)	(1.47)	(4.07)	(3.72)
R^2	.003	.006	.02	.01
Number of Observations	4,257	3,208	416	319

Note: The dependent variable is the population deviation of the congressional district from the statewide average. State fixed effects included but not reported. Standard errors in parentheses.
    $*p < .05$.

policy effect of malapportionment is to compare the type and magnitude of government spending that occurred before and after the court-ordered reapportionment revolution of the 1960s. The reapportionment revolution created, for the first time, a metropolitan majority in the House. By implication, this research has established that metropolitan areas were underrepresented prior to the 1960s. Ansolabehere and Snyder (2008), for example, demonstrated that government spending went to rural districts at the expense of urban districts. Following the reapportionment revolution of the 1960s, funding was equalized.

Not only was the overall level of funding unequal between districts, malapportionment also compelled Congress to emphasize certain types of policy instruments at the expense of others. For example, McCubbins and Schwartz found that federal spending on agricultural policies was substantially higher prior to the reapportionment revolution. A policy-making system that had been biased toward agricultural spending was now redirected toward transportation and regulatory policies. After 1965, wheat subsidies were reduced by almost half. Cotton and corn subsidies were reduced by more than one-third (McCubbins and Schwartz 1988, 409). Funding for food stamps and school-lunch programs increased, while funding for sugar farmers dropped precipitously (McCubbins and Schwartz 1988, 396).

Malapportionment also affected ideological alignments within the House. This can be seen by regressing the DW-Nominate score of individual representatives (which is a measure of ideological positioning based on roll-call voting) on the natural log of their district population. DW-Nominate scores range from −1 to 1, with the left side of the scale (−1) indicating a liberal roll-call voting record and the right side of the scale (+1) indicating a conservative roll-call voting record. Such a model shows that, for both Republicans and Democrats, larger districts correlated with more liberal representation. The negative coefficient one finds on the population variable indicates that smaller districts tended to have more conservative representatives, while larger districts tended to have more liberal members.

Therefore, a greater number of small districts created an overrepresentation of conservatives within the Congress—for both parties. The reapportionment revolution shifted the alignment leftward. As district populations were equalized in the 1960s, the number of liberal-leaning districts increased and shifted the ideological and policy balance of the House leftward. The consequences reverberated within the House for the next decade. Notably, the eradication of malapportionment increased the legislative numbers, and, therefore, political power, of liberal members of the Democratic caucus (see also Ansolabehere and Snyder 2008). These members eventually helped spearhead the transformational congressional reforms of the early 1970s (Rohde 1991).

Redistricting and Congressional Careerism

Differences in the timing and nature of districting also fundamentally contributed to the rise of congressional careerism. Among the most profound consequences of changing gerrymandering strategies was the development of a professionalized House. The data figures shown in chapter 7 showed just how thoroughly ambition and turnover differed between the 19th and 20th centuries. By 1920, nearly 85 percent of House incumbents were seeking reelection. Moreover, the decision to run for reelection had turned from a risky gamble to an almost sure bet. Of the incumbents who ran for reelection, the percentage who won was almost 90 percent. The increase in incumbents running for and winning reelection radically reduced the number of first-termers serving in the House. Between 1900 and 1962, the average percent of first-termers was 21 percent. Taking out the big wave of turnover caused by the Depression-era elections of 1930 and 1932 reduces this number even further. By contrast, between 1840 and 1900, the average percentage of first-termers had been 36 percent. The comparatively modest turnover pattern has remained consistent up to the present, and continues to define the House and national politics.

These trends furthered the transformation of the House from a body of amateurs to the professionalized legislature we have become accustomed to. One indicator of this transformation is presented in figure 9.6, which plots the average number of terms members had served by year. Throughout the 19th century, the average held relatively at two terms. Beginning around the turn of the 20th century, we see a sharp increase in the number of terms served. By 1960, the number had climbed to over five terms.

The modernization of the House—and, consequently, the modernization of national politics—has much of its roots in this transformation. The rise of "single-minded seekers of reelection" refashioned the institutional structure of the House, and the structure of the federal government, to facilitate their reelection chances (Fiorina 1989; Mayhew 1974a). Because of the central importance careerism holds in the modernization of American politics, finding its source has served as a major intellectual goal for students of the U.S. Congress. At least since Nelson Polsby's influential article, which traced the modernization of the House of Representatives

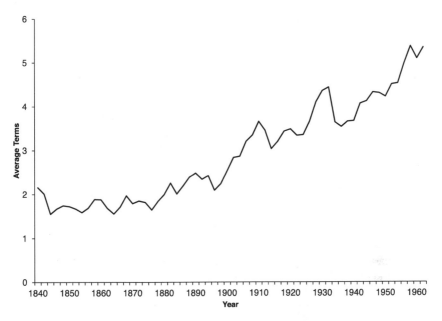

Fig. 9.6. Average number of terms served in the U.S. House, 1840–1962. The figure shows the average number of terms served by members of Congress. The solid line is a locally weighted regression line.

to the late 19th and early 20th centuries, students of institutional development have searched widely for an explanation. A number of potential answers have been given.

One prominent narrative focuses on the supposed realigning elections of 1894 and 1896. These elections, so the argument goes, eliminated two-party competition in many parts of the country. As a result, many fewer members went down to defeat via election. The supposed decline of two-party competition also influenced the voluntary decisions of incumbents to run for reelection. Knowing that their odds of winning reelection, assuming they could secure renomination, jumped up following 1896, the rates of incumbents seeking reelection naturally jumped as well.

A second narrative emphasizes the changing balance between the state capitals and the federal government. Where once, say, the Missouri state legislature may have been as relevant to party politicians as the U.S. Congress, by the turn of the 20th century the balance of power had clearly shifted to Washington. The scope and size of the national government had increased to the point that the Congress had become the keystone of the

American political system. The policy instruments at the disposal of the federal government had rapidly increased. The importance of the national government, according to this view, fueled the rise of careerism. Politicians gravitate to power. As the power of the national government rose, the gravitational pull of Washington for ambitious politicians rose as well.

Related to the growth of national government was a change in the internal politics of the House. The revolt of 1910 created a premium on seniority. By taking the discretionary power out of the hands of party leaders and locating it in an automatic process—based on seniority—members could more fully map out their career plans. The uncertainty associated with the arbitrary decision of party leaders, so the argument goes, was removed. The primary importance of seniority in making committee assignments naturally followed.

While these narratives certainly contain a good deal of truth, they are not wholly satisfying. This section argues that gerrymandering—or more appropriately, the decline of partisan gerrymandering—created an environment in which careerism could flourish. As seen in previous chapters, the frequency and fever-pitched partisanship of 19th-century gerrymandering fed the massive waves of turnover that hit the House during that era. Gerrymandering could come at any time, and it was often intensely partisan when it came. Even incumbents of the party drawing district lines often found themselves in more competitive districts as parties tried to maximize their seat share. But just as the frequency and magnitude of gerrymandering goes a long way toward explaining the rapid membership turnover of the 19th century, one might suspect that the altered gerrymandering patterns of the 20th century contributed to the decrease in turnover in the 20th century.

How did the changing nature of gerrymandering contribute to this shift? First, as we have seen, the frequency of redistricting in the 20th century declined precipitously. Many states went long stretches with stable, uninterrupted district boundaries. Hence, members of Congress had increasingly stable district boundaries. Between 1840 and 1900, the probability of a district being redrawn was 20 percent. In some states, the number was even higher. For example, during the 19th century, an Ohio congressman had a 40 percent chance of having their district redrawn in any single election. Thus, over the course of five elections, a congressman could expect to have his district redrawn more than once. It is not hard to imagine the difficulties of developing a career in the House, or a career in the constituency, with ever-shifting district boundaries.

By contrast, between 1900 and 1960, the probability of a district being redrawn was cut in half to 10 percent. And as we have seen, at certain periods (i.e., between 1914 and 1930), and in certain places, the probability of a redistricting was effectively zero. Where redistricting is less frequent, the electoral uncertainty implanted in the minds of politicians drastically recedes. Certainty facilitates planning and investment. Moreover, when redistricting happened, it tended to be less Pr partisan. This is not to say that redistricting became safe; many members still opted to retire following a redistricting. But compared to the virulent partisanship of 19th-century gerrymandering, the new politics of redistricting looked tame. One can see this manifest itself by comparing the margins of victory following a redistricting between the two centuries.

Here then is a powerful, but completely overlooked, source for the 20th-century ascent and entrenchment of congressional careerism. Members were now in a position to solidify their hold on districts in a way that was not possible in the 19th century. In the Gilded Age, a congressman from, say, Ohio, could count on having his district redrawn within a term or two with almost near certainty. It is easy to imagine the difficulties this would create in developing a political career both at home and within the House. Why try to build a home style when you know that the state legislature can, and likely will, carve up your district in two years? As Richard Fenno wrote following the reapportionment revolution, which broke the redistricting logjam, "It is this electoral uncertainty implanted in the minds of our politicians in the House of Representatives—more than policy change—that constitutes the real 'reapportionment revolution' nationally" (Fenno 1978, 12).

Why invest in a congressional career? Why invest in the institution itself—serving on committees, building the coalitions necessary for long-term legislative projects, etc.—when you face a certain redistricting in the near future? By the mid-20th century, however, congressmen could count on having the same district for long stretches of time. Building a personal vote now became a worthwhile, and achievable, investment. Coupled with other more well-known electoral reforms, such as direct primaries and secret-ballot laws, representatives could control their own fate to a much larger degree than they had in the 19th century.

Putting these two factors together suggests that the impact of changing gerrymandering strategies on career decisions can be rendered by the following probability calculus:

Seeking and Winning Reelection = f(Pr(Redistricting) × Pr(Partisan
    Gerrymander | Redistricting))

Here, the decision to seek reelection, and the likelihood of winning, is expressed as a function of the probability of a redistricting event multiplied by the probability of a partisan gerrymander given a redistricting event. As the probability of a redistricting event decreases, the likelihood of running for reelection should increase. Moreover, as the partisanship of redistricting decreases, conditional on a new map, the likelihood of running for reelection increases.

To test for differences in the impact of redistricting across the two centuries, I estimated the differential likelihood of seeking reelection following a redistricting in the two centuries. Specifically, I estimated the probability of seeking reelection in years where the incumbent's district had been redrawn. The key independent variable was a dummy variable denoting whether the election took place in the 19th or 20th century (i.e., 1 = 20th century, 0 = 19th century). The analysis ran from 1840 to 1962. The model also included control variables measuring the margin of victory in the incumbent's prior election, age (logged), and the number of terms served. The results, presented in table 9.4, column 1, strongly support the notion that redistricting had a smaller impact in the 20th century than in the 19th. The positive coefficient on the 1900 dummy variable indicates that 20th-century members were more likely to run for reelection after a redistricting than their counterparts in the 19th century.

To convert these results into substantive terms, using the estimates in table 9.4, one can calculate the probability of running for reelection in the

TABLE 9.4. The Changing Impact of Redistricting on Seeking and Winning Reelection, 1840–1962

	Seeking Reelection	Winning Reelection
After 1900 (1 = after, 0 = before)	1.25*	.72*
	(.10)	(.13)
Previous Electoral Margin	.006*	.03*
	(.002)	(.004)
Age (logged)	−.67*	−.48
	(.25)	(.36)
Number of Terms Served	−.02	−.009
	(.02)	(.03)
Log-Likelihood	−1,562.85	−833.49
Number of Observations	2916	2,043

Note: Maximum likelihood logit estimates with robust standard errors in parentheses. The first difference for seeking reelection is .24 (std. error = .02). The first difference for winning reelection is .10 (.02).

*$p < .05$.

two time periods. Setting the other variables at their median values, the probability an incumbent would seek reelection in the 19th century, after a redistricting, was .6. During the 20th century, this probability jumped to .84. This result provides support to the idea that redistricting was viewed by 20th-century politicians as less devastating than in the 19th century.

That redistricting became less disruptive to a political career is further confirmed in table 9.4, column 2. This column presents the results of a model in which the dependent variable is whether or not the incumbent won reelection, conditional on the decision to seek reelection. Again, we see that redistricting in the 20th century was less disruptive to political careerism. The positive coefficient on the 1900 dummy variable is positive, indicating that 20th-century incumbents were more likely to win reelection following a redistricting than 19th-century incumbents. Converting these results into substantive probabilities shows that the likelihood of winning reelection, following a redistricting was .76 in the 19th century. In the 20th, this likelihood grew to .86.

Overall, these results show that redistricting in the 20th century became much less doom laden for incumbents than it had been before. Incumbents were more likely to seek, and win, reelection following a redistricting. This is not to say that modern redistricting was, and is, not disruptive. Incumbents are still less likely to run following a redistricting, even now, than during more normal election years. But the results here do show that compared to the unruly gerrymandering practices of the 19th century, modern incumbents face much less disruptive districting.

Conclusion

For years, scholars have searched far and wide to explain the rise of candidate-centered politics in the 20th century without reaching a consensus. An important, but woefully neglected, piece of this puzzle can be found in changing gerrymandering strategies. The pace of redistricting, which had been frenzied in the 19th century, diminished throughout the early to mid-20th century. Because redistricting was less frequent, the average district remained undisturbed for 20 years. When redistricting did happen, the upheaval was much less drastic. The very foundation of modern congressional politics was forged out of these altered districting decisions. Members could plan for, and build, careers in the House. Both individual and aggregate turnover diminished.

Thus, by the 1960s, the essential features of the modern congressional system were in place. The vast literature on the U.S. Congress has long held that the 1960s produced a break with the past. According to this literature, incumbent reelection rates soared in the mid-1960s, ushering in an era of candidate-centered elections. Using the perks of office, according to the dominant narrative, incumbents were increasingly able to insulate themselves against adverse national electoral tides. But as this chapter has shown the foundations for these changes had already been laid well before the mid-1960s. While few would doubt that the electoral margins of incumbents spiked during the mid-1960s (i.e., Mayhew 1974b), Congress was already full of careerists. The uptick in careerism and electoral margins in the mid-1960s, so widely commented upon and analyzed, built on bedrock that had already been well established.

TEN

Gerrymandering and the Future of American Politics

In this book, I have argued for a fundamental reevaluation of gerrymandering and its impact on the evolution of American politics. The traditional narrative of political history has long centered on critical, realigning elections as the mainsprings of American politics. According to this narrative, some elections are more consequential than others. These critical elections sweep major tranches of legislators out of power and sweep in whole new classes of legislators. Critical elections produce abrupt breaks in traditional party ideological alignments and set the nation on a new policy trajectory. In short, according to this dominant narrative, critical elections are the main drivers of American electoral and policy history.

In explaining the periodic recurrence of critical elections, scholarship in this tradition has focused on mass behavior as the motor force behind realignments. Voter frustration with the status quo builds over time. These frustrations ultimately boil over, leading to a fundamental shift in party alignments and voter loyalties. Moreover, critical elections are followed by new governmental majorities who use their newfound power to fundamentally redirect the course of public policy. In short, the realignment narrative provides a sweeping explanation for the dynamics of American political history.

The realignment narrative, moreover, provides an explanation for the rise of candidate-centered politics in the 20th century. According to this view, the realignment of party ideologies following the 1896 election transformed the party coalitions of both the South and North.

Working alongside these changes in party alignments were efforts by elites, in both the South and North, to solidify their hold on political power by cutting a portion of the mass public out of the electoral process (Burnham 1965). The end result was the demise of the partisan-centered, mobilization-driven politics of the 19th century, and its replacement with the candidate-centered, advertising-driven politics of the 20th century.

The scope and power of the realignment narrative has guided a generation of scholars. The focus on rapid changes in mass behavior as the mainspring of American politics, however, has produced a radical underestimation of electoral institutions. Scholars of American political history instead have trained their attention on aspects like the ethnic basis of electoral behavior, and debates over whether certain elections meet the ever-changing benchmark of being labeled a critical election.

The focus on individual-level behavior has led to a radical underestimation of electoral institutions, in general, and gerrymandering, in particular. How citizen preferences—in the currency of votes—translate into political representation is not straightforward. Rules about how these votes are cast and counted, how they aggregate into winners and losers, and how the victors of local elections translate into political power nationally, all mediate the connection between citizen preferences and governmental outcomes. Central to this translation are the construction of electoral districts. Political decisions over whether to use geographic districts, where to place those districts, and when to redraw those districts has systematically shaped electoral politics and legislative power since the founding. Yet the importance of electoral districts in shaping political power has long been ignored by students of American political history; much to the detriment of our understanding of this history.

While political scientists are skeptical of gerrymandering, politicians throughout American history—from Elbridge Gerry to Tom DeLay—have acted as if gerrymandering presents a golden opportunity for partisan and personal gain. Politicians have deep-seated incentives to bias the translation of votes into seats. This book brings districting front and center to the narrative of American political history. For the remainder of this chapter, I first discuss the central claims made in this book. The second section turns to a discussion of how redistricting developed in the wake of the Supreme Court-led reapportionment revolution of the 1960s. I then place recent developments in redistricting politics, and scholarship, within the larger historical context uncovered in this book.

Partisan Gerrymandering and American Political Development

The U.S. Constitution delegated responsibility for election administration primarily to the states. The freedom enjoyed by the states to design electoral rules provided ample fuel for ambitious state-level politicians to further their personal and partisan goals. Perhaps nowhere have battles over electoral rules been more evident than in the design of congressional districts. The Constitution makes no mention of how states were to be divided into congressional districts, or if districts were to be used at all. Indeed, for much of the early period of American history, the choice states faced was over when and how to redistrict. Modern redistricting takes place, for the most part, according to a fixed timetable. Because congressional districts must meet the one-person, one-vote standard, states need to redraw after every census to adjust for any population changes across districts. The result has been a regularized 10-year redistricting cycle.

Nowadays, we take this cycle for granted. But within the context of the span of American history, this regularized redistricting cycle is a relatively new phenomenon. For most of American history, states could redistrict largely whenever they wanted. Some states went long stretches without drawing district boundaries. Even more dramatic was a pattern in which some states redrew more than once a decade. Ohio, for example, redistricted seven times between 1878 and 1892. Between 1862 and 1892 there was only one election cycle in which at least one state did not redraw its congressional districts. Chapter 3 showed that partisan control of state institutions drove the timing of these redistricting events. When a new party captured control of state government, and the existing districts were designed by the out party, the probability of a redistricting event spiked. When these two conditions were not present, and a state did not gain or lose seats in the federal apportionment, the probability of redistricting was almost zero. Thus, both the decision to mandate single-member districts and subsequent state-level decisions to redistrict reminds us that even the political system's most fundamental features might be molded from short-term, partisan calculations. The modern structure of the House of Representatives emerged out of these short-term calculations.

The modern redistricting process is shot through with many of the technological accoutrements of 21st century. Detailed census data, geographic information systems (GIS), and sophisticated redistricting software provide today's mapmakers with the tools to construct gerrymanders with the simple push of a button (Monmonier 2001). But as this book has demonstrated, 19th-century politicians had little trouble engineering effective partisan gerrymanders despite their technological limitations.

Much of this success can be attributed to the minimal legal and political constraints that 19th-century line drawers faced. Without a meddlesome judiciary peering over their shoulders, state legislatures were free to draw districts almost however they wanted. The pressure to protect congressional incumbents were also largely absent. The result was that mapmakers were much more willing to pursue aggressive partisan gerrymanders. Parties typically tried to maximize their seat shares by carving states into districts with minimal vote margins, even if that meant making the districts they already held less safe. The results influenced party ratios, electoral competition, and the career decisions of incumbents.

Chapter 4 showed that these maps biased political outcomes within the states and had profound consequences for party ratios in the House. Partisan plans produced an average bias of 6 percent in favor of the controlling party. Moreover, cumulating these state-level gerrymanders, I found that redistricting did, on occasion, affect party control of the House. Notably in 1878 and 1888, redistricting helped determine majority control of the House of Representatives.

These redistricting decisions also directly shaped the nature of electoral competition. With few exceptions, the national vote for Congress was very close, yet the partisan composition of the House often changed dramatically. For instance, in 1874, Republicans' percentage of House seats dropped from 69 percent to 36 percent (a loss of 94 seats) despite their national vote dropping only 6.8 percent. In 1894, Democrats lost 114 seats, while their national vote share dropped 7.4 percent. The explanation for the outsized seat swings of the 19th century have remained an unresolved puzzle for historians and political scientists.

Chapter 5 showed that partisan gerrymandering provides an important missing piece of the puzzle. State politicians fashioned congressional districts with slender, yet winnable, margins—in other words, increasing competition. Added together, these competitive districts produced a hyper-responsive electoral system where small swings in the vote produced immense swings in seats. Notably there was an overabundance of marginal Democratic seats following the 1852 and 1892 elections, and an overabundance of marginal Republican districts following the 1872 elections. In all three cases, one party dominated the drawing of districts nationwide. As a consequence, unanticipated political and economic events—the Kansas-Nebraska Act of 1854, the Panic of 1873, and the Panic of 1893—created seat swings well out of proportion to the vote swing. Although important past work has identified the presence of sharp vote-seat distortions in these eras (Brady 1985; 1988), no one has identified the essential role that partisan gerrymandering played in first constructing this hyperresponsive electoral system.

Because states often engaged in drawing highly competitive districts, this also made the career of an individual member of Congress more turbulent. Members of Congress faced a greater probability of redistricting. When it happened, it was often intensely partisan. Chapter 6 explored the impact of redistricting on congressional turnover. Members of Congress were less likely to run for reelection when their district was redrawn. Moreover, those who ran were less likely to win. The result was that in periods of intense redistricting, turnover in the House spiked. The largest periods of turnover in the 19th century, and all of American history, occurred in years when redistricting was widespread.

Overall, the politics of gerrymandering during *this* era clearly illustrates the desire, and ability, of partisan politicians to stack the electoral deck in their favor. From the initial decision in 1842 by Congress to mandate single-member districts to the politics of gerrymandering during the Gilded Age, 19th-century politicians took full advantage of institutional manipulation. Gerrymandering shaped the competitiveness of congressional elections, the partisan composition of state congressional delegations, and at times, helped determine party control of the House of Representatives.

Throughout the book, I have also pointed to cases where the alteration of party balances in the House also influenced the outcomes of legislative battles. From the Louisiana Purchase to the Kansas-Nebraska Act to tariff policy in the late 19th century, the strategic construction of district lines played a central role in providing the necessary majorities to pass these transformational pieces of legislation. It is important to note, however, that the majority of lawmaking cases examined in this book involved legislation that actually passed. Here majorities, partially manufactured by gerrymandering, pushed through legislation that may not have passed without the aid of strategic redistricting. But one might also wonder about cases where legislation was delayed, or blocked outright, because of manufactured majorities. In other words, were there "dogs that didn't bark"? Of course, systematically identifying instances of legislation that did not pass because of districting is difficult. How does one know the set of legislation that would have passed if partisan majorities had been different? Because we do not get to observe this counterfactual, it becomes incredibly difficult to empirically identify the dogs that did not bark. Such empirical difficulties are not unique to this study, and have remained a longstanding challenge for students of lawmaking. Nevertheless, one can point to illustrative examples to show that the impact of gerrymandering may not have been limited to just those pieces of legislation that were enacted.

For example, one area where gerrymandering influenced legislative outcomes without the necessity of enacting legislation was civil rights. The close partisan balance in the national government following the Civil War put the House of Representatives front and center in the battle over civil rights and enforcement of Reconstruction. Because Republicans had a near lock on both the Senate and the presidency, the fate of civil rights legislation often hinged on partisan control of the House. When Democrats controlled the House, their general strategy was to zero out funding for enforcement of civil rights in Southern elections. Enacting new legislation was not necessary. As long as Democrats could "veto" the ideal level of appropriations sought by Republicans, they could dramatically influence the nature and amount of civil rights enforcement in the South.

Similarly, in the 20th century, changes in districting strategies produced a distinct bias in favor of rural districts. During the 20th century, state legislatures opted to redistrict less. The result was rapid growth in malapportionment. As the population of the country grew, legislative districts failed to keep pace. By the early 1960s, congressional districts varied greatly in size. The result was a massive structural inequality that favored rural areas at the expense of metropolitan interests.

The Past and Present of Gerrymandering

The Supreme Court radically upended the system described above in a sweeping series of decisions handed down in the 1960s. Breaking from their standing doctrine of judicial noninterference in the political process, the Supreme Court ruled in 1962 that state legislative districting in Tennessee violated the Equal Protection Clause of the Constitution, and was, therefore, justiciable. The case, *Baker v. Carr*, represented the first salvo in a decade long judicial attack on malapportionment. In a series of follow-up cases, the Supreme Court implemented the new doctrine of one-person, one-vote by overturning districting plans in states and localities. Two years later, the Supreme Court extended the one-person, one-vote doctrine to U.S. House districts. The case, *Wesberry v. Sanders* (1964), involved congressional districts in Georgia which had not been redrawn since 1931. By 1961, the 5th District (which included all of Atlanta) had a population of 823,680, while the rural 9th District had a population of 272,154. Districts in Georgia had last been drawn in 1934. It was no coincidence that on the eve of the reapportionment revolution the longest serving member of the House—Carl Vinson—was from Georgia. Vinson was serving in his 26th term, having first been elected to the House in 1914.

The consequences of the reapportionment decisions were rapid and immense. By the end of the 1960s, malapportionment had essentially been eradicated in both congressional and state legislative districts. The result was a radical redrawing of legislative districts, and a reshuffling of political power, across the country (cf. Ansolabehere and Snyder 2008; Cox and Katz 2002). Beyond the immediate short-term consequences of the reapportionment revolution, the transformation of court doctrine fundamentally changed the redistricting game as played in the state legislatures. Notably, the reapportionment decisions injected the courts directly into the political thicket. Overseeing the redistricting process is a role the judiciary plays to this day. Notably, the courts ensure adherence to the requirement of equal apportionment of districts. The creation of congressional districts with equal population has now become required. More controversial, however, has been the courts role in using districts to enhance the representation of racial minorities in Congress and state legislatures.

Racial Gerrymandering

The reapportionment cases of the 1960s were not the only major transformation in the American electoral structure to take place during this period. Notably, Congress passed the Voting Rights Act of 1965 with the goal of reversing the systematic disenfranchisement of African Americans, primarily in the South. Certainly one of the most consequential pieces of legislation ever passed by Congress, the Voting Rights Act helped pave the way for a radical transformation of southern society and national politics. Central to federal intervention in the electoral process was federal oversight of electoral districts. Over the course of the next 30 years the issue of voting rights and redistricting would become intimately intertwined (Canon 1999).

The legal connection between districting and minority rights gained further steam in the 1980s and early 1990s in the wake of a series of path-breaking Supreme Court decisions. In 1986, the Supreme Court ruled in *Thornburg v. Gingles* that the Voting Rights Act implied legislative districts should not discriminate against racial minorities. In the wake of legislative districting in North Carolina, following the 1982 reapportionment, African-American voters sued arguing that the districts diluted their voting power and ran afoul of Section 2 of the Voting Rights Act. The court agreed with the plaintiffs and ruled the districting plan invalid. This decision was construed as a prod for state legislatures to draw legislative districts that made it feasible for minorities to get elected. In practice, state legislatures, with further prodding from the U.S. Department of Justice, took this to mean creating districts where an ethnic minority comprised a majority of the district. The driving idea was that majority-minority districts will be able to elect minorities into the legislature and thereby boost minority representation.

As state legislatures began carrying out this goal in the early 1990s, it produced considerable legal and political backlash. Creative geography in North Carolina, for example, produced the famous 12th District, which knitted together parts of Durham and Charlotte into a single district, although those two cities are more than 150 miles apart. Much of the district was comprised of little more than stretches of Interstate 85. In 1993, the Supreme Court ruled, in *Shaw v. Reno*, that race cannot be the only justification for creating a district; especially if it leads to bizarrely shaped districts like North Carolina's 12th. As a result, the court ruled that the North Carolina district needed to be redrawn. It is worth noting that the 12th District elected the first African American to Congress from North Carolina since the end of Reconstruction.

Two years later, the Supreme Court further reined in racial gerrymandering in *Miller v. Johnson*. Here the court argued that race can be a factor in creating a district, but it cannot be the predominant factor. Neither the *Shaw* or *Miller* decisions, however, completely reversed *Thornburg*. Race can still be a factor in drawing districts as long as the primary motive is partisanship rather than race, per se. Given that African Americans and Latinos are predominantly Democratic voters, the court has in effect allowed for the continued use of implicit racial gerrymandering. Nevertheless, the decisions of the more conservative Supreme Court of the 1990s have further reduced the scope for race to be a dominant factor in designing districts. But again, this is still unsettled legal doctrine and continues to be the basis for widespread litigation.

Also unsettled is the extent to which racial gerrymandering actually benefitted one party or another. Because minority voters overwhelmingly tend to vote Democratic, concentrating these voters into minority-majority districts may actually benefit Republicans. To put this in the language of efficient gerrymandering, majority-minority districts may reduce the efficiency with which Democratic votes translate into seats nationally. Gary Jacobson, for example, notes that "racial gerrymandering was responsible for as many as ten of the seats Republicans gained in the South in 1992 and 1994" (Jacobson 2009, 14). Other scholars have been more skeptical, arguing that any benefit to Republicans from majority-minority districts were overwhelmed by the immense pro-Republican national tide of 1994.

Thus, whether or not majority-minority districts benefit one party at the expense of the other party remains an open question. But read against the larger backdrop of gerrymandering history presented in this book, the push to use district design to boost the representation of ethnic minorities must be seen as nothing short of ironic. As we have seen, gerrymandering in the 19th century was a weapon. In particular, a weapon aimed at disenfranchising African Americans in the South. Democratic gerrymanders, in the North and South, in the 1870s, notably, brought to power a Democratic majority bent on reversing reconstruction. The sweeping Democratic victory in the House elections of 1874 put Democrats in a position to undermine federal Reconstruction. The strategic use of the appropriations process allowed Democrats to starve the enforcement of Reconstruction.

Party Bias

While the Supreme Court has been willing to rule on gerrymandering in the areas of malapportionment and minority rights, the justices have remained reluctant to rule directly on the partisan impact of redistricting. Over the subsequent decades, the judiciary has elaborated and refined legal doctrine surrounding the districting process. But it is worth noting that this court supervision only extends to certain areas of the districting process. While malapportioned districts violate current legal doctrine, the Supreme Court has yet to rule a plan unconstitutional on the grounds of being an unfair partisan gerrymandering. Indeed, in a dissenting opinion in *Wesberry v. Sanders*, Justice Harlan argued that focusing on the size of districts ignored the bigger picture. The great oversight of the majority opinion in *Wesberry*, according to Harlan, was that parties could still use districting to engineer unfair political outcomes.

The Supreme Court, however, has, over time, stepped close to the line of ruling a redistricting plan unconstitutional on the basis of partisan gerrymandering. Notably, in *Davis v. Bandamer* (1986), the court ruled that partisan gerrymandering was justiciable. Yet, the majority opinion also ruled that the plaintiffs would need to show discriminatory vote dilution to reach the level of an Equal Protection Clause violation. The court argued, in *Davis*, that this threshold had not been met. More recently, in *Vieth v. Jubelirer* (2004), the court again dealt with the constitutionality of partisan gerrymandering. In a plurality decision, this time the court ruled that partisan gerrymandering was not justiciable. The plurality opinion concluded that while partisan gerrymandering may, in principle, violate the Equal Protection Clause, it would be impossible for courts to empirically validate whether a map had met the threshold of a partisan gerrymander—or even to establish what that threshold should be. This decision, however, failed to completely turnover the precedent set in *Davis v. Bandamer.* Justice Kennedy, writing in a concurring opinion, argued that gerrymandering might still be justiciable. However, the Supreme Court has yet to define a standard that would rule a gerrymander unconstitutional.

The upshot of these decisions is that there still is still plenty of legal room for partisan mapmakers to exploit districting for partisan advantage. One result of this legal opening is a firestorm of commentary every 10 years about the supposed evils of redistricting. Reflecting on the incendiary redistricting battles of the early 2000s, the *New York Times* published an editorial, "Democracy Takes a Hit." The editorial summarized the view of redistricting held by most political observers, stating that "Partisan gerrymandering . . . has reached a crisis point. Because of increased partisanship and improvements in technology used to determine district lines, legislators now regularly create districts that all but ensure victory for the party that controls the districting process" (*New York Times*, April 29, 2004). This perspective, however, was not unique to the editorial pages of the *New York Times.* The traditionally more conservative editorial page of the *Wall Street Journal* proffered similar comments, writing that modern gerrymandering demonstrates "the lengths, widths and depths to which the politicians have gone to create invincible incumbents and disenfranchise millions of voters" (*Wall Street Journal*, March 11, 2005).

Thus, for commentators along the political spectrum, allowing politicians to write the rules that determine their future success represents one of the fundamental drawbacks of the Constitution. Draw the boundaries one way, and Democrats are in power. Draw the lines another way, and suddenly Republicans are in power. The result of modern redistricting efforts, according to these commentators, has been to produce "elections with no meaning" (*New York Times*, February 21, 2004).

These fears, however, are not new. Hand-wringing over the potential evils of redistricting can be found throughout American history. The very phrase "gerrymander" was coined in 1812 by those who felt aggrieved by what they saw as the unfair abuse of the districting process. And angst over the use and abuse of redistricting has not stopped. In 1892, to take one example, the *Atlantic Monthly* equated redistricting with nothing less than

"Legal Disenfranchisment" (*Atlantic Monthly*, April 1892). Democratic voters in Kansas, the article went on to say, "have no more hope of being represented in Congress at Washington than if they had no vote at all; they have but the shadow of liberty, - the substance being denied them as much as it is the Russian peasant or the Indian ryot" (quoted in Argersinger 1989, 63).

Jump forward to the 21st century and one continues to hear many of the same concerns. Political observers across the spectrum—including legal scholars, journalists, reform groups, and even the general public—trace many of the perceived ills of American democracy to gerrymandering. For example, some legal scholars have argued that letting politicians draw district lines fundamentally undermines the health of American democracy. Some have likened modern mapmaking to letting the "foxes guard the henhouse" (e.g., Gerken 2010). Others draw their analogies from economics, likening bipartisan gerrymandering to duopolistic cartels (e.g., Issacharoff 2002).

These concerns have also found expression in more popular outlets. In a provocative 2003 *New Yorker* article, Jeffrey Toobin excoriated redistricting as it is currently practiced in the states. The title itself—"The Great Election Grab"—signaled the widespread fear of politician-led redistricting. The image conveyed is one of politicians, in effect, stealing elections through mapmaking. Similarly, a recent book written by a professional geographer, and written for a popular audience, carried the subtitle "How Politicians Manipulate Electronic Maps and Census Data to Win Elections" (Monmonier 2001).

This anxiety surrounding politician-drawn district maps has also led to efforts to change the rules surrounding redistricting. Reform groups in a number of states, fed up with partisan polarization and legislative gridlock, have trained their sights on redistricting. This has led some states to remove redistricting from state legislators and hand it over to independent citizen-based commissions. For example, California voters recently chose to create a citizen-based redistricting commission responsible for drawing both state legislative and U.S. House district maps. The hope among reformers is that nonpartisan maps will produce more competitive elections and less polarized legislators.

Against this avalanche of worry, it is therefore very interesting to read the political science literature on redistricting. With few, if important, exceptions, research in political science offers a much more benign perspective. In fact, the dominant theme of the political-science literature is that the supposed dangers of redistricting are vastly overblown. Gerrymanders may bias political outcomes here and there, but the overall impact of gerrymandering on the national balance of power is modest (e.g., Cain and Butler 1991; Campagna and Grofman 1990; Niemi and Abramowitz 1994; Seabrook 2010; Swain, Reed, and Borelli 1998). Similarly, the modern growth of incumbent reelection rates and victory margins, it is argued, has little to do with bipartisan redistricting (e.g., Abramowitz, Alexander and Gunning 2006; Ansolabehere and Snyder 2008; Friedman and Holden 2009). Nor have scholars found much evidence linking gerrymandering to the rise of party polarization in Congress (e.g., McCarty, Poole, and Rosenthal 2009; Oppenheimer 2005; Theriault 2008).

There is no consensus, however, as to why redistricting appears to have minimal impact. One possibility is that the legal rules surrounding redistricting prevent politicians from pulling off full-blown gerrymanders. States must conform to the one-person, one-vote doctrine and adhere to the Voting Rights Act, which protects minority interests in the electoral process (e.g., Shotts 2001). Even the most notorious gerrymander of recent memory—the Texas remap of 2004, for example—had two of its districts thrown out for violating the Voting Right Act. These limits, enforced by an ever-watchful judiciary, narrow the range of options that parties can choose from when drawing new boundaries and thereby blunt the impact of gerrymandering.

A second possibility is that the gains to be had from gerrymandering are simply limited to begin with. According to this view, too many factors prevent mapmakers from meaningfully biasing electoral outcomes. The value of incumbents and seniority in Congress mute the motivations of state legislators to pursue out-and-out partisan gerrymanders. Even when states try to gerrymander, pro-Democratic gerrymanders in some states often cancel out pro-Republican gerrymanders in other states. Moreover, shifting voting patterns can quickly undermine even the most carefully crafted map (Rush 1993).

This book has shown that gerrymandering can, and has, dramatically shifted the political balance of power in national politics at critical junctures in American history. Throughout the 19th century, gerrymandering biased partisan seat distributions, and, on occasion, even decided majority control of the chamber. At this point, one might wonder to what extent the scales of power can be tipped by gerrymandering. How far can the national balance of power be tipped by the strategic design of districts? The narrative provided in this book suggests that the extent to which gerrymandering can tip the scales is highly conditional on the political context in which redistricting takes place. For much of the 19th century, with some notable exceptions, the political universe was highly polarized. At both the state and national level, the balance between the two major parties was often quite close. This was especially true in the years after the Civil War and the reentry of the South into the Union. Because party control of the House was often razor thin, both the incentives to gerrymander and its impact increased sizably. When party control of the House was almost a foregone conclusion, as it was for much of the post–World War II era, the incentives to aggressively pursue gerrymanders receded. Thus, one lesson of this book is the importance of taking into account the larger political context in which gerrymandering strategies are pursued.

Moreover, although this book has emphasized those instances in which gerrymandering demonstrably influenced outcomes, it should not be concluded that political outcomes were solely fashioned by politicians manipulating district design for personal gain. The American democratic system contains mechanisms that provide for a degree of self-correction and has prevented partisan politicians from converting elections into winner-take-all affairs. First, gains made in one state can be cancelled by countervailing gains in another state. Second, even when states were able to manufacture winner-take-all systems—such as those found in Indiana, Ohio, and Maine—these highly efficient gerrymanders carried with them substantial risks. A small electoral breeze in the wrong direction could spell disaster for a majority party. And as we saw with in the elections of 1854, 1874, and 1894, big gambles turned into massive losses. Finally, the larger constitutional system designed by the framers explicitly built mechanisms to work against winner-take-all politics. The separation of powers and staggered elections provides both the president and the Senate with a separate electoral base. The separation of purpose that can arise when either the Senate or the president is controlled by a party different than the House of Representatives provides a further bulwark against full-blown winner-take-all politics.

Electoral Competition

Alongside their reluctance to rule on party bias, Supreme Court justices have also been unwilling to declare a redistricting plan invalid on the grounds that it violates a constitutional standard of political competition. Indeed, some have argued that the periodic redistricting required by the reapportionment doctrines has only further dampened electoral competition. Because politicians are naturally interested in self-preservation, the regular redistricting cycle affords politicians a regular opportunity to readjust district boundaries in a way that preserves their electoral security. These supposedly incumbent-protection acts have then been blamed for the rising rates of incumbent reelection rates and rising victory margins.

Political science research, however, is far from reaching a consensus on whether redistricting can serve as a plausible explanation for declining rates of competition in House elections. Indeed, identifying the connection, if any, between gerrymandering and electoral competition has been one of the front-burner questions occupying students of congressional elections for the past 30 years. Some have argued, echoing Tufte (1973), that modern redistricting has been captured by House incumbents who demand, and receive, safe congressional districts.

This stream of research lays much of the blame for declining competitiveness at the feet of redistricting (e.g., Cox and Katz 2002; Hirsch 2003; Carson and Crespin 2004). Another strand of the literature, argues that redistricting as a causal explanation for reducing competition has more bark than bite (e.g., Ferejohn 1977; Ansolabehere, Snyder, and Stewart 2000; Oppenheimer 2005). According to this line of thought, factors such as incumbency, modern residential patterns (e.g., the increasing partisan homogeneity of cities and suburbs), and fluctuating party loyalty strongly outweigh any independent effect that incumbent-friendly gerrymandering may have.

Here we can see the power of paying attention to a much longer time frame. One of the major differences between modern redistricting and this earlier era is the nature of redistricting plans drawn by state legislators. This book has shown that in the 19th century, when a single party was in charge of creating congressional districts, they were much more likely than their modern counterparts to draw competitive congressional districts in an attempt to maximize the number of seats their party could win on Election Day.

In evaluating the impact of contemporary redistricting on competition, it is essential to consider the full range of counterfactuals. One might ask: what if gerrymandering was conducted by 19th-century standards? While the naysayers may very well be right that redistricting has little marginal impact on electoral competition, it is crucial to also consider the "base." What would competition look like if gerrymandering returned to 19th-century standards?

As one illustration of the differences between redistricting then and now, consider the case of Ohio. Specifically, I want to consider the congressional district plans drawn by the Ohio state legislature for the election of 1882 to those for the 2002 election. This is a valuable comparison because the two rounds of redistricting share many common features. First, in both cases, Republicans had unified control of the redistricting process.[1] Second, the division of the statewide vote was roughly the same in both cases. In 1880, Democrats' share of the two-party presidential vote was 47.6 percent, and in 2000 it was 48.2 percent. So, in both eras, heading into the redistricting cycle the state as a whole was very competitive.

Yet when we turn our attention to the actual congressional districts that were drawn, stark differences appear. To compare the two redistricting plans, I used the presidential vote from 1880 and 2000 respectively, and aggregate this vote into the new congressional districts. In 1880, for example, I used the Democratic percentage of the two-party vote by county. Because Ohio's congressional districts in this era were comprised of one or more whole counties, I aggregated the presidential vote into the newly created congressional districts by consulting historical district maps (Martis 1982). For the 2000 cycle, the task was much easier. The *Almanac of American Politics* (2004) reports the 2000 presidential vote aggregated into the new districts that were created for the 2002 election. Thus, for both eras, we have a general exogenous measure of the underlying competitiveness of congressional districts.

TABLE 10.1 Comparing Redistricting Plans in Ohio, 1882 and 2002

District	Vote in New Congressional Districts, 1882	Vote in New Congressional Districts, 2002
1	47.5%	47.4%
2	48.9%	35.1%
3	48.3%	46.4%
4	60.7%	36.1%
5	57.8%	38.5%
6	49.8%	48.9%
7	47.5%	42.7%
8	44.2%	37.1%
9	47.6%	57.3%
10	50.1%	55.8%
11	44.1%	81.4%
12	48.4%	47.4%
13	54.4%	54.6%
14	45.0%	45.8%
15	47.9%	45.8%
16	55.1%	44.2%
17	44.9%	63.1%
18	44.5%	42.7%
19	30.7%	—
20	44.7%	—
21	42.6%	—
Average Democratic %	47.9%	48.4%
Average Margin	4.8%	16.5%
% of Districts between 45% and 55%	52% (11/21)	39% (7/18)

Note: The numbers in columns 1 and 2 are the two-party percentage of the district-level presidential vote with the exception of Districts 1 and 2 in 1882. Both of these districts were in Hamilton County, which prevented identifying the presidential vote since I do not have precinct-level data for this particular election. Since these two districts were essentially unchanged from 1880, I report the congressional vote in 1880 for these districts.

The results of this exercise are presented in table 10.1. The columns list the two-party presidential vote by district for the two plans. At the bottom of the table are summary statistics. One can clearly see the rather dramatic differences between the two districting plans. In the 1882 redistricting plan, the average district margin was 4.8 percent, while in 2002 the average district margin was a much larger 16.5 percent. Similarly, simply counting the number of districts that had a two-party vote between 45 percent and 55 percent, we again find major differences. In 1882, nearly half of Ohio's 21 districts (11 out of 21) would be considered marginal.[2] By contrast, in 2002 only 38.8 percent fall into the marginal range (7 out of 18). So, here we have a comparison where many of the surface features are the same: a single party controlling the districting process and healthy competition at the statewide level. Yet, the congressional districts drawn by state legislators in the two eras produced two starkly different results. These results, albeit for one state, suggest that the debate over redistricting and electoral competition needs to be reframed. In considering this debate, one needs to ask not just what marginal changes redistricting produces, but what would redistricting look like if we returned to 19th-century standards. Looking at redistricting from the latter perspective strongly suggests that district design does indeed influence modern electoral competition. But it is only by turning to the past and expanding our knowledge of redistricting that this insight emerges.

This book has examined the causes and consequences of gerrymandering throughout U.S. history. But the incentives that motivated the party politicians of the 19th and early 20th century have not stopped. Politicians continue to fervently seek election and seek the capture of national government. The incentives and constraints that politicians face have only grown more complex with the entry of the judiciary into the redistricting process. But political science and history have underestimated the importance of gerrymandering in shaping the dynamics of American party history. Gerrymandering has profoundly shaped party alignments and individual career trajectories throughout history. Districting determined who held political power in the Congress and fundamentally altered the course of public policy. The reverberations of these battles continue to stir American politics. In evaluating the consequences of legal doctrine and potential reforms to the contemporary redistricting process, therefore, it is essential to have a firm understanding of the history of gerrymandering in America.

Notes

CHAPTER 1

1. The practice of judicial noninterference would later become codified in Felix Frankfurter's opinion in *Colegrove v. Green* (1946) which enunciated the "political thicket doctrine." But this opinion merely formalized what had already been the long-standing practice of judicial restraint toward redistricting (Ansolabehere and Snyder 2008).

2. Cited in Cooter 2000, 182.

3. In addition, two states—New York and Pennsylvania—had multimember districts. The 1842 law also outlawed this practice.

CHAPTER 2

1. Some recent historical scholarship on this episode argues that Madison's district was not quite the gerrymander that its contemporary critics claimed (Hunter 2011).

2. Cumulating or "plumping" votes (i.e., giving more than one vote to a single candidate) was not allowed.

3. I started in 1800 because, prior to this election, party labels were still in flux in certain parts of the country, and not all members of Congress clearly identified with one party (or faction) (see Hoadley 1986). Moreover, data on party ratios in the state legislatures before 1800 is spotty at best (see Dubin 2007).

4. Pennsylvania did, however, opt to use a few multi-member districts.

5. Beginning with the Apportionment Act of 1872, Congress allowed states to elect any newly gained seats in at-large elections if, for some reason, they failed to redistrict. In calculating the proportion of Democratic seats, I excluded at-large seats. Including them does not change the results.

6. Bias is calibrated to what would have happened if the vote were split 50-50.

Thus, the bias estimates reported in table 2.2 are the result of passing λ through the following equation: $\exp[\lambda]/(\exp[\lambda] + 1) - 0.5$.

7. States with only one seat, or states that elect their entire delegation at-large, are excluded.

8. For more on the electoral rationale for Republican and Federalist flip-flops on the issue of expansion, see Theriault 2006.

CHAPTER 3

1. A month after his inauguration, Harrison died of pneumonia and was succeeded by Vice President John Tyler. Nominally a Whig, Tyler was a former Jacksonian, strong supporter of states' rights, and a strict constructionist. He subsequently became a thorn in the side of congressional Whigs and vetoed their cherished banking legislation. Tyler was subsequently read out of the party (Holt 1999).

2. See Shields 1985.

3. Tyler attached a message upon signing the bill voicing his displeasure with the content. Whigs in the House were furious, and, led by John Quincy Adams, initiated a resolution calling for an official rebuke of the president's actions (Shields 1985, 367).

4. This provision also meant that multimember congressional districts, which were used on a limited basis in New York, Maryland, and Pennsylvania, were no longer allowed.

5. Three of the Georgia Whig delegation resigned mid-session, and were replaced by Democrats. Thus, at the time of the vote on the Apportionment Act, Georgia had a mixed delegation of six Whigs and three Democrats.

6. The Democrats won the gubernatorial election 55 percent to 43 percent, and control of both legislative chambers.

7. Since then Congress has occasionally granted exceptions, sometimes allowing states to elect one member at-large, or exempting the districting requirement for states who fail to agree on a districting plan after a new apportionment. For example, in 1932, Congress allowed states losing seats in the federal apportionment to elect their members via general ticket, but only for that one election.

CHAPTER 4

1. *Washington Post*, October 14, 2004.

2. While upholding the bulk of the plan, the Supreme Court struck down two of the newly drawn districts on grounds that they violated sections of the Voting Rights Act.

3. Cox and Katz 2002 provide evidence that the initial wave of redistricting following the Supreme Court decisions of the mid-1960s had substantial partisan consequences (largely in favor of the Democratic Party).

4. These provisions are based on various federal statutes. See Martis 1982, 7.

5. The Supreme Court in *Smiley v. Holm* (1932) declared that the legal reversions of the 1911 Apportionment were still in force even though Congress did not explicitly include them in the 1929 Act.

6. The 1862 Apportionment Act explicitly exempted California and Illinois from the single-member district requirement and allowed them to elect their delegations by general ticket.

7. Negotiating a new district plan, appeasing congressional incumbents, satisfying local party organizations, and agreeing on how best to allocate partisans into new districts were among the many transaction and opportunity costs that had to enter into any party's utility calculation.

8. This case eventually ended up in the U.S. Supreme Court. The Court decided in *Smiley v. Holm* (1932) that the legislature had to abide by the statute-making prescriptions specified in Minnesota's state constitution, and therefore declared the governor's veto valid.

CHAPTER 5

1. Beginning with the Apportionment Act of 1872, Congress allowed states to elect any newly gained seats in at-large elections if for some reason they failed to redistrict. In calculating the proportion of Democratic seats, I excluded at-large seats. Including them does not change the results.

2. In this analysis, I use the statewide total Democratic vote. Using the total vote, as opposed to the average across districts, captures biases arising from both the distribution of voters and from malapportionment (Grofman, Koetzle, Brunell 1997). I explore the magnitude of malapportionment, and its impact on elections, in chapter 8. To foreshadow, malapportionment accounts for only a small percentage of the bias.

3. States with only one seat or states that elect their entire delegation at-large are excluded.

4. The estimates in Brady and Grofman 1991 show an average swing ratio of 3.98 in the 19th century (1850 to 1900) and 2.13 in the 20th century (1900 to 1980). Engstrom and Kernell (2005, 542) estimate an average swing ratio of 4.64 between 1840 and the 1890s (in non-Southern states). This dropped to 3.48 after widespread adoption of the Australian ballot (the analysis stops at 1940).

5. In almost all of these cases, I used either state-legislative election returns or the presidential votes reported at the ward and town level. These sources are available upon request. In some instances, I was also able to use contemporary reports from the *New York Times* for corroboration. The only case I was forced to exclude was the Massachusetts redistricting of 1892 because the district lines cut across too many county boundaries.

6. As a comparison, Born (1985, 312–13) estimates a coefficient of .771 for the period 1952 to 1982, and .668 when he restricts the sample to the period after the reapportionment revolution (1966–82).

7. Models including state and year fixed effects produced largely similar results. Using the presidential vote, instead of the congressional vote, predicted the intended change slightly worse and the actual outcomes slightly better than the congressional vote, but also contained an occasional large miss (i.e., when the most recent presidential election was four years prior to the redistricting). I preferred to use the most recent electoral results possible since the politicians drawing the maps likely used them.

CHAPTER 6

1. More recently, Cox and Katz 2002 have provided a partial rehabilitation of the Tufte thesis as applied to the reapportionment revolution of the 1960s. They showed that victory margins increased in Republican-held districts, but not Democratic-held districts. The notion of a conditional partisan impact of redistricting, as applied to the 19th century, is one I examine in more depth later (see also Cain 1985).

2. I have run the results with bipartisan plans included. The estimates for these plans are always considerably lower than for partisan plans, as one would expect, but because of the small number of observations the standard errors are substantial.

3. To control for third-party movements, I also estimated the model including the statewide minor party vote as an independent variable. The estimates for the swing ratio were largely unchanged.

4. I also considered estimating separate state-by-state swing ratios using the method proposed by Gelman and King 1994. The Gelman and King method relies on a two-step method. First, estimate a model of district-level vote shares. Second, simulate vote outcomes under different scenarios (e.g., different national vote swings). Finally, estimate seat swings under these different scenarios. Because the regressions for states with small House delegations produced very noisy forecasts of district-level vote shares, I opted instead to estimate the average swing ratio.

5. This election actually took place over the calendar years of 1854 and 1855. Congressional elections in this period were not all held in November of even-numbered years; some states held elections prior to November, while others held elections the following year. For ease of presentation, I will simply refer to this election period as the "Election of 1854."

6. The 31 Democratic districts above 70 percent were all located in the South.

CHAPTER 7

1. I have also run the model with year-fixed effects instead. The results for the redistricting coefficient remain largely the same. Moreover, running the model with state-fixed effects had minimal effect on the results.

2. The expectations for this variable are not necessarily straightforward. The reason is that not all congressional elections occurred at the same time as the presidential election. Throughout this period, some states held congressional elections in non-November months. The potential impact, if any, of nonconcurrent elections on surge and decline effects in this era remains understudied.

CHAPTER 8

1. The court allowed the original map to be used for the 2002 election because the primary elections had already been held. A redrawn map was then put into place for the 2004 elections and remained in place through the 2010 elections. The redistricting map eventually ended up in front of the Supreme Court (*Vieth v. Jubelirer* 2004). In a plurality opinion, the court upheld the plan arguing that they could not come up with a justiciable standard for determining whether a partisan gerrymander violated the Equal Protection Clause of the Constitution.

2. The partisan and policy consequence of malapportionment in the Senate has

been the subject of a handful of studies (Lee and Oppenheimer 1999; Riker 1955; Stewart and Weingast 1992). There is also research on the apportionment of House seats across states and the particular methods for calculating how many seats each state receives in the decennial apportionment (Balinski and Young 1982; Eagles 1990; Kromkowski 2002). Here I am focusing on the intrastate apportionment of House seats.

3. This example draws heavily from Grofman, Koetzle, and Brunell 1997.

4. Data on district-level population comes from Parsons, Beach, and Dubin 1986; and Parsons, Dubin, and Parsons 1990.

5. As a comparison, on the eve of the reapportionment revolution in 1962, the average difference between smallest and largest districts had surged to 270,000 people.

6. These differences, however, pale in comparison to the Senate. The current ratio of inequality in the Senate is a whopping 69 (California versus Wyoming).

7. Here I use the absolute value. In the later analysis, I use the actual value to measure deviations above and below the state average.

8. Although substantial, these inequalities pale in comparison to many state legislatures. For example, Argersinger (1992, 78) reports that the Rhode Island senate in 1900 had an average deviation of 111.

9. Another obvious cleavage was rural versus urban districts, which, in some cases, correlated with party divisions, but at other times cut across the parties (e.g., Eagles 1990). Here I am mainly concerned with partisan cleavages.

10. The town-based apportionment scheme of the lower house gave Republicans a virtual lock on that chamber. From here they had an institutional veto to prevent any redistribution of either the state or congressional districts that might benefit Democrats.

11. I also ran an analysis with the entire sample and included a term for those years right after a redistricting that was also interacted with the other terms in the equation. The years immediately following a redistricting did not differ significantly from other years in predicting deviations, so it was left out of the final equations.

CHAPTER 9

1. For those keeping track, this means that between 1842 and 1962 Connecticut had only two congressional district maps.

CHAPTER 10

1. In 2001–2002, Republicans in Ohio held both the state legislature and the governor's office. Because the legislature failed to act before January 2002, under the state constitution, they needed a 2/3 majority in both houses for a new law to take effect in 2002. Thus, Republicans had to gain the votes of a handful of Democrats. Nevertheless, the plan was considered a Republican gerrymander (see Barone and Cohen 2003, 1246).

2. This is a conservative estimate. If one were to round off, then the 16th, 17th, 18th, and 20th Districts would also make the cut, increasing the total number to 15 (or 71 percent).

References

Abramowitz, Alan I. 1983. "Partisan Redistricting and the 1982 Congressional Elections." *Journal of Politics* 45:776–70.

Abramowitz, Alan I., Brad Alexander, and Matthew Gunning. 2006. "Incumbency, Redistricting, and the Decline of Competition in U.S. House Elections." *Journal of Politics* 68:75–88.

Aldrich, John. 1995. *Why Parties?* Chicago: University of Chicago Press.

Altman, Micah. 1998. "Traditional Districting Principles: Judicial Myths vs. Reality." *Social Science History* 22:159–200.

Ansolabehere, Stephen, and James M. Snyder. 2008. *The End of Inequality: One Person, One Vote and the Transformation of American Politics.* New York: W.W. Norton.

Ansolabehere, Stephen, Alan Gerber, and James Snyder. 2002. "Equal Votes, Equal Money: Court-Ordered Redistricting and Public Expenditures in the American States." *American Political Science Review* 96:767–78.

Ansolabehere, Stephen, James Snyder, and Charles Stewart. 2000. "Old Voters, New Voters, and the Personal Vote: Using Redistricting to Measure the Incumbency Advantage." *American Journal of Political Science* 44:17–34.

Argersinger, Peter. 1992. *Structure, Process, and Party: Essays in American Political History.* Armonk, NY: M.E. Sharpe.

Argersinger, Peter H. 1985–86. "New Perspectives on Election Fraud in the Gilded Age." *Political Science Quarterly* 110:669–87.

Balinski, Michael L., and H. Peyton Young. 1982. *Fair Representation.* New Haven: Yale University Press.

Baker v. Carr, 369 U.S. 186 (1962).

Barone, Michael, and Richard E. Cohen. 2003. *The Almanac of American Politics, 2004.* Washington, DC: National Journal Group.

Bawn, Kathleen. 1993. "The Logic of Institutional Preferences: German Electoral Law as a Social Choice Outcome." *American Journal of Political Science* 37:965–89.

Beck, Nathaniel, Jonathan N. Katz, and Richard Tucker. 1998. "Taking Time Seriously: Time-Series Cross-Section Analysis with a Binary Dependent Variable." *American Journal of Political Science* 42:1260–88.

Bensel, Richard Franklin. 2004. *The American Ballot Box in the Mid-Nineteenth Century*. Cambridge: Cambridge University Press.

Berman, Mitchell. 2004. "Putting Fairness on the Map: The High Court Has a Chance to Ease Flagrant Partisan Gerrymandering." *Los Angeles Times*, May 28.

Binder, Sarah A. 1997. *Majority Rights, Minority Rule: Partisanship and the Development of Congress*. Cambridge: Cambridge University Press.

Book of the States. 1942–2010. Lexington, KY: Council of State Governments.

Born, Richard. 1985. "Partisan Intentions and Election Day Realities in the Congressional Districting Process." *American Political Science Review* 79:305–19.

Brady, David. 1988. *Critical Elections and Congressional Policymaking*. Stanford: Stanford University Press.

Brady, David. 1985. "A Reevaluation of Realignments in American Politics: Evidence from the House of Representatives." *American Political Science Review* 79:28–49.

Brady, David, and Bernard Grofman. 1991. "Sectional Differences in Partisan Bias and Electoral Responsiveness in U.S. House Elections, 1850–1980." *British Journal of Political Science* 21:247–56.

Brady, David, Kara Buckley, and Douglas Rivers. 1999. "The Roots of Careerism in the U.S. House of Representatives." *Legislative Studies Quarterly* 24:489–510.

Burnham, Walter Dean. 1970. *Critical Elections and the Mainsprings of American Politics*. New York: W.W. Norton.

Burnham, Walter Dean. 1974. "Rejoinder to "Comments' by Philip Converse and Jerrold Rusk." *American Political Science Review* 68:1050–57.

Burnham, Walter Dean. 1982. "The Appearance and Disappearance of the American Voter." In *The Current Crisis in American Politics*, edited by Walter Dean Burnham. New York: Oxford University Press.

Burnham, Walter Dean. 1985. *Partisan Division of American State Governments, 1834–1985*. [Computer File] Conducted by Massachusetts Institute of Technology. ICPSR, ed. Ann Arbor, MI: Inter-University Consortium for Political and Social Research [producer and distributor].

Butler, David, and Bruce Cain. 1992. *Congressional Redistricting*. New York: Macmillan.

Cain, Bruce. 1984. *The Reapportionment Puzzle*. Berkeley and Los Angeles: University of California Press.

Cain, Bruce E. 1985. "Assessing the Partisan Effects of Redistricting." *American Political Science Review* 79:320–33.

Cain, Bruce E., and David Butler. 1991. "Redistricting Myths Are at Odds with Evidence." *Public Affairs Report, Institute of Governmental Studies, University of California, Berkeley* 32, no. 5.

Calabrese, Stephen. 2000. "Multimember District Congressional Elections." *Legislative Studies Quarterly* 25:611–43.

Calabrese, Stephen. 2006. "An Explanation of the Continuing Federal Government Mandate of Single-Member Congressional Districts." *Public Choice* 130:23–40.

Campagna, Janet, and Bernard Grofman. 1990. "Party Control and Partisan Bias in the 1980's Congressional Redistricting." *Journal of Politics* 52:1242–57.

Canon, David T. 1999. *Race, Redistricting, and Representation*. Chicago: University of Chicago Press.

Carson, Jamie L., and Michael Crespin. 2004. "The Effect of State Redistricting Methods on Electoral Competition in the United States House of Representatives." *State Politics and Policy Quarterly* 21:455–69.

Carson, Jamie L., Erik J. Engstrom, and Jason M. Roberts. 2006. "Redistricting, Candidate Entry, and the Politics of Nineteenth-Century House Elections." *American Journal of Political Science* 50:283–93.

Carson, Jamie L., Erik J. Engstrom, and Jason Roberts. 2007. "Candidate Quality, the Personal Vote, and the Incumbency Advantage in Congress." *American Political Science Review* 101:289–302.

Carson, Jamie L., Jeffery A. Jenkins, David W. Rohde, and Mark A. Souva. 2001. "The Impact of National Tides and District-Level Effects on Electoral Outcomes: The U.S. Congressional Elections of 1862–63." *American Journal of Political Science* 45:887–98.

Carson, Jamie L., and Jason M. Roberts. 2005. "Strategic Politicians and U.S. House Elections, 1874–1914." *Journal of Politics* 67:474–96.

Clubb, Jerome, William Flanigan, and Nancy Zingale. 1987. *Electoral Data for Counties in the United States: Presidential and Congressional Races, 1840–1972*. Computer File, ICPSR # 8611.

Colegrove v. Green, 328 U.S. 549 (1946).

Cooter, Robert D. 2000. *The Strategic Constitution*. Princeton: Princeton University Press.

Cox, Adam. 2004. "Partisan Fairness and Redistricting Politics." *New York University Law Review* 79:751–802.

Cox, Gary W. 1997. *Making Votes Count*. Cambridge: Cambridge University Press.

Cox, Gary W., and Jonathan N. Katz. 1999. "The Reapportionment Revolution and Bias in U.S. Congressional Elections." *American Journal of Political Science* 43:812–40.

Cox, Gary W., and Jonathan Katz. 2002. *Elbridge Gerry's Salamander*. Cambridge: Cambridge University Press.

Cox, Gary W., and J. Morgan Kousser. 1981. "Turnout and Rural Corruption: New York as a Test Case." *American Journal of Political Science* 25:646–63.

Cunningham, Noble E., Jr. 1963. *The Jeffersonian Republicans in Power: Party Operations, 1801–1809*. Chapel Hill: University of North Carolina Press.

Davis v. Bandemer, 478 U.S. 109 (1986).

DeBats, Donald. 1974. *Elites and Masses: Political Structure, Communication and Behavior in Ante-Bellum Georgia*. PhD diss, University of Wisconsin.

DeConde, Alexander. 1976. *This Affair of Louisiana*. New York: Charles Scribner's Sons.

Dubin, Michael J. 2007. *Party Affiliations in the State Legislatures: A Year by Year Summary, 1796–2006*. Jefferson, NC: McFarland and Company.

Eagles, Charles W. 1990. *Democracy Delayed: Congressional Reapportionment and Urban-Rural Conflict in the 1920's*. Athens: University of Georgia Press.

Engstrom, Erik J., and Samuel Kernell. 2005. "Manufactured Responsiveness: The Impact of State Electoral Laws on Unified Party Control of the Presidency and the House of Representatives, 1840–1940." *American Journal of Political Science* 49:531–49.

Erikson, Robert S. 1972. "Malapportionment, Gerrymandering, and Party Fortunes in Congressional Elections." *American Political Science Review* 66:1234–45.

Feller, Daniel. 2004. "The Bank War." In *The American Congress: The Building of Democracy*, edited by Julian E. Zelizer. Boston and New York: Houghton Mifflin.

Fenno, Richard. 1978. *Home Style: House Members in Their Districts*. Glenview, IL: Scott, Foresman.

Ferejohn, John. 1977. "On the Decline of Competitive Congressional Elections." *American Political Science Review* 71:166–76.

Fiorina, Morris, David Rohde, and Peter Wissel. 1975. "Historical Change in House Turnover." In *Congress in Change*, edited by Norman Ornstein. New York: Praeger.

Fredman, Lionel E. 1968. *The Australian Ballot: The Story of an American Reform*. East Lansing: Michigan State University Press.

Friedman, John N., and Richard T. Holden. 2009. "The Rising Incumbent Reelection Rate: What's Gerrymandering Got to Do With It?" *Journal of Politics* 71 (April):593–611.

Garand, James and Donald Gross. 1984. "Changes in the Vote Margins for Congressional Candidates: A Specification of Historical Trends." *American Political Science Review* 78:17–30.

Gelman, Andrew, and Gary King. 1994. "Enhancing Democracy Through Legislative Redistricting." *American Political Science Review* 88:541–59.

Gerken, Heather. 2010. "Getting from Here to There in Redistricting Reform." *Duke Journal of Constitutional Law and Public Policy* 5:1–15.

Gienapp, William E. 1987. *The Origins of the Republican Party, 1852–1856*. New York: Oxford University Press.

Glad, Paul W. 1964. *McKinley, Bryan, and the People*. Philadelphia and New York: J.B. Lippincott.

Glazer, Amahai, Bernard Grofman, and Marc Roberts. 1987. "Partisan and Incumbency Effects of 1970's Redistricting." *American Journal of Political Science* 31:680–707.

Griffith, Elmer C. 1907. *The Rise and Development of the Gerrymander*. Chicago: Scott, Foresman.

Grofman, Bernard. 1983. "Measures of Bias and Proportionality in Seats-Votes Relationships." *Political Methodology* 9:278–95.

Grofman, Bernard, William Koetzle, and Thomas Brunell. 1997. "An Integrated Perspective on the Three Potential Sources of Partisan Bias: Malapportionment, Turnout Differences, and the Geographic Distribution of the Party Vote." *Electoral Studies* 16:454–70.

Hirsch, Sam. 2003. "The United States House of Unrepresentatives: What Went Wrong in the Latest Round of Congressional Redistricting." *Election Law Journal* 2 (2):179–216.

Hoadley, John F. 1986. *Origins of American Political Parties, 1789–1803*. Lexington: University Press of Kentucky.

Holt, Michael F. 1983. *The Political Crisis of the 1850's*. New York: W. W. Norton.

Holt, Michael F. 1984. "The Election of 1840, Voter Mobilization, and the Emergence of the Second American Party System: A Reappraisal of Jacksonian Voting Behavior." In *A Master's Due*, edited by William Cooper, Michael Holt, and John McCardell. Baton Rouge: Louisiana State University Press.

Holt, Michael F. 1999. *The Rise and Fall of the American Whig Party: Jacksonian Politics and the Onset of the Civil War*. New York: Oxford University Press.

Hunter, Thomas Rogers. 2011. "The First Gerrymander? Patrick Henry, James Madison, James Monroe, and Virginia's 1788 Congressional Districting." *Early American Studies: An Interdisciplinary Journal* 9:781–820.

Inter-University Consortium for Political and Social Research, and Carroll McKibbin. 1997. *Roster of United States Congressional Officeholders and Biographical Characteristics of Members of the United States Congress, 1789–1996: Merged Data* [Computer file]. 10th ICPSR ed. Ann Arbor, MI: Inter-University Consortium for Political and Social Research [producer and distributor].

Issacharoff, Samuel. 2002. "Gerrymandering and Political Cartels." *Harvard Law Review* 116:593–648.

Jacobson, Gary C. 2009. *The Politics of Congressional Elections, 7th Edition*. New York: Pearson/Longman.

Jenkins, Jeffrey, and Charles Stewart III. 2001. "Sophisticated Behavior and Speakership Elections: The Elections of 1849 and 1855–56." Paper presented at the Annual Meeting of the Midwestern Political Science Association.

Katz, Jonathan, and Brian Sala. 1996. "Careerism, Committee Assignments, and the Electoral Connection." *American Political Science Review* 90:21–33.

Katznelson, Ira, and Quinn Mulroy. 2012. "Was the South Pivotal? Situated Partisanship and Policy Coalitions During the New Deal and Fair Deal." *Journal of Politics* 74 (April): 604–20.

Kernell, Samuel. 1977. "Toward Understanding 19th Century Congressional Careers: Ambition, Competition, and Rotation." *American Journal of Political Science* 21:669–93.

Kernell, Samuel. 1986. "The Early Nationalization of Political News in America." *Studies in American Political Development* 1 (1):255–78.

Kernell, Samuel. 2003. "To Stay, To Quit or To Move Up: Explaining the Growth of Careerism in the House of Representatives, 1878–1940." Presented at the Annual Meetings of the American Political Science Association, Philadelphia, August 28–31.

Kernell, Samuel, and Michael P. McDonald. 1999. "Congress and America's Political Development: The Transformation of the Post Office from Patronage to Service." *American Journal of Political Science* 43:792–811.

Ketcham, Ralph. 1971. *James Madison: A Biography*. Charlottesville: University of Virginia Press.

Key, V. O. 1955. "A Theory of Critical Elections." *Journal of Politics* 17:3–18.

Key, V. O. 1956. *American State Politics*. New York: Knopf.

Kiewiet, D. Roderick, and Langche Zeng. 1993. "An Analysis of Congressional

Career Decisions, 1947–1986." *The American Political Science Review* 87 (4):928–41.

King, Gary. 1989. "Representation through Legislative Redistricting: A Stochastic Model." *American Journal of Political Science* 33:787–824.

King, Gary. 1998. *Unifying Political Methodology: The Likelihood Theory of Statistical Inference.* Cambridge: Cambridge University Press.

King, Gary, and Robert X. Browning. 1987. "Democratic Representation and Partisan Bias in Congressional Elections." *American Political Science Review* 81:125–73.

Kousser, J. Morgan. 1974. *The Shaping of Southern Politics.* New Haven: Yale University Press.

Kousser, J. Morgan. 1992. "The Voting Rights Act and the Two Reconstructions." In *Controversies in Minority Voting*, edited by Bernard Grofman and Chandler Davidson. Washington, DC: Brookings Institution.

Kousser, J. Morgan. 1996. "Estimating the Partisan Consequences of Redistricting Plans—Simply." *Legislative Studies Quarterly* 21 (November):521–41.

Kromkowski, Charles A. 2002. *Recreating the American Republic: Rules of Apportionment, Constitutional Change, and American Political Development, 1700–1870.* Cambridge: Cambridge University Press.

Kruman, Marc W. 1983. *Parties and Politics in North Carolina, 1836–1865.* Baton Rouge: Louisiana State University Press.

Lax, Jeffrey R., and Mathew D. McCubbins. 2006. "Courts, Congress, and Public Policy, Part II: The Impact of the Reapportionment Revolution on Congress and State Legislatures." *Journal of Contemporary Legal Issues* 15:199–218.

Lee, Francis E., and Bruce I. Oppenheimer. 1999. *Sizing up the Senate: The Unequal Consequences of Equal Representation.* Chicago: University of Chicago Press.

Levine, Peter D. 1977. *The Behavior of State Legislative Parties in the Jacksonian Era: New Jersey, 1829–1844.* Cranbury, NJ: Associated University Presses.

League of United Latin American Citizens v. Perry, 548 U. S. 399 (2006).

Martis, Kenneth. 1982. *The Historical Atlas of United States Congressional Districts, 1789–1983.* New York: Free Press.

Martis, Kenneth. 2008. "The Original Gerrymander." *Political Geography* 27:833–39.

Mayer, George H. 1951. *The Political Career of Floyd B. Olson.* Minneapolis: University of Minnesota Press.

Mayhew, David R. 1974a. *Congress: The Electoral Connection.* New Haven: Yale University Press.

Mayhew, David R. 1974b. "Congressional Elections: The Case of the Vanishing Marginals." *Polity* 6:295–317.

Mayhew, David R. 2002. *Electoral Realignments: A Critique of an American Genre.* New Haven: Yale University Press.

McCarty, Nolan, Keith T. Poole, and Howard Rosenthal. 2009. "Does Gerrymandering Cause Polarization?" *American Journal of Political Science* 53:666–80.

McCormick, Richard P. 1953. *The History of Voting in New Jersey.* New Brunswick, NJ: Rutgers University Press.

McCormick, Richard P. 1966. *The Second American Party System: Party Formation in the Jacksonian Era.* Chapel Hill: University of North Carolina Press.

McCormick, Richard P. 1975. "Political Development and the Second Party System." In *The American Party System*, edited by William Nesbit Chambers and Walter Dean Burnham. New York: Oxford University Press.

McCubbins, Mathew D., and Thomas Schwartz. 1988. "Congress, the Courts, and Public Policy: Consequences of the One Man, One Vote Rule." *American Journal of Political Science* 32:388–415.

McDonald, Michael P. 2006. "Drawing the Line on District Competition." *PS: Political Science and Politics* 39:91–94.

McMillan, Malcolm Cook. 1978. *Constitutional Development in Alabama, 1798–1901*. Spartanburg, SC: The Reprint Company.

McSeveney, Samuel T. 1972. *The Politics of Depression: Political Behavior in the Northeast, 1893-1896*. New York: Oxford University Press.

Miller, John C. 1960. *The Federalist Era, 1789–1801*. New York: Harper and Row.

Mitchell, Franklin D. 1968. *Embattled Democracy: Missouri Democratic Politics, 1919–1932*. Columbia: University of Missouri Press.

Monmonier, Mark S. 2001. *Bushmanders and Bullwinkles: How Politicians Manipulate Electronic Maps and Census Data to Win Elections*. Chicago: University of Chicago Press.

Nevins, Allan. 1924. *The American States During and After the Revolution, 1775–1789*. New York: Macmillan.

Niemi, Richard G., and Alan I. Abramowitz. 1994. "Partisan Redistricting and the 1992 Congressional Elections." *Journal of Politics* 56 (3):811–17.

Niemi, Richard, and Laura Winsky. 1992. "The Persistence of Partisan Redistricting Effects in Congressional Elections in the 1970's and 1980's." *Journal of Politics* 54:565–72.

Oppenheimer, Bruce I. 2005. "Deep Red and Blue Congressional Districts: The Causes and Consequences of Declining Party Competitiveness." In *Congress Reconsidered*, edited by Lawrence C. Dodd and Bruce I. Oppenheimer, 135–58. Washington, DC: CQ Press.

Oppenheimer, Bruce, James Stimson, and Richard Waterman. 1986. "Interpreting U.S. Congressional Elections: The Exposure Thesis." *Legislative Studies Quarterly*. 11:227–47.

Ornstein, Norman J., Thomas E. Mann, and Michael J. Malbin. 2008. *Vital Statistics on Congress, 2008*. Washington, DC: Brookings Institution Press.

Owen, Guillermo, and Bernard Grofman. 1988. "Optimal Partisan Gerrymandering." *Political Geography Quarterly* 7 (January):5–22.

Parsons, Stanley B., William W. Beach, and Michael J. Dubin. 1986. *United States Congressional Districts and Data, 1843–1883*. New York: Greenwood Press.

Parsons, Stanley B., Michael J. Dubin, and Karen Toombs Parsons. 1990. *United States Congressional Districts, 1883–1913*. New York: Greenwood Press.

Perman, Michael. 1984. *The Road to Redemption: Southern Politics, 1869–1879*. Chapel Hill: University of North Carolina Press.

Polsby, Nelson. 1968. "The Institutionalization of the U.S. House of Representatives." *American Political Science Review* 68:144–68.

Polsby, Nelson, Miriam Gallaher, and Barry Rundquist. 1969. "The Growth of the Seniority System in the U.S. House of Representatives." *American Political Science Review* 63:787–807.

Price, H. Douglas. 1975. "Congress and the Evolution of Legislative 'Professional-ism.'" In *Congress in Change: Evolution and Reform*, edited by Norman J. Ornstein. New York: Praeger.

Price, H. Douglas. 1998. *Explorations in the Evolution of Congress*. Berkeley: Institute of Governmental Studies Press.

Rae, Douglas. 1967. *The Political Consequences of Electoral Laws*. New Haven: Yale University Press.

Remini, Robert V. 1967. *Andrew Jackson and the Bank War*. New York: W. W. Norton.

Remington, Thomas F., and Steven S. Smith. 1996. "Political Goals, Institutional Context, and the Choice of an Electoral System: The Russian Parliamentary Election Law." *American Journal of Political Science* 40:1253–79.

Reynolds v. Sims, 377 U.S. 533 (1964).

Riker, William H. 1955. "The Senate and American Federalism." *American Political Science Review* 49:452–69.

Rush, Mark E. 1993. *Does Redistricting Make a Difference? Partisan Representation and Electoral Behavior*. Baltimore: Johns Hopkins University Press.

Rusk, Jerrold. 1970. "The Effect of the Australian Ballot Reform on Split-Ticket Voting: 1876–1908." *American Political Science Review* 64:1220–38.

Rusk, Jerrold. 2001. *A Statistical History of the American Electorate*. Washington, DC: Congressional Quarterly Press.

Scarrow, Harold. 1999. "The Impact of At-Large Elections: Vote Dilution or Choice Dilution?" *Electoral Studies* 18:557–68.

Schattschneider, E. E. 1960. *The Semisovereign People*. Hinsdale, IL: Dryden Press.

Schickler, Eric. 2001. *Disjointed Pluralism: Institutional Innovation and the Development of the U.S. Congress*. Princeton: Princeton University Press.

Schmeckebier, Laurence F. 1941. *Congressional Apportionment*. Washington, DC: Brookings Institution.

Seabrook, Nicholas R. 2010. "The Limits of Partisan Gerrymandering: Looking Ahead to the 2010 Congressional Redistricting Cycle." *The Forum* 8 (2).

Shepsle, Kenneth A. 2001. "A Comment on Institutional Change." *Journal of Theoretical Politics* 13:321–25.

Shields, Johanna Nicol. 1985. "Whigs Reform the 'Bear Garden': Representation and the Apportionment Act of 1842." *Journal of the Early Republic* 5:355–82.

Shotts, Kenneth W. 2001. "The Effect of Majority-Minority Mandates on Partisan Gerrymandering." *American Journal of Political Science* 45:120–35.

Sickels, Robert J. 1966. "Dragons, Bacon Strips and Dumbbells—Who's Afraid of Reapportionment?" *Yale Law Journal* 75:1300–1308.

Silbey, Joel A. 1977. *A Respectable Minority: The Democratic Party in the Civil War Era*. New York: W.W. Norton.

Silbey, Joel A. 1991. *The American Political Nation, 1838–1893*. Stanford: Stanford University Press.

Smiley v. Holm, 285 U.S. 355 (1932).

Stampp, Kenneth M. 1965. *The Era of Reconstruction, 1865–1877*. New York: Alfred A. Knopf.

Stewart, Charles III. 1991. "Lessons from the Post-Civil War Era." In *The Politics of Divided Government*, edited by Gary W. Cox and Samuel Kernell. Boulder, CO: Westview Press.

References   221

Stewart, Charles III, and Barry R. Weingast. 1992. "Stacking the Senate, Changing the Nation: Republican Rotten Boroughs, Statehood Politics, and American Political Development." *Studies in American Political Development* 6:223–71.
Strahan, Randall. 2007. *Leading Representatives: The Agency of Leaders in the Politics of the U.S. House*. Baltimore: Johns Hopkins University Press.
Summers, Mark Wahlgren. 2004. *Party Games: Getting, Keeping, and Using Power in Gilded Age Politics*. Chapel Hill: University of North Carolina Press.
Sundquist, James L. 1983. *Dynamics of the Party System: Alignment and Realignment of Political Parties in the United States*. Washington, DC: Brookings Institution.
Swain, John W., Stephen A. Borrelli, and Brian C. Reed. 1998. "Partisan Consequences of the Post-1990 Redistricting for the U.S. House of Representatives." *Political Research Quarterly* 51:945–67.
Taussig, F.W. 1931. *The Tariff History of the United States*. New York & London: G. P. Putnam and Sons.
Theriault, Sean M. 2006. "Party Politics during the Louisiana Purchase." *Social Science History* 2:293–304.
Theriault, Sean M. 2008. *Party Polarization in Congress*. Cambridge: Cambridge University Press.
Thornton, J. Mills. 1978. *Power and Politics in a Slave Society*. Baton Rouge: Louisiana State University.
Tinkcom, Harry Marlin. 1950. *The Republicans and Federalists in Pennsylvania, 1790–1801*. Harrisburg, PA: Pennsylvania Historical and Museum Commission.
Tomz, Michael, Jason Wittenberg, and Gary King. 2000. *CLARIFY: Software for Interpreting and Presenting Statistical Results. Version 1.2.2*. Cambridge, MA: Harvard University, March 3. http://gking.harvard.edu/.
Toobin, Jeffrey. 2003. "The Great Election Grab." *New Yorker*, December 8.
Tufte, Edward R. 1973. "The Relationship between Votes and Seats in Two-Party Systems." *American Political Science Review* 67:540–54.
Tyler, Gus. 1962. "Court Versus Legislature: The Socio-Politics of Malapportionment." *Law and Contemporary Problems* 27:390–407.
Valelly, Richard M. 2009. "The Reed Rules and Republican Party Building: A New Look." *Studies in American Political Development* 23:115–42.
Vieth v. Jubelirer, 541 U.S. 267 (2004).
Walsh, Justin. 1987. *The Centennial History of the Indiana General Assembly, 1816–1978*. Indianapolis: The Select Committee on the Centennial History of the Indiana General Assembly.
Wang, Xi. 1997. *The Trial of Democracy: Black Suffrage and Northern Republicans, 1860–1910*. Athens: University of Georgia Press.
Wesberry v. Sanders, 376 U.S. 1 (1964).
Wood v. Broom, 287 U.S. 1 (1932).
Yearley, C. K. 1970. *The Money Machines: The Breakdown and Reform of Governmental and Party Finance in the North, 1860–1920*. Albany: State University of New York Press.
Yoshinaka, Antoine, and Chad Murphy. 2009. "Are Mapmakers Able to Target and Protect Congressional Incumbents? The Institutional Dynamics of Electoral Competition." *American Politics Research* 37:955–82.
Zagarri, Rosemarie. 1987. *The Politics of Size: Representation in the United States, 1776–1850*. Ithaca: Cornell University Press.

Index